MW01028374

THE SUMMA DOMESTICA

THE
SUMMA
DOMESTICA

Order and Wonder in Family Life

⊰❊ VOL. 3 ❊⊱

Housekeeping

LEILA M. LAWLER

Illustrations by Deirdre M. Folley

SOPHIA INSTITUTE PRESS
Manchester, New Hampshire

Sophia Institute Press
Box 5284, Manchester, NH 03108
1-800-888-9344

www.SophiaInstitute.com

Sophia Institute Press® is a registered trademark of Sophia Institute.

hardcover ISBN 978-1-64413-398-9

ebook ISBN 978-1-64413-399-6

Library of Congress Control Number: 2021940523

Second printing

CONTENTS

THE SUMMA DOMESTICA

Order and Wonder in Homemaking

To an open house in the evening
Home shall men come,
To an older place than Eden
And a taller town than Rome.
To the end of the way of the wandering star,
To the things that cannot be and that are,
To the place where God was homeless
And all men are at home.

G. K. CHESTERTON, "THE HOUSE OF CHRISTMAS"

rder means first things first. For the family, first things are the journey on earth toward heaven in the company of those we love; first things are also mundane realities such as making sure the kids are fed on a regular basis and have something to wear, while keeping clutter from swallowing us with nary a trace.

I myself have gone on a journey of discovery about order and wonder in the home, and it has led me to the importance of trying to do one's best with what one has. When our children were very little, on the other side of the wall in the side-by-side duplex house we lived in was a lovely couple who had never had children. They were old enough to be my parents, and they were friendly. Bert would come over on some neighborly pretext, and before I knew it, he would be neatening up all the reading material on my coffee table, which was a lot—magazines, mail, books—everything just thrown on there, as was my habit. He would make tidy stacks of all my stuff, even putting toys in the baskets; only then would he sit down and chat with whoever was around. He loved the children.

I noticed something, even as I interiorly demurred at what I saw as the uselessness of his effort: tidying the piles made my living room look instantly better. I started tidying them myself (rather than waiting for my odd middle-aged gentleman neighbor to do it for me, you ask? Yes, I reply, humbly). It took someone literally meddling in my affairs (as opposed to telling me to do it or ignoring it until I figured it out) for me finally to assimilate that such a detail made a difference.

Much of what I write here is taken up with so many seemingly mundane details of *order*, such as menu planning, laundry organization, cleaning methods, and even frugality tips, that the reader might be forgiven for not seeing the connection with educating children, which is the underlying motivation of these volumes, after all. But let's think: if you sincerely want to educate your children, but if, on any given actual day, you don't know what is for supper by suppertime, how will you have the peace of mind to help your children explore the world with delight? If anyone asks me how to go about homeschooling, I always want to answer, "Are you at peace with your duties? Have you fed your children recently? Washed their faces? Gotten up on time? Read a book of your own, having made time for such a pursuit?"

There are indeed many amazing facts for children to learn. But how can they learn them if you, the person they rely on for an environment in which to learn, are frazzled by the exigencies of survival?

Without a peaceful, orderly home, we have short tempers, crankiness, and most importantly for the strict understanding of education (even when the children attend conventional school) no mental space for oversight of what is being learned and what needs to be learned. Many a parent laments that his child is falling through the cracks and doesn't see that the disorderliness at home is the cause—or at least isn't aware of the necessary (if, granted, insufficient) condition for a flourishing life.

As you read, keep in mind that I wrote almost all of this one bit at a time, to help the woman who feels incompetent gradually to find her way to keeping her own home the way that suits her and gives her a sense of accomplishment, of mastery, and of creativity. I have tried to keep that incremental approach intact while also delivering a complete volume. I hope that you will find real encouragement in these pages, even where topics seem to overlap; my aim is to help you discover in a gradual and peaceful way, the wonder of the hidden life of *home* in the satisfaction of living its order.

PART 1
On Making a Home

Much of my writing has been to encourage people who are not naturally tidy, clean, or prone to decorating to find satisfaction in creating order. If someone who has trouble with being orderly resolves to improve, that person might start with the particulars of cleaning, organization and so on—and might find the task overwhelming. In a development that may strike some as paradoxical, making things beautiful (or, as I like to say, pretty—it seems less stressful) can be the motivation to find that order and the means by which it can be done without feeling suffocated by the sheer amount of work involved and the paralysis of not knowing where to start.

Sometimes the incentive to do necessary work—even drudgery—comes from a creative vision, and then the slog, the long march through the swamps of housewifery, becomes a joy—or at least not so bad as we feared.

Xenophon, ancient philosopher and chronicler of history, wrote of the beauty of order in his book *The Economist*, "After all, my wife, there is nothing in human life so serviceable, naught so beautiful as order." His narrator, Ischomachus, recounts the pleasing arrangement of things on a merchant ship:

> There is no time left, you know, ... when God makes a tempest in the great deep, to set about searching for what you want, or to be giving out anything which is not snug and shipshape in its place. God threatens and chastises sluggards. If only He destroy not innocent with guilty, a man may be content; or if He turn and save all hands aboard that render right good service, thanks be to Heaven.[1]

---

[1] Xenophon, *The Economist*, trans. H. G. Dakyns, chap. 8. I am indebted to John Cuddeback for introducing me to this ancient author's domestic musings.

He turns from the ship to the home, where he extols the same order, not only for the sake of being ready for danger, but for something higher:

> let me harp upon the string of beauty — image a fair scene: the boots and shoes and sandals, and so forth, all laid in order row upon row; the cloaks, the mantles, and the rest of the apparel stowed in their own places; the coverlets and bedding; the copper cauldrons; and all the articles for table use! Nay, though it well may raise a smile of ridicule (not on the lips of a grave man perhaps, but of some facetious witling) to hear me say it, a beauty like the cadence of sweet music dwells even in pots and pans set out in neat array: and so, in general, fair things ever show more fair when orderly bestowed.[2]

I think if we can bring some of this "sweet music" into our lives, some harmony and order, we will find the same sort of pleasure and enjoyment — in the *home*.

[2] Ibid.

Competence versus Perfectionism

Whoever is diligent will soon be cheerful.

— GEORGE MACDONALD, *THE PRINCESS AND CURDIE*

There is simply no way that you don't have *more* ability than I to make a home, with all that *making a home* entails. I fail every day, at that and at many other things. I started writing about how to do things because I suspected that the perfect images we see online are a bit defeating. When I began, I had the vision that maybe it would help to see someone *just doing her best*, with a little competence.

I've always posted photos on my blog, with the aim of drawing people into the text. Sometimes it has happened that the photos did the opposite: they functioned to make readers think that I was far, far more competent than they. This is partly because the pictures are taken from a certain point of view, so that you don't see what I don't want you to see (though

Heaven knows, I thought the pictures were humble enough). Partly it's due to the fact that the only child I had as I began the blog was the one who wondered why on earth I don't sweep the hearth after putting logs in the fire—and then did it for me.

It wasn't always thus, as you can imagine. It was just like it is at your house if you are a little conflicted, easily distracted by books, and prone to flights of fancy regarding what your true destiny might be. Only, worse, because I'm not actually driven by any obsession to cleanliness—just to a sort of good-enough order.

However, in the interest of slaying vanity disguised as false modesty, I will say that I seemed to have shown that I am able to get readers of the blog to tackle some of their problems. I found that I just took a guess at what those things were—probably based on what I myself was reading on the Internet at the time—and left it to them to take what I said in that spirit of random projection. I was always amazed when someone would comment that I had addressed *just* their issue at the time.

Above all, my hope was that they came away from the posts knowing that the stuff *they* need to deal with is their very *own*. That is, I always tried to keep from making my problems the readers' problems; my aim has always been to facilitate a good look at oneself, whatever the circumstances might be and however little I could imagine them. Sort of an operating principle, if you will, to be applied as necessary to specific cases.

Speaking of what ultimately is about our relationship with God—this tricky ability to figure out what our very own struggle is, and not continually make other people's our own—a while ago I read a blog post, the author of which was embarking on the project of finding out what God's will for her could be.

She thought that finding God's will for her was going to be a vast, immense project. As I remember, she was allotting a year, maybe more, to get the job done. She even left home in order to devote herself to the search, as if God is in a certain place (but that place is never where we are, when we approach the search this way).

Do you sometimes feel as if you have no idea what God's will for you is? That you would need to take time off and go away to focus on that one problem in order to make head or tails of it?

What would you think if I told you that you could find out *right now* what His will is? That it's a "problem" of a day or an hour, not years? His will for you, specifically? (And I'm not going to trick you by saying that God's will for you turns out to be "love everyone," or "work for world peace," or even "lock and load"!)

It's not really a secret, and it's so simple that it seems as if it couldn't possibly be true. It's just this: trying to do all what you must do, *today*, with a loving heart—not everything you could possibly do but what you *must* do.

Knowing what those things might be couldn't be simpler, and it counts as the most meaningful prayer and also the *remedy* for the distraction of *other people's priorities*. In God's presence, think of *your* obligations; most importantly, the people to whom you are obligated.

You have obligations to God, and again, they are quite simple. He doesn't ask for much: worship Him on Sundays, give thanks, ask Him for your needs and desires, keep His commandments.

You have obligations to your husband. He has obligations to you too, and the best way to get him to live up to them is to live up to yours; don't fall into the trap of thinking he has to go first.

You have obligations to your children—it's all you! They owe you nothing until they can learn the Fourth Commandment,[3] and even then it's a work in progress.

You have obligations to a boss, if you have one. The newsletter for the committee if you said you'd do it. A class if you're teaching one.

And you have obligations to yourself: to take a shower, get some rest, eat a proper meal, and stop running around like a crazy person.

You could sit down right now and make a list of these things. If it's just what you *have* to do, *today*, it won't take long, especially if you take into account your limitations: illness, nursing a baby, tiredness, importunate toddlers, someone unpleasant you must deal with …

There's a word for all these things, one that isn't often used these days, and it's "duty"—the thing you should be doing today, the *one* thing, for the ones God has given you to serve.

[3] Honor your father and your mother.

Duty. An elusive, if not repellent, word. I mean, we feel repelled when we haven't been doing it, our duty. It hides itself behind strange ideas that come from nowhere and everywhere, thoughts such as looking for God's will somewhere other than *here*.

But I've noticed a paradox, perhaps embedded in the Gospel injunction that we must die to live and that the stone that was rejected becomes the cornerstone: that when you joyfully and wholeheartedly do *the things you have to do* as coming directly from the hand of God, then other unforeseen other things open up, and you discover the big picture, the adventure, the outrageously perfect plan God has for you—if adventure is what you wanted. If not, you discover the marvelous rest God has for you!

In other words, you find your heart's desire—so don't be afraid!

Therefore, while you are waiting for the big reveal from on high and thinking, "If only, if only!" (the number-one sentence starter for losing your bearings: If only I lived somewhere else! If only I were married to someone else! If only my children were like those children! If only I could do things easily like that person!), and wondering *what* in Heaven's name God's will for you could be, and whether you should go reform the slums or climb a Peruvian mountain or rescue flood victims—and maybe those are things you should do, for all I know, it's not up to me—just make a little list, a teensy list of things that you should do *today where you are*: get supper ready, make sure everyone has something clean to wear tomorrow, make the bed, give the baby a bath, call the doctor to make an appointment, wash the dishes.

Don't be like Dickens's Mrs. Jellyby in Bleak House, whose eyes "could see nothing nearer than Africa!" "It must be very good of Mrs Jellyby to take such pains about a scheme for the benefit of natives—and yet—Peepy and the housekeeping!" Maybe it was just that she didn't *know how* to take care of anything nearer. Maybe she wasn't *competent*. I happen to think that trying to be competent helps you have a loving heart for God's will!

I think that you love what you do *when you know how to do it!* Whether it's something the world sees as important *or* something it sees as drudgery, what's stopping you from tackling the stuff you have to do is not really knowing how to do it, how to get started, how to make it a habit.

Not only cleaning a bedroom but doing a good job of it, because you just know how. And clean it you must.

Getting a good supper together, on time, frugally; there's a satisfaction in that, not pride in a bad sense. I think it's the same good feeling you would have for anyone who did that, as when you say you are proud of your child for a good job. You are allowed to be proud of yourself in that same way, you know.

Love your neighbor as yourself means sometimes taking pleasure in a job well done just as if someone else did it, and this very pleasure glorifies God when it's offered to Him. I think there's some confusion on this very point.

On the one hand, you could demand a perfectionism in the daily round that would get in the way of more important things. Losing peace over a messy room just isn't worth it. And it is pride to think that our worth is bound up in how other people view us. Perfectionism often has its roots in a sense of inferiority, as if we lose our standing with others if we show a crack or flaw.

But that's not realistic. There are valid things that interfere. I remember times I just had to go shopping because the need for underwear had become acute! That meant the cleaning was put off. Or if someone dropped by, the priority at that moment was serving a hospitable meal, not whisking away toys. (Someone who doesn't have a lot of kids around can hardly imagine these problems, but there's a critical mass of humanity that makes the smallest errand or chore turn into a bog of quicksand.) At those moments, we have to console ourselves with the knowledge that tomorrow is another day to make another list and try again.

On the other hand, there's a scorn for doing things competently, as if there's something almost shameful in knowing how to keep things clean or teaching a child to read—as if real, intelligent, loving moms shouldn't care about home and children and husband! (Unless they can be shown to be dabbling in a high-priced way—"I used my *fabulous* designer squeegee to get this window *fabulously* clean—now, off to the resort with the *hoi poloi!*") But a daily commitment, usually without benefit of any kind of designer anything, is not going to be appreciated by many.

Maybe the confusion is not seeing that the Gospel injunction "be ye perfect" means, I think, that God wants our perfection in love. I think it's consoling to know that He is more patient than we can imagine with imperfections in everything else. There really can't be perfection in material things—they are just too prone to entropy. So don't you see the go-ahead there, written into the natural order of things, just to do a humble, competent job when it comes to the "everything else"?

Do your best to do each thing competently (not perfectly), and add your own little touches for your own and the Lord's enjoyment. Enjoying life's order is something God Himself did, on that seventh day, and this restful attitude can be reflected in the smallest things we do.

Don't get frustrated or negative with yourself if your duties are not carried out perfectly, but don't think it doesn't matter. If taking care of your home, your husband, your children doesn't matter, what does? But what's important is the effort and the sort of "background love" that goes into becoming the sort of person who really wants to do the given job.

And maybe that little list really will be all, as far as God's will goes, and you will be given the knowledge that it is. On the other hand, maybe there will be another thought of something He's trying to tell you, and that thought will be a quiet inspiration from the Holy Spirit. And, don't worry, it will be clear quite soon, either way—no need to run away from home to find out! And know that, with this calm determination to do what you ought, you can be serene in knowing that you are following God's will.

Beauty

he English philosopher Roger Scruton points out that there are two kinds of beauty: (1) the individual, expressive, and revealing gesture, and (2) ordinary harmony and fittingness:

> In everyday life it is the second kind of beauty that is important, and it is exemplified in home building, gardening and the design of squares, houses and streets. It is important because it expresses and amplifies the human desire for settlement, for an environment in which things fit together and people too. It is an instrument of peace.

Summer is winding down here. The bees are working hard, but there won't be a large harvest this year; the weather was too dry. The grass in my backyard has recovered somewhat; in the front, it's still pretty stressed. However, it was never impressive, even on its best days.

I see all the weeds I haven't pulled. I see them clearly. I see my plans, and how I didn't get to many of them. The garden is what it is. I dream in June, and I pick what I can in September: plenty of tomatoes this year, kale always, and raspberries—which are just a treat!

Inside, there are shelves to put up in the laundry room. We could have done that job over Labor Day weekend, but we went to a wedding and took advantage of the proximity to children and grandchildren to make the rounds of their houses. And certainly, that is all good!

I feel the urge coming on to make some quilts, but I'm not quite ready to get started. Hopefully I will be soon; maybe when the cooler weather settles in for real and the tomatoes are safely inside.

Scruton speaks of how ordinary beauty is imperfect, unlike the perfection of the grand gesture. But it reconciles us to our own imperfection while allowing us to remember that there is perfection, giving us a home in the world while reminding us of something beyond.

I believe that these words resonate particularly with the mother and the father of the family, however large or small that family may be. If we serenely pursue this *ordinary* beauty in everyday things and relationships, we build our home. This beauty gives us what Scruton calls settlement, and it gives others settlement as well. It gives them a glimpse of what they can have, themselves, without the anxiety of thinking they must somehow be perfect; paradoxically, it's that very homelikeness, the imperfection, that most reminds them, and us, of the perfection of Heaven.

Take the Reality Test and Straighten Out Your Life

What follows is actually one of my most loved and read posts—not because it's so profoundly written, but just because it's my pep talk about something you don't often hear, which is doing the *least* you can do, not the *most!* The advice in this book is aimed at just this: helping you figure out the details of the two things you simply must get control over in your home—the least you can do—before you can start implementing your life's dreams.

A Practical Resolution

Do you make a bunch of New Year's resolutions every January—resolutions about being a more loving wife and mother, taking care of your husband, keeping your home, and raising your children better? Do you feel a little twinge of doubt (maybe even anxiety) about whether you will keep those resolutions?

I'm going to tell you the secret to doing better. It won't sound like much. But it really works, and I know it does because it's how an overintellectual yet undereducated, impractical, and undisciplined person like me has been able to keep house for all ten of us—not as you see in a magazine; not as you see on some blogs; but enough to be called housekeeping, and on a tight budget too!

And here it is, the incredible secret that no one but me will tell you (unless you call up the friend who told me), and it's really amazing in its simplicity:

> Do better in the minimum that anyone can expect from you, and you will do better in everything else.

This counterintuitive revelation was vouchsafed to me one time when I was really sick. I had given birth to my dear Will, my sixth child. It was a very difficult time that left me recovering from major surgery and double pneumonia. And then I got the flu.

As I lay on the sofa, cradling the phone, lamenting to my friend (whom we call Auntie Sue) about my seriously miserable condition and the mountains of duties beckoning to me—no, hurling themselves at me—and especially the fussy baby who was not quite getting enough milk due to my illness, and my phenomenally, epically, heroically messy, dirty house, she told me this: basically your family needs food and clean laundry from you right now.

Just think about tackling those two things. Just two little tasks that the minimum in housekeeping comprises.

Now, maybe you are not sick and not recovering from a major trauma, and maybe you don't have a passel of kids. And maybe you are sort of a perfectionist and want things really clean and nice, as in a magazine. And maybe you are great at all that and should write a book.

But just maybe you are sort of keeping things going by dint of a boom-and-bust cycle, and no one really knows where you will land today. Maybe you are the way I was, and things are sort of okay but not really the way you want them to be. They will never be perfect—you know that—but they could be better.

Maybe you are like me, and can manage with functioning appliances from the last decade; maybe you don't really care whether things are brand spanking new. But as you look around, the dismalness is starting to get to you.

If the foregoing is the case, I can help you!

Let me ask you: When you are making your resolutions, do you have at the top of your list these two items: feeding and clothing your particular horde? Because if you do, things will go well for you this year. And this is why: no matter what other duties you have, the two biggest challenges you will face will be—ta da!—cooking dinner and doing the laundry.

Conversely, if you have a grip on these two areas—if you have serenity when contemplating the dining table or the washing machine—you will be rational in your approach to all other areas of your life: losing weight, saving money, cleaning up, using your time well, loving your family more, having reading time with your kids, teaching them Latin—you name it! It will all go better if you have order in these two fundamental duties. Or at least our inevitable failures even in this minimum won't upset the peace of our family as much, when we find ourselves knee-deep in horticulture or building violas da gamba or whatever our real passion might be.

I call these duties for a reason. Some mothers look at dinner and clean clothes as chores assigned by a particularly demanding, even cruel parent. This attitude, of course, begs the question of who that parent is! At the same time, in their heart of hearts, these mothers consider the basic duties to be optional.

They whine! They complain! They live with a laundry room that has piles of dirty laundry, and a master bedroom that has baskets of unsorted clean laundry! They get annoyed because their kids are hungry! They hate cooking supper!

They think that someone else will come and fix all this for them (perhaps that invisible yet demanding parent)! They spend money, the household's hard-earned cash, on takeout dinners, or frozen dinners, or drive-through dinners, because they can't figure out what to have for supper; and on new clothes, because the old ones are dirty! And then they say they have to work because they don't like being home and the family is not able to live on one income.

Does this describe you, perhaps a little? Then only you can solve this problem, the problem of your life; and this is the year to do it! I will show you how! Now, I can't show you how to make your home like what you see

21

in a magazine. Can we all remind ourselves that our design mavens may actually have no family and that a crew, perhaps several crews and a staff, make their every whim a reality?

If I can do it, so can you! If a girl (I was nineteen, after all) who got married without really knowing how to sweep can keep house, so can you! If a girl who thought that *Mastering the Art of French Cooking* was a good manual for meal planning can keep three squares on the table within a budget, so can you! If little old me, who would rather read a novel than scrub a toilet (and I don't think I'm alone in this), and who shorted out a whole apartment building ironing a shirt the first year of her marriage, can do it, so can you!

Look at it this way: if you had the profession of managing, say, a hotel, you would be darn sure that, first and foremost, you had a plan, a system, and a clear idea of how you would provide food, clean sheets, and a warm atmosphere for your customers. You would not whine. You would pat yourself on the back for having such a great career! If you did not do this, you would be fired!

Oops—are we in danger of being fired from our jobs as moms? (Hmmm … while pondering our resolutions, we probably should add one to be grateful to the long-suffering good humor of our families!)

Now, I know you are actually not like those babies I describe above, those terrible whiners. And you probably have a better work ethic than I do. But still, have you achieved clarity in these two important areas of your home-keeping duties? That's where I come in, with the clarity.

You know, your whole life is preparation for one thing or another. Jumping forward to when you find yourself a mama, you replace your sponge so that your kitchen will be clean. Your kitchen needs to be clean so that you can cook in it peacefully (and not get people sick or grossed out).

Your baby needs to be nursed (held, cuddled, fed) so that you start a good relationship with him so that later, when you give him a needed punishment, he knows you love him and learns to obey.

He needs to obey you so that he will stay alive long enough for you to tell him a few important things he needs to know before moving out—such as, that he can escape being whipped around by his moods and by his desires (see volume 1).

You plan meals so that you aren't surprised every day by the necessity of making dinner, so that, by the time your kids are old enough to sit at the table and listen, having learned enough manners not to roll their eyes so that they can participate in an actual conversation, your mind is just clear enough to realize that you need your husband there too so that the kids will listen to him, since you can't remember what it is you wanted to say, though you know it was important. Clearly, I am not the expert on these things, but one thing I do know: these are things you must figure out quickly so that you will be ready for the next challenge.

I see many people thinking that those things (cooking, cleaning, laundry, and the rest of the details of order) are ends in themselves, and they aren't. They are some of the practical things that go into mothering and making a home, but they are all for a purpose. Even making a home is for a purpose: so that we have a place in which to find out what God's will for us is and are able to take a stab at carrying it out.

Since one can wear dirty clothes, but one can't last long without food, I will start our journey to Order and Wonder with meals.

PART 2
Menus and Food

Meals don't just appear; food doesn't just buy itself! Nor can we simply be told, "Plan your meals" and know what to do. You need (well, I needed) exact directions and specific strategies. Feeding a family turns out to be a complex enterprise requiring thought and skill—and time.

Becoming competent in this area will happen and I will help.

How to Make Dinner
Every Day and Like It

I have dished up enough grub to satisfy up to eleven people on a regular basis—five of them hungry teenage boys (those were the days when we hosted a couple of boarders too!). I've fed my own seven children, husband, and mother, day in and day out, shopping for them with a bunch of them in tow. (Joys of homeschooling!) And I've been doing this in a semi-quasi-mostly-orderly way for about a quarter of a century.

I've planned meals while pregnant, nursing, convalescent, on the run, and under the weather. I don't always do a great job. Sometimes my family members have looked at me with a "this is your idea of dinner?" look, but usually it gets done, it's usually tasty, it doesn't break the bank—and those are my credentials.

And if you've read volume 1, you can see now how important it is to eat dinner together, at your own table at home, on a regular basis. But making this happen isn't magic, especially when you've also seen the importance of living on one income.

So we will start out here with the most basic issue of this whole project, and hold at bay all provisos and quid pro quos, as the Genie in *Aladdin* says. We will refine. We will be frugal. We will get fancy. We will discuss the ins and outs of deep freezing. We will discuss the true pitfall: eating out.

But for now, let's grapple with the first step.

This step is simply not covered in any of the guides or books or manuals that I have read. Everyone else starts by saying, "Make a week's menus to create a shopping list." That's like saying, "Make a dress for the ball from a pattern" to someone who doesn't know how to sew! They've skipped the important part.

Or these helpful experts give you their menus, which maybe you (or more likely your family) have no interest in; very importantly, as you will see, their menus certainly have nothing to do with what's on sale at your grocery store and don't take into account the schedules of a busy family.

Make Your Menus: The Secret to Successful Meal Planning

How did I come by this secret knowledge? Well, I'm the kind of person who could be found, long ago, *either* serving up Farce de Porc, Pointes d'Asperges au Beurre, and Soubise, *or* staring blankly at a package of frozen ground beef at 5:15 p.m., wondering what the heck to do with it. Not very practical, either way!

Then a more experienced friend told me that I simply had to know what I was going to have for dinner by 10:00 every morning. Good advice.

And then the long-suffering Phil pointed out to me that "we" were spending six hundred dollars a month on groceries. In 1984. For the five of us, three of whom were babies. I cried that day.

But it must have been an angel who whispered to me that if I planned my menus for the week, I'd do better. And I'm here to tell you that if you do nothing else but this one little step, and shop accordingly, you will cut your grocery bill by at least a third.

I once read that the average single American woman buys chicken breasts, broccoli, lettuce, and yogurt. And that's it. Granted, that was single women, but perhaps some of us haven't quite made the transition. Does frozen pizza count as variety if you have a family? I'm afraid not.

Others give you ideas for individual dishes, but I find that whole meals, all planned out, are what make the difference between failure and success. But don't be overwhelmed, because they will be *your* menus, and you won't have to wrack your brains every week to come up with them.

My secret, the key to success at last, is to have a master list of menus (most of which will be fairly simple, even humble) that you created along with your very own family, and you can consult it whenever you need to. You will be confident, knowing that when you plan out this week's offerings, everyone will be pleased, you will use your pantry and other food stores well, and you will shop efficiently.

Simply ask your family and yourself what they like to eat, and write it down! You don't do this every day, of course. No—once and for all, you all brainstorm together and create a Master Menu List. Then you use that to make your weekly or monthly lists, without troubling your family any further, except occasionally when you see their tastes changing or you become inspired.

If you think you get it, then go! If you would like more detail, excruciating detail *and* step-by-step instructions, keep reading.

Eating Out

But first, let me say a few words about eating out, and why your menus need to include things you would normally order in a restaurant.

Eating out (all the time, I mean, and all of these comments include takeout and delivery as well) is … well, it's sort of a snare and a delusion. You think that you can afford it, but that's because you don't put it in your grocery budget. If you did, you'd be appalled.

If you charge your meals, you are probably still paying for things you ate years ago! At normal credit card interest rates, if you carry a balance on your credit card, you might be paying many times what the meal originally cost you. Eating out has ruined many a family's finances. At least if you charge a chair, it isn't gone the next day!

Yet there's something so enticing about being enveloped in the warm, cozy, food-swathed environment of the restaurant. Something so appealing about letting the kids choose what they want. Something so comforting about not having to think about cooking. It makes you so happy.

Eating out is a nice treat—I'm not against it. But let's examine it as a way of life.

Think of what you are missing when you eat or order out several times a week. Let's leave aside the money issue. Let's even leave aside the health issue, important as that is. Let's look only at what we are missing when we don't interact on a daily basis at home.

Kids need to be served balanced, nutritious meals that they basically have to eat without complaining. They shouldn't have choices at a particular meal. (You will ask them their favorite menus—and I will explain this below—and that's enough.) The discipline of eating what's set before you turns your mind to other, more important issues.

Sitting together at home, the whole family is discussing matters of consequence or laughing over common experiences. The members are interacting and getting to know each other (including children getting to know their mother and father!), which also means putting up with each other. Soon the family is making decisions together and building a life together. These are priceless times, incredibly formative, and all too fleeting—and a whole lot of them happen at the dinner table.

Someone, and that someone is you, has to make that all happen, and that means staying out of eateries unless the trip is planned, affordable, and all the more enjoyable. I think that because you also have to taxi people around, go to games, check homework, and do the laundry, a little part of you feels that it's not decisive if you eat out a lot. Please reconsider this. All those other things serve this one thing, your time together, bonding as a family.

But it's true that we are tired and haven't planned well. So let's do that now!

You know what? I found out I could make cheesesteaks (one of my favorite eat-out choices)! I found out I could make guacamole, fish tacos, breadsticks, and onion rings (using the deep fryer I got at a yard sale for seventy-five cents)! I found out my kids love my homemade pizza! I even made a creditable stab at the eggplant salad we had at the divine Persian restaurant in the city.

We don't need no stinkin' restaurants to be happy. We will enjoy these things if we do go out, but as long as I plan well, we can also be happy right here at home.

Master Menu Work Plan

This part is fun and almost feels like work avoidance. Everyone will help you, unlike in the next steps, where you will use the information they have given you so that you always know what your family will be eating and when.

Creating Your Family's Master Menu List

You will need a pen and a few sheets of paper. Any piece of paper will work.

Sit down with your family—all of them. I tend to think things will go better if you haven't just eaten something. On the other hand, it would also help if everyone isn't so hungry that they can't concentrate on talking about food without getting upset.

Ask them this simple question: What are your favorite meals? We'll concentrate on the main meal for now. Stick with me, because this is a process that builds on itself.

Do try to get your family to tell you the whole menu, not just a certain dish. A complete menu means a meal with all its components. This could be three or four dishes in the traditional sense (meat, starch, salad, rolls, for instance) or something more one-dish (spinach lasagna—but don't forget the breadsticks if that is their favorite part). Write all their ideas down.

Getting all this information might take more questions, but it's worth it. Perhaps the family will be most helpful if you make it a game.

Here are some prompts to get everyone to tell you just about everything they like to eat. Let them go right through one category before you ask the next prompt.

- What are your favorite meals right now? (Make sure you write them all down! Make them wait while you do: it helps them remember more.)

- What were your favorite meals when you were young? (This applies more to your husband and you than to the eight-year-old, but I bet the eight-year-old has something to contribute!) What unusual or special meals did your family have growing up? What did your pals growing up have that you remember? Taco salad? Oyster stew at Christmas? Grilled fish? Chicken and dumplings? What did you have with that? Applesauce? Fritters? Squash? Corn on the cob?

- What are your favorite ethnic meals? Chinese? Italian? Greek? Portuguese? Your family includes certain ethnic traditions, I'll wager: be sure to include those, whatever they may be, with whatever goes with them. Since I grew up with a lot of Egyptian food, I include my favorite dishes, and they have become my family's favorites also. My husband is quite Irish, and we enjoy a boiled supper with brown bread as well as some old Boston favorites (baked beans, fish pie).

- When you went to a friend's house, what were you served that you enjoyed, that maybe we don't usually have? A casserole? Fried chicken? Soup? What did the mom serve with that? Biscuits?

- What meals in books or movies appeal to you? (Think *Farmer Boy*, Dickens, *Anne of Green Gables*, Dorothy Sayers, *Big Night*, etc.)

- When you go to a restaurant, what do you most like to order? If you could go to any restaurant, what type would it be? If you could order anything without regard to cost, what would it be?

Onion rings? Chicken Caesar salad? Beef Kempinski? Duck à l'Orange? Cheesesteak? Shrimp cocktail? The last few times you went to a restaurant, what did you order that you really liked? Fajitas? A deep-fried onion flower? A cheeseburger?

- What are your favorite "easy" supper meals (that are not spaghetti or pizza)? Sloppy joes? Hot dogs? Breakfast for supper? Fish tacos?
- What are your favorite fancy meals? Roast beef with Yorkshire pudding? Salmon and peas? A turkey dinner? Peking duck?

When you are finished, you should have a fairly long list of menu ideas. Take your list and sit quietly by yourself. If any menu reminds you of another menu, write that one down too (for instance, if a lasagna dinner reminds you of a baked ziti dinner, write that one down). It's very important that you try to put them in menu form. If someone says "spaghetti," try to get him to tell you if he would like salad or green beans, garlic bread or rolls with that. Don't stress out; you can easily add ideas later as they occur to you.

Now as a final step, you could put all this data into the computer and organize it by type, or you can wait for the next step in the plan, which has more tips, to do that.

I got myself a durable and waterproof binder and some of those nifty plastic sleeves to put papers in, and I made a place for all my food info. Don't worry, we'll come back to this. And remember: yes, if I can do it, so can you!

Congratulations! This was the hard part, and it was fun!

Why My Menu Planning Is Different

It took me a while to realize that I needed to write down detailed menus when planning meals for the week, which is why I emphasize this method here. For a long time, I'd just jot down "pork chops" and then stand in the produce aisle, getting all wound up inside my head, probably thanks to dear Julia Child, that culinary paragon who both taught me to cook via her *Mastering the Art of French Cooking* and rendered me a bit of an overthinker in the kitchen.

Sometimes you just need to write down "broccoli" next to your "Chicken casserole" so that you can move on with your life as lived in the grocery store. Sometimes you are in such a broccoli rut that you need to write down "salad with pear, blue cheese, and pecans" or even "chou-fleur blanchi" if you remember what that means, so that your poor family can move on with *their* lives at the dinner table.

For shopping purposes, you also need to be able to see at a glance of your list of menus just how many heads of lettuce you will need (because you have actually scheduled salad for four out of the seven nights) and whether to check the cornmeal supply (because you want cornbread with your chili, days from now). Those items won't turn up if you haven't thought out the whole menu, and efficiency will suffer.

After working on this menu making, we will have learned about ourselves that we can't look at a package of chicken thighs in the grocery store and somehow, at that moment, know what to do with them and what to serve them with — not while quelling two toddlers and figuring out unit prices of boneless versus boned, we can't.

The grocery store is not where we magically become inspired.

Do you realize that everything — *everything* — hinges on knowing what is for dinner?

What is the difference between a reasonably tidy home and living in a pit dug out by spatially challenged warthogs? Between being able to have a good homeschooling day and feeling as if you are in charge of a bunch of illiterate savages who figure out the speed of passing trains with knotted ropes and their fingers? Between starting a creative project of any kind, working on it, and finishing it, and feeling as if all you do is go in and out of the grocery store?

The difference is knowing that dinner is under control.

Why is this? Because, and I realize this might be news to you, so hang on: *dinner happens every day.*

Now, one reason I started writing for others about my menu system is that I often read elsewhere about people's meal ideas, and they always amount to something like, "Make your menus, shop, and cook." It did seem as if *something* was left out.

On the other hand, I was somewhat daunted by the amazing proliferation of really wonderful blogs, magazines, and books with barges of recipes.

Yet recipes are not really the issue, since the chances are slim that you have the ingredients on hand to make something truly different and exciting, and how can you either rely solely on "things you have on hand" or shop effectively for more variety without knowing which recipe or sort of food you will make on which day?

In a nutshell, I'm telling you that it's not enough to say, as articles I have read do say, "Monday we'll have spaghetti; Tuesday we'll have rotisserie chicken from the grocery store; Wednesday we'll eat out; Thursday we'll have pasta; Friday we'll have leftovers; Saturday I get the day off from cooking; and Sunday my mother will rescue me."

We can see that the expert here is hardly cooking at all. Going by this list, she's spending a lot of money on prepared food, planning on eating out because of her inadequate plan, and leaving herself open to an emergency trip to the store or yet another restaurant outing with that deceptive "leftovers" entry.

Another source tells you simply to come up with a bunch of menus without regard to the day of the week. As I contemplate a different schedule every day, brought on by the plethora of children around me, I wonder what her life is like. I also wonder if her plan is too much cooking, since, with my detailed plan, I can *schedule* making chicken, broccoli, and rice one day and using the extra I've planned on in a casserole a few days later. Now that's "leftovers."

Most "weekly" menu plans I have seen factor in a day *or more* of eating out. Maybe those writers are living in New York City, where eating out is a must, as far as I can tell; or maybe they just can't imagine cooking seven days a week, or maybe they haven't checked their credit card statement lately. But a family living on one income doesn't plan to eat out once a week. That is not a hardship, however. Once you learn to plan, you eat very well and come to see normal restaurant fare as not worth the expense.

Think of it this way: Taking three children to a fast-food restaurant is the equivalent of purchasing a couple of nice steaks—the ultimate fast food at home!—grilling them, and serve them sliced with baked potatoes, salad, and garlic bread, with money to spare. And there would be leftover steak for sandwiches the next day.

Or if time is the issue, purchasing a bunch of cold cuts and making subs to go would leave you with plenty of dollars left over for your ice cream fund. Buy cashews, dried apricots, and string cheese, and everyone would be satisfied until they reach home, with money and extra snacks to spare.

Anyway, try using my plan for making the week's menus. The key is not to think up things all the time. Spend some quality time planning and render them already thought up.

Menus versus Mixing and Matching

Why do I insist on spelling out a menu for each day's dinner? Wouldn't it be just as easy to sort of mix and match, putting together a week's worth of ideas and then just deciding at the moment what to make?

Maybe for some people it is, and building in flexibility can only help you, but if you have a busy household, try to follow the liturgical calendar, and also have a tendency to space out over a good book or phone conversation with a distant friend, my way, where you think out all the elements in advance, might be for you.

Remember, you don't have to make the same menus I do. After you have made your very own basic menus, as described earlier, according to your own preferences, you'll find that you make better use of all the inspiration that surrounds us in the form of magazines, online sites, and cookbooks.

Perhaps your whole family is invited out for dinner. Lucky you! You get an extra day in your meal planning! Push everything down the list or skip over one of the night's menus.

Some flexibility comes from *unexpected* leftovers. If you end up with enough food from one night to carry you through another, that's a bonus day in your menu plan (distinct from planned leftovers). Another use for unforeseen leftovers is to pool them for "leftovers day," aka "bits and pieces," "fab buffet," or whatever name you give this meal for maximum family approval. Pull out everything, warm up what needs to be warmed, arrange it tastefully and appealingly, and let people take what they want.

Supplement with a good loaf of homemade bread, butter, and cheese if you need it. Again, just juggle your days and pocket the bonus.

Cheap and Not Cheap

The next step in making that master plan isn't maybe what you are thinking.

The next step is to get these menus sorted out into "cheap" and "not cheap" (or use any words that appeal to you—you might prefer "affordable" and "fancy" or something less abrupt), because when you are managing a household on one income, you need to have good control over your food expenses. You need many thrifty menu ideas, meals that appeal but don't cost much. And they need to be written down in advance, because the enemy of thrift is last-minute deciding, which always defaults to spending more.

The exercises below will explain it to you if you'd like more information, and there are examples.

Simply think about what you would make if you had only a small amount of money to spend, and put those menus in one list. Think about what's more elegant, special, and expensive, and put those in another list. It helps to do it in a computer document so you can shuffle them around.

That's all there is to this step, but it's an important one.

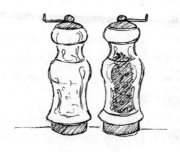

Menu Planning

Now that you have that list of menus or at least a few grudgingly imparted vague ideas garnered from your family, and you've begun to ponder the importance of eating meals at home, at the table, together, do some brainstorming. Get out your recipe clippings and your cooking magazines. Open up your inspiration file or site. Flip through and write down anything that seems as if it would work for a family meal. Make sure whatever you write down is in complete menu form, for the *menu* is the key to good planning.

And as I said, as you go through your list, try to figure out which menus seem to be fairly inexpensive. These will all go into one document (do it on your computer if you want and file it under "recipes" as "cheap menus").

In this section I will give you examples. They tend to the very traditional "American" sort of category because those are the tried-and-true backbone of feeding a family in our country.

Believe me, I can get just as fancy, global, and eclectic as the next person, but in my examples, I have kept it somewhat plain so that you can see that not every meal has to be super inventive. My sense is that the consumerist-driven food industry has exhausted us by making us feel that every meal must be some sort of culinary epiphany, when really, what is important is that the food is of good quality and the company is loving. These are just examples—in your own mind you can easily translate them into what you have come up with and what your own cultural background suggests as "plain family fare."

Thrifty Menus

Here are some examples from my own "Cheap Menus" list—meals designed to make the most, especially, of a small amount of meat or none at all, and still be nutritious and tasty:

Sausages or hot dogs
Baked beans
Cole slaw
Brown bread

Chicken Caesar Salad
Oven fries
Garlic bread

Chicken enchiladas
Orange and romaine salad
Cornbread

Spaghetti and meatballs
Green salad
Bread

Spinach lasagna
Mixed stir-fry vegetables with ginger and soy sauce
Bread

Chicken and broccoli stir-fry
Rice

Quiche
Three-bean salad
Rolls

Cannellini bean, sausage, and kale soup
Grilled cheese sandwiches

Chicken noodle soup
Pumpkin muffins and cheddar cheese

Pizza (homemade, of course—"bought" is not cheap!)
Salad

Chili
Cornbread
Zucchini in cheese sauce
Rice

Bean burritos
Corn
Guacamole

Do you get the idea of how these are thrifty menus? One chicken breast can be plunked down in front of one person, and then it will serve only that person. *Or* you can put it in a big salad or an enchilada casserole, and it will serve three or four people.

Notice that I have included everything I would serve at that meal. Notice that every meal includes bread, pretty much. In a large family, this is a must. You will avoid a lot of grief if you are not worried that your child is starving by having only a taste of each dish; the bread and butter will see him through. Your teenagers need rolls and butter.

Of course, you can swap things out, but believe me, food planning is simply easier if you start with menus, rather than individual dishes. If you can arrange the menus by type (Italian, Chinese, bean, chicken, and so forth) the process is even easier.

Regular Menus

You can also think in terms of the season. Many of these menus I've mentioned seem suited to the school year and cold weather. When summer comes, you will add to the list with all the great grilled foods, salads, and cold suppers you will suddenly think of (and inspiration for which will be all around you in magazines and on food sites).

And that's another thing about menu making: often I've found that I just can't think of anything to make for supper—have drawn a complete blank on any foods at all—because the season is changing and I just haven't realized it. At the end of summer, I get energized for menu making if I stop thinking about grilled chicken and start thinking about soup—and vice versa.

Make a list of "regular" menus with main dishes such as stew, pot roast, pork roast, chicken bake, roast chicken, and so on—menus with meat as the main course, so not thrifty in themselves—and be sure to add the sides that you enjoy.

Here are some examples of less cheap weekday menus, which I would suggest alternating with the more frugal ones:

Pork chops with apples and onions
Green beans
Roasted squash
Rolls

Honey-ginger chicken
Rice
Broccoli
Rolls

Beef stew with potatoes and carrots
Green salad
Rolls

Grilled steak tips
Garlic mashed potatoes
Grilled Italian vegetables
Focaccia

Pulled-pork sandwiches
Cole slaw
Oven fries

Special-Occasion Menus

Next, make a list of the special-occasion menus that you and your family have come up with; they are more Sunday fare or menus you would make only for holidays or other special occasions. Keeping a record of your festive meals makes menu planning much easier the next time you do it.

Here is an example of a restaurant meal that would be a little pricier than your normal home-cooked fare and takes a lot more preparation for each element. Note, however, that making it at home costs a fraction of what you would pay at the restaurant.

T-bone steak
Mushrooms and onions
Salad with blue cheese dressing
Twice-baked potatoes
Parker House rolls

Here is a Thanksgiving menu (my own Thanksgiving menu has many more dishes, but this is the basic thing we mean when we say "turkey dinner"):

Roasted turkey with gravy
Cranberry sauce
Squash
Mashed potatoes
Brussels sprouts with chestnuts
Potato rolls

Here are two Sunday menus:

Baked ham
Roasted sweet potatoes
Green beans
Applesauce
Biscuits

Roasted chicken
Roasted squash
Kale salad
Rolls

Any menus that you make need to be what you and your family like. I would also encourage you to make them doable. If you like to get fancy (and I often do), you can embellish, of course. But so often with a busy family, we are rushing and tired; keeping expectations (for yourself!) reasonable is the difference between success and failure.

Cookbooks such as *Joy of Cooking* and the *Better Homes and Gardens Cookbook* have menu sections, and you should consult them—they have gotten me out of a rut many a time. However, those books have to appeal to a wide range of tastes and unknown desires, whereas you are free to leave out things that no one in your family likes and put high on the list things they do like! It's your own personal compendium, and no two families' lists will be the same.

These menu lists are the backbone of your weekly menu planning. For a while, you should consult them faithfully, and then, voilà! you will have memorized them!

Writing Your Menus for a Given Week

You want to make menus for *at least* a week. It's more than possible, as you get good at the process, to make them for two weeks or a month. But for now, let's just get the week under our belt, on the theory that it's a doable goal that won't overwhelm you.

With your menu lists in hand, all printed out, make your plan for the week. Yes, you are ready to do it. And it won't be that hard, because you already have a "stockpile" of ideas that you know your family likes.

What do you need to do this? You could use an Excel spreadsheet, a PowerPoint presentation, a PDF file that you download off an organizational website, or any other technologically advanced method you choose. But I usually grab a scrap of paper and jot down:

M:

T:

W:

Th:

F:

S:

S:

M:

I like to make them for one extra day so that I have that leeway if I don't get to the store. I can always roll the plan for that day into the next weekly list.

Then I look at my calendar to see which days I'll be in the car at four in the afternoon rather than able to be cooking at home; which days I know I'll be tired because I have a meeting the night before; and which days I know I will have time to bake or roll up tortillas or something like that.

Then I choose my menus accordingly. In another section, I will go into depth on what I call "Save a Step Cooking"—making extra of various things and then using them at various times. For now, let's just go through the week together.

Here's my thought process, which I hope will give you the idea of how to make a week's worth of menus that will fit your schedule, pantry, and energy level like a glove:

Monday: This is a day I when spend a lot of time in the morning cleaning up from the weekend and making sure I am up to date on my bills and checking account. Mondays are a day of anxiety over the coming week's demands or at least a sense of extreme busyness for most people, so it's good to have something easy and hearty for dinner. I usually have an Italian-American type of dish on this day. Knowing that I will probably be making spaghetti with meatballs (that I have already frozen) or pasta with meat sauce or easy no-boil lasagna makes this day a cinch.

- Spaghetti with meat sauce: I've already frozen my browned and seasoned meat that I did in one big session—more on that later.
- Salad: if my stores of fresh veggies have gone down, I can easily serve carrot sticks instead.
- Garlic bread: I stockpile enough bread to know I can pull a loaf out of the freezer, and if I'm short on time, a nice warm loaf without the garlic is fine too, if a bit disappointing.

Tuesday: On this day I teach a religion class in the late afternoon. I can do my grocery shopping in the morning, but I can't do any cooking in the afternoon. I like to use something left over from Sunday on this day.

- Leftover stew: I make enough for my Sunday meal and for at least one more meal.
- Noodles (the stew goes further if you serve it *over* the noodles; just make sure you have lots of gravy)
- Green beans tossed with olive oil and salt
- Bread: I make all our bread other than bagels and pita—and sometimes I make the pita!— and usually have a bunch in the freezer. If not, I can easily make biscuits.

Wednesday: I like to serve soup on Wednesdays. It's a good way to be simple in our eating habits, and it leaves me time to bake and do other things on this day when I don't *have* to go out until 3:30. When you serve soup, you might want to have some little nibbly things such as a bowl of peanuts, tortilla chips and hummus, and cheese and crackers out on the counter for the older ones who need more calories. Those things can be added to the table after the littles have had some soup and bread.

- Split pea soup (using a hambone from the freezer)
- Cornbread

Thursday: Since our meals have been simple for the first days of the week, I tend to be more elaborate on Thursdays. Kids are ready for a hearty meal, and its leftovers are helpful on the weekend, when more people are around. However, we have a lot going on on Thursdays. I have a busy afternoon that never ends. It's also a good day for a chicken menu, most of which can be popped into the oven and left to roast without much oversight.

- Roasted chicken: Never, ever roast just one chicken! The leftover meat can be frozen and pulled out of the freezer another day; the carcasses can go into the stockpot for broth.
- Squash or roasted yams: leftover from Sunday, or roast along with the chicken in their own pan.
- Salad
- Biscuits, made from my homemade mix (found in the breakfast recipes in the appendices)

Friday: We go meatless on Fridays except during the Octave of Easter and on solemnities. Almost always we have homemade pizza and salad. Occasionally we have a fish dish or a pasta dish, so I'm highlighting that here.

- Salmon cakes with yogurt cumin sauce: I keep canned salmon in the pantry for this simple meal; the sauce is just plain yogurt with cumin and lemon juice.
- Waldorf salad: all the ingredients store very well for when you're low on fresh veggies: apples, walnuts or pecans, celery, raisins or dried cranberries, tossed with a little mayo, vinegar, and salt.
- Rice
- Pita bread

Saturday: Usually we have leftover pizza for lunch, which is pretty hearty (I make an extra one with meat on Friday night for this purpose). So, by Saturday night, we don't need anything too filling or complicated. In addition, I've usually worked hard on chores and don't want to cook! My husband grew up having hot dogs and baked beans on Saturdays. I'm not a huge fan, but it *is* easy! If we have lots of leftovers, we'll have a "bits and pieces" night—meaning a meal in which I bring out all the little leftovers there may be and set them out, along with good bread and an assortment of cheeses, saving those hot dogs for a busy day when I really can't cook.

- Hot dogs with buns
- Baked beans (homemade or from a can)
- Cole slaw (homemade)
- Oven fries

Sunday: It's worth it to do a traditional big Sunday dinner. You will get at least one more meal out of it in the coming busy week; maybe more, if you play your cards right. More importantly (and sometimes we do have something very simple), it's good to have a family day, emphasizing being together and resting. A roast is restful to make — more so than a casserole! Try to make something with bones you can use for soup another day. To make your Sunday even more restful, prep the work on Saturday so that all you have to do is turn on the oven.

- Pork roast: Make extra for barbecued-pork sandwiches later in the week.
- Mashed potatoes: Make extra for shepherd's pie later in the week; use cooking water for bread making.
- Broccoli: Make double for broccoli soup for lunches.
- Rolls: Keep a lot of homemade rolls in the freezer!

Monday: I like to make a "weekly" menu of a little more than a week, in case I get thrown off somewhere. Having an extra meal up your sleeve without any extra preparation really helps.

- Chili: It's easy to make a large amount and freeze what's left over; serve with sour cream and cheese.
- Rice
- Orange slices
- Guacamole
- Tortilla chips

These menus are what the Lawler Family tends to eat when we are not being fancy. You can certainly use them, but you should feel free to make menus that reflect what *your* family likes to eat, for that is the entire point of being successful at menu making!

An Example of Planning Menus around Activities

I'll show you why I like to assign a specific menu to a specific day, going so far as to write down, in my menu plan, what is going on that day—in other words, making the menus part of the activity calendar. Here's how I prepared for a week in the life of one spacey mom, when I still had children at home and many activities. Imagine we're sitting down on Sunday evening, March 15, to make the menus for a Monday shopping trip:

Tuesday, March 17, is St. Patrick's Day, and I will be out in the late afternoon, not coming home until 5:30. I'll be making what I always make on this day: corned beef dinner and Irish soda bread. But I spell it out on my menu, because if I don't possess cabbage, red potatoes, and buttermilk, then this simple dinner will not come off! The detailed menu enables me to make a detailed shopping list *without having to rethink everything.*

Wednesday, March 18, is my son Will's birthday. I have to remember to ask him what he wants for dinner (I guess I'll catch him after his soccer practice), and I have to schedule baking a cake. I also have to get Bridget from choir practice to dance practice and won't be home until 7:15 p.m.

Thursday is the feast of St. Joseph. This glorious saint, wonderful protector of the family, of virgins, of the Church, of the soul—intercessor to God for all our daily needs—deserves a proper commemoration. I want to prepare for that. But it's a day when I have a religion class to teach in the afternoon and Bridget's dance class from 6:00 until 7:30 with a half-hour drive each way. And I have to be at a committee meeting at 7 p.m. in the next town. Great! I'll bilocate! I can do this! Or maybe not. All right, I'll have a lasagna in the oven and good ice cream in the freezer.

On Friday, we will have a Lenten supper with friends. Again, simple: I can make soup and bread, and people will bring things to contribute—but I'd better be ready. I'll be gone all morning with Bridget's orchestra.

And this schedule represents only the ridiculous activities of two children, one of whom can drive himself! I remember when I had five children playing soccer (three on travel teams), three in dance (obviously they overlapped, but still) and on and on. And on top of everything, I'm someone who exhorts others not to overschedule children. Dinner must be served, though.

What do you do about games, meetings, classes, and errands? We simply cannot afford drive-through for those days. No wonder people think they can't afford to give up the wife's income: they are spending it all on activities and fast food.

I know that on Saturday I won't want to be cooking anything complicated. It will be a day for franks and beans (which my husband loves, luckily!).

Sunday we will have another family visit for dinner. I want to make the ham-and-leek pie that came out so well on the feast of St. David (patron of Wales). The ham and the pie crust are in the freezer, but I have to put leeks on the grocery list.

Sure, there can be interchangeability, both in the days and in the dishes. Just because you wrote "salad" doesn't mean you can't do green beans. But if you have the plan written out according to the activities and events you have on the roster, you will experience the satisfaction of order.

Plan for a Week or a Month?

I suggest beginning by planning a week's worth of meals, but once you are used to working this way, going by the month might work better. When I had all my family about me, I planned menus for a month. It was more effective in terms of effort to put in the work all at once, and by not starting from scratch every time but working from your trusty menu list, you soon realize that the meals are on a basic rotation that makes planning ahead easy.

Lunches

Lunch is a touchy subject for me because I detest it. I can hardly even say it. Are you ready for "br-lunch?" "su-lunch?" I am always blurting. I like breakfast and supper. I don't like lunch!

So, as with all the other resisted-yet-unavoidable things we do, we need a plan. Those of us at home eat leftovers that aren't earmarked for future suppers. That third of a pan of lasagna, a bit of meat and a bunch of rice that can be heated up together, a few meatballs that can be sliced up and tossed on leftover pasta. If you don't like making sandwiches, it's *even more* important to make more than you plan on eating at supper so that you have something to eat the next day at lunch.

Important note: these little tidbits are not dreary at all if they were well cooked to begin with, and crucially, *if the first meal had not been previously frozen.* Leftovers of food that was already not fresh will indeed be dreary. This fact is one of the main reasons that I endorse what I call Save a Step Cooking as opposed to freezer cooking, but more on that below.

A big pot of macaroni and cheese will be supper and lunch for a few days.

Soup is a great lunch dish; it's very flexible, as you can always add a little water, broth, or milk to stretch it.

The occasional quesadilla or salad rounds out the menu plan here. And yes, sometimes I make sandwiches, grumble, grumble.

On Saturdays, when I would rather walk barefoot on tiny swords than make lunch (as opposed to my normal weekday aversion), we have leftover pizza from the night before. Making that one extra pizza is so worth it for the next day, when you are knee-deep in chores and errands. And if takeout pizza is your fallback during the week (because you didn't plan menus), it will be enjoyed. It can be rounded out with other leftovers or a peanut-butter sandwich for a still-hungry child.

Again, make your grocery list with *your* favorite lunch menus in mind. You should know how many loaves of bread you need in a week (and if you make bread, how many sacks of flour!), how much ham, how many blocks of cheese, how many cans of tuna, how many packages of pasta—the things you need for each lunch each day.

On Packing Lunches: A Secret to Keeping Your Sanity

When the kids were packing lunches for school, and I had up to six people heading out the door with a brown bag, I realized something important: don't expect to make lunches during breakfast. It's a bad idea.

The counters are already strewn with bagels, butter, eggs, cereal, and milk. Add to that mayo, ham, plastic bags, chips, and all the rest, and you will spend the rest of the morning just putting things away. And you'll be cranky while you do it and after everyone leaves, because the breakfast- and lunch-making scene is so unpleasant and chaotic.

No. Make lunch at lunchtime, the day before. While you are making sandwiches for those at home, make them for the next day as well! While you are heating soup, get lunches ready for the brown-baggers! At the very least, make them at night before bed. Do whatever it takes to avoid the morning chaos.

I like to make them myself or delegate the task to a responsible older child, because it's the most efficient and frugal use of the food for me to oversee and manage the preparations. The children can't be expected to use that last chicken breast to make chicken salad. No kid is going to know to put the extra half a slice of ham on each sandwich to avoid leaving behind a slice and a half, good for nothing. Something will end up shoved to the back of the refrigerator if you are not there to supervise.

But, once the sandwiches (or at least chicken salad) are made and wrapped or discussed with a competent executor, it's up to your children to get a bag and put into it a piece of fruit, some snacks, a cookie, and the sandwich. Keep a good supply of brown bags in a handy spot. You children can even get a napkin. They can do it.

And they have to be sternly warned never to throw good food away! "Give that sandwich to a classmate and then tell me if you are getting too much or don't like something." (Not that they are allowed to be super picky, but if there is a genuine distaste for mustard or meatloaf, they'd better let me know and not just throw it away!)

Frugal Grocery-List Making

ow we somehow have to get from a nice, tidy menu list to having food in the house with which to prepare all those meals. And if you're like me, with a strong preference for reading a book, taking a nap, or really anything other than figuring this stuff out, and, to boot, you have a bunch of kids, no money, and a fair amount of homeschooling thrown in, you might like to know how to approach the grocery list.

Buy Low, Sell (Eat) High

First, when I'm making the menus, I start with those that *must* be made this week because (1) something needs to be eaten or it will spoil, (2) someone needs some particular dish or *he* will expire ("Make meatball subs or I will expire"), or (3) something in my freezer might as well be taken advantage of because nothing like it is on sale this week.

In my mind, this way of doing things is related to the economic principle that one must buy low, sell high. Just as you don't go out and buy stocks when they are at their highest price—necessitating a sale later when the price is low—so you don't use food willy-nilly but try to always make the most of the lowest-priced food you can obtain or have obtained so that you can eat high (eat well!). Since we consume food (and thus can't sell it later for a profit), it's a little different, but this is how I think of it. That roast that's in the freezer, the one you bought on sale three months ago, will serve you well this week when there is no sale roast to be had in the stores.

So much for what's already on hand. To make my weekly menu, I need the flyers for the grocery stores I know I want to go to—the ones I know have reasonable and not inflated prices across the board. I make my remaining menus based on what is on sale. (Remember, as you do this, that your master list is so you don't churn your wheels every week, getting deeper into a rut of not knowing what's for dinner. Pull it out every time you plan your weekly menus and shopping. I often have to remind myself that I have already thought things through, and making menus shouldn't be a new experience every week!)

Aha! I see my handy local market has ham for seventy-nine cents a pound; we are having ham for Sunday dinner next week for sure, and I am confident I have several ways to use it on my master list. If nothing else, buy at least one for the freezer so that you can buy low and sell (eat) high another day. (In the section on organizing food, I will address the issue of where to store all this food.)

You should quickly be able to fill your menu list with foods that you already have on hand that you "bought low" *and* with things you will "buy low" this week. In a few weeks, you should have a good enough stockpile, in pantry and freezer, to be able to do most of your shopping with sale items only, or at least at your targeted low price. And that is how you permanently lower your food budget while eating very well.

If you have no extra money to spare for this project, put the money you save by buying sale items into your next week's budget. Then use that little extra to buy more sale items. That way, you will soon be ahead of your budget.

Now examine every item on every menu. Do you have enough flour to make this week's bread? Do you have enough beans for the soups you've planned? Celery? Noodles? And so on down the list. Your menu plan will be derailed if it turns out that you can't make something because you lack an essential ingredient.

Once you have all the items for your menus, go over your needs for other meals and snacks. You should have some idea of how many eggs, gallons of milk, boxes of crackers, and so forth you go through during the week. If you don't have any idea, that's something for you to observe in the next month and ascertain. All that goes on the list, and off you go!

This trip is your main shopping at the store that has the best overall prices. You can stop at a store for some specials if it is more or less on your way to somewhere else.

Every week, I stop at a store that has good unadvertised markdowns on meat, but I know that bargains on other items await me elsewhere.

If you are lucky, you have a child who enjoys scouring the flyers for good prices, understands unit pricing, and gets the "lowest regular price" idea. His reward is that he will come across something he wants that you might have overlooked, and he can put it on your list. One of my children helped me like this, and it made list making so much easier! (He went on to be an economics journalist!)

Keep in mind that if you are spending hundreds of dollars a month on groceries, you need to think big. Saving a buck here or there isn't as important as saving on *everything* you buy. It's also not as important as getting a real bargain *all* the time on *all* your meat or produce.

Don't wear yourself out and use up a lot of fuel running around, and don't go to a place just because it's closest or is a big-box store. The pasta at my local big-box store is more than 20 percent higher per pound than at my local market, and the tuna too. But the dog food is much cheaper. Don't be tricked by their tricky flyers. Use your common sense and your price notebook! (Do take note of a particular store that has a low price on, for instance, milk, but not much else. Perhaps your husband can make a stop once a week to stock up just on milk.)

Start-Up Costs; or, Don't
Use Up Your Pantry Supplies

Your motivating idea should be to buy low (get stuff on sale, marked down, on clearance, at a good price—consistently) and sell high. Again, the sell-high bit doesn't exactly apply, because you aren't selling your food; you are eating it. But to me it just means "eat high"—eat well despite high prices—and "time is money"—consider your time something you have to buy at a high cost, and use it well.

Here's another economics principle for you: keep start-up costs low. Start-up costs are the up-front expenditures made in a business before delivering the product to the customer. You are the business. The customer is your family. The product is the meal. The costs are in dollars and time!

Now to this one, there are two parts. One we have talked about, and it's mainly about time: saving a step every time you cook. But there are other start-up costs that are real costs, in actual dollars.

Adding to Your Stores

Does it make sense to use up your pantry items entirely?

Sometimes I read the advice, supposedly frugal, to use up everything you have on hand before buying more food. And I don't think this is actually frugal in the long run.

Now, to be clear, I realize that it happens that you are at the end of the money and have to be clever. I've been there too, and I think it's worthwhile to know how, in an emergency, to get by for a while on what you have.

The problem, though, with using up all the beans, rice, and onions you have as a regular practice, before buying anything more, is that very soon you will need those things and not necessarily be able to get them at a good price! You will have to start up your process of building the pantry all over again, which costs too much in time as well as money.

So I want to talk about the normal case, which is that you have a certain limited amount to spend every month, and you need to make the most of it.

For long-term frugality, constantly adding to your stores by buying low is the best way to squeeze every penny. It has to do with start-up costs! You have to look at everything you buy as representing a certain amount of time and effort as well as money. You hunted down the best price for flour, sugar, beans, coffee, canned tomatoes, pasta, oil, and so on. You invested in a certain quantity of these things—more than you need for the present moment, to tide you over to the next sale—with the idea of saving money overall.

With the money you save buying these things at a low price, you are able to buy other things at a low price as well, stocking up on meat, vegetables in season, and fancy things like nuts, chocolate, dried fruits, and so on. Very likely there will be a time lag between getting them into your pantry and the next time the price will be right.

Meanwhile, you do your weekly shopping, continuing to roll your extra money (gained from stocking up on low-priced items) over into supplies for future meals. And it's essential that you do this if you are able to, because every week there will be some things that are priced low that you can stock up on. Some weeks are better than others, and it is true that you can spend more or less depending on how good the prices are, if you are willing to use what you have.

Saving Money Takes Time

It's hard to start doing all this. It takes effort. You have to change your thinking. You have to research prices. It's a start-up cost.

It gets easier if you don't have to do it all at once. It's easier if you don't have to get the machinery grinding up from zero each time!

Now, your menu plans, in addition to the goal of providing interesting, nutritious dishes for your family in a timely manner, should also take into consideration this ongoing process of using your own stores of food to the best possible advantage ("selling high").

If there are bags of frozen broccoli (from when you cooked extra when making a side dish) at the bottom of your freezer (I will tell you below how to organize your deep freezer!), *and* whole chickens are on sale this week, then I would plan to make a big pot of broccoli soup. That way, you take advantage of both the stash you have and the bargain you can get.

Your menus shouldn't just be a reflection of what you feel like eating that week but also a judicious use of what you have on hand and what's on sale this week.

More on Lists and Shopping

Time to examine your list. It's essential to organize your list in the order you will shop for things, *not* in the order they occur to you. Arrange your list by aisle and fill in categories as you think of them. If you have a random list going, take a moment to rewrite it by grocery-store aisle; it will save you lots of time at the store. You have a mental picture of the store (enhance it by looking at those signs they have hanging over each aisle). You don't need a specially printed list; you just need to make your list visual.

If something is on sale, buy a few extra at least—if the price is below the lowest *normal* price for the item (see "Price Notebook," below). Your pantry should have depth to it, so that you are not always shopping for staples, but replenishing when sale prices are good. This is the backbone of saving money on groceries, and you won't see the effect for many months. But then your food budget will stabilize at a lower level.

When turkeys are on sale at Thanksgiving, buy a frozen one and put it in your deep freezer (at the bottom). When ground beef is on sale, buy twice as much as you need for that week. When zipper freezer bags are on sale, buy extra so that you have freezer bags to store your ground beef in!

When tomato paste is on sale, buy twice as much as you need—more if your budget allows for it—and store it in your pantry.

Beware of the sneak attack, price-wise, in the staples department. If you save on ground beef but at the same store pay much more for flour, sugar, canned beans, canned tomatoes, bread, milk, and so forth, then you haven't saved, and it would be worth it to shop where the basics are lower, even if the ground beef isn't on sale.

Big-Box Stores

I used to shop at the big-box store when I had more people to buy for. If your household is little, it's not worth the membership fee, unless you have a pet (pet food is a lot cheaper there) or the store sells alcohol (the ones near us don't). When I had enough shopping for both the big-box store and the supermarket, I could discipline myself to buy only the things that are truly cheaper at each. If you do all your shopping in a big-box store, you will spend much more. As an example, the last time I checked, although flour and sugar were cheaper there, pasta, rice, and other staples were considerably more. (This depends on your region, of course.)

Since right nearby is a good, large, cheap grocery store, I make the special trip to that one to get my large quantities, figuring that the membership fee goes a long way in paper products and other things I would have saved on.

Again, if you have a large family and pets, it could be worth it to go there. How to tell? You must know your prices!

Price Notebook

Do you know your grocery stores' prices well? To save money, you must know your prices! You do this by keeping a price notebook (until you eventually memorize the prices). Why? Let's work through it.

Grocery store A has a name that is designed to appeal to people like you and me, making us think we will save money there—something like "Super Thrifty" or "Cheapo's." And indeed, their flyer prominently displays seemingly amazing deals. Pork chops for ninety-nine cents? Chicken legs for thirty-five cents? Cheap. (Well, around here it is.) But I'm telling you, everything else in that store is much more than even at "Elegant Market"!

That means that unless you are willing to go there for the pork chops and go to another store where you know the prices on all the other things you need are 20 percent on average cheaper, you will end up spending more.

For instance, the same store advertising the cheap chicken legs has the mayonnaise you usually buy, and it's fifty cents *more* there than at store B. And the same for 90 percent of what you are going to put in your cart. Store A even advertises that mayo in its flyer *as if* it's a bargain! It's a total mind game—they are counting on your *not knowing* how much you pay for all those other things, the hundred little things you fill your cart with. They put the price of a dozen eggs in that flyer, as if it's a low price. They are assuming you don't know the average price of eggs in your area! Do you?

If you did your weekly shopping at this store, you would spend a lot more than anywhere else, regardless of the bargains. And I bet those pork chops are not cut right. Stay away from this type of place; it's simply not worth your time.

Keep a price notebook. Write down in a small notebook the *unit* price (price per pound, per ounce, per liter, per hundred, or what have you) of the things you buy. What kind of things? Everything, but especially the pricier things. Yes, there are bargains in beans, but you really need to know the *regular* prices of ground beef, flour, sugar, broccoli, bananas, apples, pork roasts, condiments, cans of tuna, bottles of ketchup, and so on. This is especially important for buying from Amazon, because Amazon doesn't list its prices by unit in a way that items can be efficiently compared, frustratingly. It's up to you to figure it out, which can take a lot of work—and your time is worth something!

Keep in mind that things such as eggs are tricky to figure out, because one dozen eggs does not necessarily equal another, even though each carton contains twelve eggs. You might need two small eggs to equal one jumbo, and on top of that, some stores' "large" eggs are another store's "small"! Really, eggs should be sold by the pound, and even that wouldn't work, since the shells of different-size eggs would weigh different amounts, not to get too picky about this. So you have to get smart on how you compare them, and intuition is sometimes needed.

I have noticed a trend in selling vegetables such as red peppers individually priced ("by the each," as they sometimes hilariously say!) rather than by the pound, which is incredibly obnoxious. Feel free to take them over to the scale and weigh them—then mark down the per-pound price in your notebook. Soon you will know what a good price on peppers is.

For most things, go by the amount in that orange square on the sticker on the shelf, not the price for the box, bottle, and so forth.

Start to note approximately how much snacks cost, for instance. White flour, oats, and sugar are in the one-dollar-a-pound region, and butter is in the two-dollars-a-pound region. But boxed prepared snacks can be from four to ten dollars a pound! Sometimes everyone needs to buy a box of granola bars, but it's really important to your budget to know how much you are paying for them *per pound* and to have it in your mind that, for instance, ribeye steak might be in the same price region! (Let's see, which would I prefer, a granola bar or a ribeye steak?)

Non-Food-Item Pricing

There's another area of price awareness that has to do with nongrocery items that you buy sometimes at the grocery store and sometimes elsewhere: toilet paper, laundry detergent, lotion, toothpaste, and so forth. Sometimes the grocery store has sales on these things; you might save yourself money and an extra trip by buying them at the grocery store, but you need to know the prices.

One of the very hardest items to price is toilet paper. In theory, there is a unit price, but unit of what? Squares? But the thickness of the paper affects how many squares one uses. And then there are fat rolls and tiny rolls and super soft rolls. Sometimes you are to be forgiven for not knowing how much you are paying, but do your best.

Spend a few weeks *paying attention* and *writing down*. Keep updating your notebook. Eventually you will know the prices by heart, and this will save you time when you are deciding whether a sale is really a sale or just a come-on. It will help when you are somewhere unusual and see a putative bargain. Things are tricky out there in grocery-store land. Sometimes the larger box of an item isn't cheaper, per unit, than the smaller, counterintuitively. Sometimes a discount store is expensive. Sometimes even a coupon doesn't make the purchase worth it, if you compare with the store brand.

The only way to navigate these waters is to know your prices.

Save a Step Cooking

 cook very few dinners completely from scratch on a given day, although all my cooking is from "scratch." This talent is what I have come to call Save a Step Cooking!

Make menus with an eye to the little extra things you can squirrel away for another meal as you go about your normal cooking routine. Getting into this habit of saving steps will streamline your dinner preparations and make the kind of cooking that moms of big families have to do enjoyable—or at least not burdensome.

If you are clever, you can schedule your week so that you put in a big cooking effort on only one or two days—at the most—and usually you will take advantage of some time-saving steps you've done when it's convenient and efficient. You still make everything you want from scratch, but efficiently!

I think of this as "buy low, sell [use] high" as applied to the precious commodity of time. Use your time when it's plentiful—say, on a day when you are home for at least a morning, rather than doing errands all day—to build up a food stash for a day when you have little time (when time is "expensive" for you). Use the hour that you are already making a roast chicken to roast two chickens (or three!). This costs you no more in time for the actual roasting and only a little more for cutting the extra cooked chicken up and adding the bones to the stockpot. Later, when you need cooked chicken or chicken stock for a recipe, it will already be there for you.

To use another economics image: you are applying efficiencies and economies of scale by using your means of production to increase output. So, for instance, if you are already making bread, you increase the dough and make a couple of loaves to freeze. Even an extra pan of rolls in the freezer will take the edge off the work of a future meal. Your setup and cleanup are not significantly more, but you end up with a lot more of the product.

See, when you have put "meatloaf, mashed potatoes, peas, applesauce, rolls" on your menu list, you can make the menu lists of future weeks a lot easier if you make enough to produce two meatloaves plus a tray of meatballs and freeze what you aren't eating that day.

Save a Step versus Bulk Cooking

In contrast, the idea of bulk cooking that is often written about and promoted has you taking many steps all at once—shopping for many meals, cooking many kinds of foods—for later. Realities of life in a large busy family don't get factored in—nursing a baby, illness, extra guests ...

No matter how many articles I read about it, it's never going to happen that I get all my food using coupons or that I cook once a month and freeze all my meals. In forty years of doing this, it hasn't happened. But I'm still frugal, and I'm still fast. (I'm almost never on time, but I am fast.)

I'm committed to fresh, simple, delicious food, and I'm very efficiency-minded, being an engineer's daughter. If I find a coupon, I'll use it, because I like saving money, but coupons are not a system—not a food system. They don't get your dinner made every single day!

Bulk cooking is efficient in one way, but it doesn't address certain issues. One is that if you are like me, you get tired easily. (I bet you are stronger than I am, though!) Food is better made fresh, for the most part. So I just can't imagine my entire meal (as opposed to components of that meal) being defrosted. And I don't think one person with a very large family can do it all in one or two days.

I don't like the boom-and-bust way of doing things, perhaps because I'm too prone to burning out and then getting depressed. I like to be on an even keel, knowing that each day will have its own pace. Everyone experiences days of nonstop activity, but I'd rather not force myself into such days as part of a long-term plan.

If I cooked for a solid day or more (apart from the many hours it takes for a holiday dinner or another special occasion), I would not recover in time for the next bout! And then, what about nursing the baby, reading to the kids, and taking a nap? I couldn't have spent two days not doing *those* things!

Worst of all is the recommendation to prepare for the week ahead with a bulk cooking marathon on Sunday, when Sunday has enough for moms to do, and we, too, have to rest on Sundays!

I think it's a healthy thing for kids to know that Mom will usually be in the kitchen at a certain time getting things ready. They help, of course, and they also have those great free moments that seem like hours, with the smells wafting around them as they play or read. They need an opportunity to find you there, busy but also able to talk.

Those are great memories for them! Do we really want to eliminate that part of life? To do so would have the unfortunate consequence of enabling the frantic, activity-oriented child-rearing we see today, something that I am devoting this book to alleviating.

With Save a Step Cooking, you do *whatever you are already doing*, only you see how you can use the existing setup to give yourself a little edge later. The devoted mother does need to be organized and efficient; that calm presence in the kitchen relies on having set up a good rhythm in household management. In just a couple of short weeks, this system will pay off, and you will have even more free time to create efficiencies in even more areas as they occur to you.

By the way, my friend Sue wrote a ditty for our readers, since Save A Step Cooking is her idea, which I stole (well, I stole the name and most of our conversations). She is the most frugal person I know, and someday she will write a funny book in which she recounts to you the doings of her family of ten children. Meantime, this is what she offers you:

> Make ahead,
> Do the prep,
> Double up.
> Save a Step.

Use Your Menu Planning

Now, concretely, the menu planning stage is the place to do most of this thinking. I find it interesting that mothers of the past did what I'm suggesting as a matter of course, because they were very busy with many activities, many children, and few resources. Mothers like Ma Ingalls of the Little House books would make their roast (if they had one) on Sunday and then use what was left from it in the coming week. Even without freezers, they had a stash of preserved food, stale bread, and what have you that awaited clever use in many dishes. They used up the less stable items first, and then moved on to those that kept. They had common sense!

Here are some ways to get started on this today. You will think of lots of others. My point is this: Don't do all your work all at once. Work and stash as you go, saving your steps along the way.

1. *Plan for roasts at least two Sundays a month.* It's fairly easy to do, and everyone loves a roast with gravy. The frugal way to do this is to make whatever roast or large piece of meat is on sale. Try to get one that is at least a few pounds larger than what you would normally buy, or two chickens if you usually roast one, three if you usually roast two. It will repay you many times in the coming days! You can prevent people from eating too much meat by serving enough side dishes, along with hearty rolls. Make them take those first! (This strategy is behind such foods as Yorkshire puddings, the idea being that working men needed a little filling up with tasty gravy-soaked morsels—eggs and flour, for instance, being easier to come by than standing roasts—before they moved on to the meat. Wisdom.)

You don't have to take care of the leftovers right away. You can cover the pan with foil, put the whole thing in the fridge (if you have enough room; I do think a second fridge is worth the cost in a big, busy household), and deal with it the next day. Meat is easier to cut up when it's cold anyway.

I have been known to set a pot (with a tight-fitting lid, of course) out in the cold garage on the workbench when my fridge is full. However, once you get used to cooking this way, you will find it doesn't take very long to divide leftover meat into slices, chunks, and bones.

Wrap the meat up separately, labeling each package clearly. (Have supplies for this activity at your work station.) Many times I even divide leftover meat into categories based on the size of the chunk and whether it's white or dark meat. Label a package of small bits of ham "ham for soup" and one of lamb "roasted lamb for shepherd's pie."

Either wrap the bone up for freezing, or go ahead and start a stockpot as your family helps you clear up after dinner. Just throw the bones and any handy onion, carrot, and celery in, cover with water, and set to a boil. If you want, you can just do the bones and add vegetables at another stage. You can add leftover gravy if you won't be using it in the next two days. Certainly scrape any pan juices and drippings into the pot. All of that will enrich the broth nicely. There is not really any precision to this! Set the timer for two hours. Many is the time I've boiled down and burnt a pot of broth after leaving the kitchen! That's not thrifty!

Once the broth has cooked (the bones will be soft or, in the case of big meat bones, all the connective tissue will have boiled into the liquid, and any meat in there will be bland to the taste), pour it through a colander into a bowl large enough to allow quick cooling. Put it in the refrigerator until the next day. If you have ever tried vainly to get liquid fat out of a bowl of stock in a rush, you will thank yourself many times over for doing it this way. The next day (or the day after, up to a week—no rush), scrape off the fat (or lift it off in one piece, depending on the type of broth) and throw it away. Note: Some fat is well worth saving in a clean jar in the fridge: snow-white pork fat, duck fat, beef fat. You can roast your potatoes in it, and that will be lovely. Since I always have at least two jars of bacon grease in my fridge, I do not keep chicken fat.

Spoon the congealed broth into containers, leaving headroom (at least an inch, for expansion as the liquid freezes), and label them clearly. I write with a Sharpie right on my plastic containers. New writing goes right over the old. These containers can go in the freezer. Broth in the fridge that doesn't have a seal of fat on top will keep for about two days. With its layer of fat, it will keep for a week. This broth will be the lynchpin of your food stash, saving you many steps in the coming weeks.

Now, any recipes on your handy Master Menu List that call for cooked meat will be a breeze for you. Barbequed-pork sandwiches? Check. Chicken enchiladas? No problem. Ham and bean soup? Yup. Turkey potpie? Got it. Minestrone? The broth is already in the freezer, as are the ham pieces. You won't have everything you need for a given dish, of course, but you will be well on your way, without having knocked yourself out on an all-day cooking spree.

2. *Make more of whatever you are making.* Let's say that you have scheduled roast sweet potatoes in their jackets for a side this week. (Sweet potatoes are my favorite food. I love them so! Nothing could be easier, either. Just choose a bunch of uniform size, put them on a sheet of tinfoil on a baking tray, and roast them at 425 degrees. They make an awful mess as they ooze their sugars, so do use the foil. Then serve, split open, with a little butter and salt. Heaven!) Roast twice as many as you need, and let the extras cool completely. Then remove their skins, slice them into a container, and freeze. Another day you can have sweet potatoes as a side dish, premixed with butter and salt, without the hot oven or the messy tin foil.

Making a potpie? Can you make another one, even if it's smaller? I could never face making potpies on a day I was also making every other meal for the month, but if I'm already making one, it's not that hard to make another.

Making more is particularly important with baking. Making a pie? Make an extra crust or two—it will freeze perfectly if wrapped well, and then your potpie will be that much closer to realization.

Homemade bread freezes beautifully. Make sure the loaf has cooled completely—at least a couple of hours on a cooling rack. Sometimes I leave loaves out all night if I bake them at night—after all, bakeries do that! Then freeze, well wrapped. When it's defrosted, it tastes as if you baked it that day. You can wrap it in paper towel and microwave it in a pinch, and it will be just fine. It's always worth it to freeze at least a loaf or enough rolls for a meal.

If you are making cookies, scrutinize the recipe. It's almost not worth doing if you are not going to make extra. It takes so much time to get the ingredients out and mix them. Go ahead and make a quadruple batch! You can freeze the dough if you can't get to baking all the cookies now.

A lot of things can be frozen that you wouldn't expect, and it's easy enough to search online to find the answer. Ask yourself if you can make more for later, and then do!

3. *Save a Step on basic recipe building blocks.* Don't get caught without bread crumbs. Not only do you used them in many recipes, but any otherwise lame dish can be made so much more appealing with a topping of bread crumbs.

Save all the bread bits and bobs, and put them in the food processor. I used to balk at doing this because I didn't want to have to wash the processor out after such an insignificant use. Then I realized that either the crumbs are so dry and inert in terms of anything else I would put in the processor that a simple wipe would do, or I was going to use the processor soon after for something that would not be affected by my having processed crumbs in there; I could wash it afterward. (If the bread is very hard, use the blender instead. Don't forget that you can use a regular-mouth mason jar: the blade assembly fits and then your crumbs are already in the jar! Leave off the rubber gasket for dry grinding, as with crumbs, it tends to get pulled into the jar to disastrous effect.)

Put the crumbs in a ziplock bag, press out the air, and keep them in the freezer.

Almost every conceivable savory dish calls for chopped onion, minced garlic, and perhaps chopped peppers. Sauté up double, triple, or more, freezing the extra for next time. Go another step: if the recipe calls for doing all this with ground beef, cook a large amount and freeze the extra!

I can't count how many times my skin was saved, dinner-wise, by having this mixture in the freezer, ready to go. You can make spaghetti with meat sauce, chili, sloppy joes, meat enchiladas, burritos—all without firing up the skillet.

Most recipes using boneless chicken breasts are enhanced by pounding the breasts first. If I'm making boneless chicken breasts, it's almost certain that I'm in a rush! So when I buy them, I take them out of the package, pound them all, and repackage them in sets of three with a layer of plastic wrap in between the sets. They store all flat in a ziplock bag and are ready to go right out of the freezer—much better than trying to handle them half frozen and all bunched up.

You can also skip pounding, the object of which is to make the breasts an even thickness, by simply slicing into each breast partway to even up the thickness and opening it up like a book or fanning it out a bit so that heat can be distributed evenly.

Chopping nuts for a recipe? Why chop half a cup? Chop the whole package, and then freeze the extra. (Buy two packages if you think you will need whole nuts for something else.)

Even cutting up carrots and celery can get you a step ahead when you make your broth. Pop the bits you've trimmed (assuming they are not rotten) in a ziplock bag in the freezer. You will be all ready to go on Sunday evening when you get out that stockpot for the bones from your roast. By the way, mushroom stems, parsley stems, and parmesan cheese rinds are great additions to the stockpot. Just pop them in that same handy bag as you acquire them.

Making mashed potatoes? Drain the cooking water into a bowl, and then transfer it to a clean jar. Any bread recipe is enhanced by substituting potato water for some of the liquid. If it's salted, remember to adjust your recipe a bit. It keeps for a week or so in the fridge.

Cooking bacon? We have bacon at least once a week. That's a lot of bacon fat to throw away! Drain the fat into a clean jar and keep covered in the fridge (not in a can on the counter, no matter what your grandpa did). Use it to make your pancakes and as the shortening in savory pie crusts. If you decide one day to do a deep fry, use the bacon fat! It's so tasty.

4. *Store things well so they will help you later.* Make it a priority to do the best you can with what you have. If you buy a lot of broccoli, cook it all right away. Cooked vegetables save their freshness better than raw. You can use the leftovers in soups and casseroles or just reheat it if you didn't overcook them to start with, but a bunch of raw broccoli in the fridge will lose its savor pretty quickly.

Stocks and broths that have been strained into a bowl will keep very well under their seal of fat in the fridge for a week or so. But they won't keep forever! So keep track of what you have.

Put whole grains, nuts, flours, and spices in the freezer, well labeled. Left out, they go rancid and stale quickly.

If you are not inspired now, store the item in question for maximum freshness and decide later. You may come across just the right idea when you least expect it.

Do a little more when you can, not all at once. Now you are getting the idea. If you are cooking something anyway, think ahead and cook some more of that particular thing. Choose your dishes to produce other dishes another day.

Don't be afraid of leftovers. As long as they are handled correctly, leftovers are the goal here! Don't be afraid to build your stash and Save a Step!

Twelve Things to Stash
That Will Help You Get
Supper on the Table

Some people (who write articles you might see) scoff at the idea that you need to plan a week or more's worth of menus, or even that you can do it at all. They say you just need good recipes and nice fresh food. But these people, whom I sure we would find delightfully spontaneous and witty, should we ever meet them, simply don't have as many small children or teenagers as we do, and they undoubtedly have a sushi cart rolling right by them as they type. I bite my thumb at these people!

You really don't need recipes, which are all around you—you need menus.

How are you going to go shopping, efficiently, if you don't know *just* what to make? And how will you know just what to make if you don't figure out, once and for all, what you and your own particular family actually like to eat?

Yes, someday you will be so experienced that you can pull things together using what's on hand, at least some of the time; and certainly when the garden or farmer's market is burgeoning with fresh produce, supper seems to make itself and inspiration is just floating in the air, ready to be plucked and put to work. That's great, and you'll be happy knowing that you still know how to plan menus for meals if you need to.

Another thing: sometimes the menu doesn't work, no matter how careful you were to plan it with your day's activities in mind. Someone is sick, you forgot to defrost, you ran out of a key ingredient, someone ate the very thing you were counting on—these things happen!

You Need a Thought-Out Stash

So you do need a few things up your sleeve and in your stash—"anytime" resources that can be relied upon to fill the gaps. Once you understand how building a stash works, you can collect these resources as you move through your day in the kitchen and at the store.

One day, I had bread dough rising in the fridge, as I often do, and then I remembered about it and put it on the wood-burning stove, which I had just lit, so that it could come to room temperature and be baked.

Then I went into the other room, because experience has shown that I will definitely remember that I have something going on in the kitchen when I'm elsewhere, and nothing stupid will happen.

When I came back into the kitchen, the fire was roaring and the dough was risen, all right. In fact, the bottom half of it had started to bake (in the inadequately greased pan). What to do?

Well, I might be doomed to repeat some mistakes, but I knew that I could get something out of this mini disaster. Not a nicely baked big loaf of bread, but something. So I gently pulled off the part of the dough that wasn't already baking, formed it into a little focaccia-like lump, put it on a properly greased baking dish, and popped it into the oven, letting it continue its rise as the oven pre-heated. It was fine as a little bit of bread for the family at supper; actually, they loved it, which is so sweet of them and why I don't give up entirely in the face of my distractedness.

The other bit, the part in the pan, I just baked as it was. It was not lovely, and it was impossible to get out of the pan without serious hacking and muttering. The substance itself tasted fine and not even sour, as I thought it might after being prebaked on the wood stove. I could have used it for Breakfast Casserole (see the recipes in the appendices) or bread pudding, but I chose to make it into bread crumbs to stash away for another day.

Later and unrelatedly, one of my daughters remarked on how I am able to "pull out" things from the fridge, such as bread crumbs, to get supper together. Now that she's seeing it from her own perspective as a homemaker, she was wondering how it's done.

I kept reassuring her that it's something that comes with experience and, to be fair, definitely results from having a certain number of people around to cause the build-up of food you can later use in this seemingly magical way. Save a Step cooking (delved into above) is the best, most painless way to keep from having to come up with a meal from scratch every day or go broke trying.

I'm not going to list the usual things you find in magazines about what to have in your pantry. I take it for granted that we all know we shouldn't buy pasta one box at a time, and that jarred tomato sauce has its place. You have your cans of tuna and beans (or maybe some beans you've soaked and popped in the freezer). You understand that you need to have a supply of milk and eggs. You have rice.

But what else would be helpful to have around? I will tell you:

1. *Pie crust.* When you make a pie, make extra crust by doubling the recipe, form it into a disk, and stash it in the freezer well wrapped and labeled. A pie crust makes a small amount of stew (beef or chicken pieces with potato, carrot, and peas or really any braised meat and vegetables) into that wonderful, magical, filling substance known as potpie. One pie crust, rolled out thin, can make a tasty galette (an open tart piled with any little tidbits and free-formed by folding the edges of the crust back over the top) that rounds out a pot of soup or some leftover slices of meat or what have you. Sweet-potato galette with sage, onions, and goat cheese is delicious. Just pile the ingredients on your pie crust in layers and bake.

2. *Pieces of ham.* A reader asked me what kinds of things I would make with the little bits, since I'm always referencing them. *What wouldn't you make?*

Soup is better with bits of ham. Mac and cheese becomes dinner with pieces of ham. Galette (see number 1, above) is heartier with little bits of ham strewn upon it. You can make Hawaiian pizza if you also have a can of pineapple in the pantry. You can toss pasta with ham and green beans and feed eight people with half a cup of meat. So next time you serve ham, carefully divide the leftovers into nice slices, chunks, bone, and little bits you've taken off the bone (although you don't have to be obsessive about it since the meat on the bone is good for the soup). Place each sort in its own ziplock bag, label it, and stash it away.

3. *Pieces of bacon.* You'll have to squirrel these away before the barbarians attack breakfast, but even two slices (I always get thick-cut bacon) will crumble up nicely on a salad with blue-cheese dressing. That galette I mentioned above will be lovely with bacon. You can add crumbled bacon to mayo to make lettuce, cheese, and tomato sandwiches that aren't BLTs but do have a sort of bacon-y aura.

4. *Stock.* When you have a roast (and making a roast on Sunday is the best way to keep work to a minimum on Sunday and still serve a nice dinner and also save plenty of steps for the weeks ahead), put all the bones in a pot with the bits of onion, carrot, and celery that you've collected along the way (see "Save a Step Cooking"; you can keep those in a plastic bag in the freezer as well, along with parsley stems and mushroom bits). Add any pan drippings if you haven't already used them for gravy or sauce.

It's not beyond me to ask the family to put their chicken bones in the pot when they're clearing their plates. Add water, and simmer it for the rest of the evening (it doesn't take days, as some think) with a tablespoon of vinegar, if you remember it. Even if you add nothing, just simmer the bones. Then strain the liquid into a bowl over a colander and set the bowl in your fridge (sometimes in winter I put the pot, with the lid on it, on the workbench in the garage; being able to handle such things is a good reason to have a second fridge but sometimes even that gets full!).

The broth will keep with its layer of undisturbed fat for a week or more. Before using or storing the broth, scrape off the fat (you can keep it if you want—I usually don't if it's chicken, as I have lots of bacon grease handy, but I keep duck and goose fat, for pâtés and roasted potatoes). Pour the stock into mason jars (leaving two inches of headroom), and freeze or use within a day or so of removing the fat. Defrost stock by putting the jar in a container of cold water, completely submerged (you can crack a jar if you only put it in only partway); after about fifteen minutes, you can slowly microwave it or add warmer water to your container.

Stock is essential. With stock you are ready for any gravy or nice sauce, and you can make good, hearty soup. The stock you buy at the store, even in the pricier organic brands, has many additives, often soy or MSG in some hidden form, to give it the umami taste that homemade has with the addition of celery or mushrooms. Homemade stock is not hard to stash (boil it down if you have space issues—you can add water later), and it's so good for you!

5. *Pieces of cooked chicken.* When your supper of roast chicken is over (and remember, you should never roast fewer than two chickens at a time), separate it into big pieces, bones, and little bits. The latter will be your special stockpile for chicken salad sandwiches, chicken Caesar salad, and chicken quesadillas. Making chicken soup with your stashed broth? Add a cup of pieces of cooked chicken at the end, and the meal will stick to your family's ribs.

6. *Cabbage, carrots, celery, and apples* in your fridge drawer. In winter especially, when you can't get to the store for fresh veggies, you can always pull out ingredients for one of my three favorite side dishes: coleslaw (shred cabbage and carrots, toss with mayo, vinegar, a little sugar, salt, and cumin), carrot sticks (obvious), and Waldorf salad (cut up celery and apple, add raisins or dried cranberries, toss with chopped nuts such as pecans, and dress like coleslaw minus the cumin, or with it, for that matter).

7. *Garlic-ginger paste.* This is easy to make by crushing equal amounts of fresh garlic and ginger and adding a teaspoon of salt for every quarter cup of the resulting paste. Keep it in the fridge. Add the paste to coleslaw along with bacon or cashews. The paste also makes stir-fry fast and extra authentic.

8. *Sausage and beef mix.* When Italian sausage and ground beef are on sale, buy extra packages of each. Then fry and drain the meat, divide it up, store it in ziplock bags, and freeze. With this mix you can make spaghetti sauce, chili, tacos, shepherd's pie—all super fast. Always make more than what you need for the dinner you're cooking, because you will use it, trust me.

9. *Cooked veggies.* Cook your green beans, sweet potatoes, squash, peas, whatever—with another meal in mind. They keep well in the fridge (make sure you know how to cook your green vegetables to the proper point and no further). Two days later, pull them out and heat them up. Most veggies (not green beans, it's true, although even those will work in minestrone or stew) freeze fine. A part of me dies a little when I see a recipe for a casserole that instructs you to cook its elements separately. That takes so long! Plan potpie after you have previously cooked the meat and veggies and want a delicious way to serve the leftovers.

10. *Frozen corn.* Suki says that corn makes everything better. It's true. You can add it to potpie, chili, or soup to stretch it out a bit as well as make it tastier. Peas and spinach are also good to have in the freezer for when you don't have another fresh veggie on hand.

11. *Bread dough* in the fridge. Almost any dough will be just fine in the fridge, rising there slowly until you are ready for it. Homemade bread makes the simplest meal seem wonderful and warm. You can always make supper of a tray of dough, spread out, topped with your sausage and beef mix (see number 8) and cheese. Cheeseburger pie! Delish!

12. *Bread crumbs.* The most ordinary casserole is just a million times better with a layer of toasty bread crumbs on top. Use any regular-mouth mason jar with your blender blade[4] to grind them. (You may be able to source a

---

[4] Don't use this blender trick with hot liquids—there's no room for expansion and the glass could break. It would be great to source a couple of plastic mason jars for this purpose. Making a frozen drink works well with this method—it's ready to drink right out of the jar. When grinding dry ingredients, leave the rubber gasket off, as it has a tendency to be pulled in and chopped up.

plastic mason jar, which would be best and safest for this purpose.) Collect all those heels of bread and leftover toast—you can keep them in a bag in the freezer until you are ready to grind them.

With bread crumbs you can quickly make chicken breasts with a thin spread of mustard, topped with buttery crumbs or mac and cheese for dinner. Your meatloaf and meatballs need them. And does your market sell thrifty bags of red peppers? Cut the peppers in half, or in quarters if they are large, and arrange them on an oiled pan. Mix some kind of cheese (goat, feta, or even cream cheese), with some bread crumbs, parsley, and maybe a small amount of finely diced tomato or sundried tomato; drop a tablespoon of the mixture onto each piece of red pepper; top with a little grated parmesan; and roast for twenty minutes at 400 degrees. Serve with a pasta dish. You can't pull that one out of a hat without bread crumbs, but you could serve it at your best dinner party!

Save a Step at Breakfast

Now that you have mastered the dinner-menu idea, let's do breakfast.

Do you wonder why your kids are crabby? Are there meltdowns at your house as you start math? Do you have a child who gets headaches? Do you feel shaky sometimes? There must be breakfast. Cereal alone doesn't cut it. Children will be better off having some protein and fat; some even need to wait a bit before eating.

Do the same thing with your breakfast menus as you did with dinner: find out what everyone really wants to eat, and add your special dash of common sense and practicality. Then make a shopping list based on your preferences.

For breakfast, the process will be simpler than for dinner, because most people eat more or less the same thing every day for breakfast. I find that I just need to have a few basic breakfasts ready to go; the creativity comes in with Sunday's breakfast, which at our house is usually quite hearty.

Breakfast must have protein, and milk alone isn't enough. Personally, I am subject to fits of low blood sugar, and I am aware of how I don't function unless well fortified.

A teacher tells about a high school student who seemed really hungry by midmorning. When the suggestion was made that the child needed to eat breakfast, the student's mom's response was a dreamy "yes, that would be a good idea"—she seemed unaware that it was her task to accomplish this goal!

If your child is involved in a sport along with other after-school activities, has a lot of homework, and goes to bed a bit later than he should, he is not going to be able to get breakfast and make himself a lunch to pack unless you make it possible by shopping and doing some of the prep work.

So there is flexibility but also the need to manage the whole process. At our house, the weekday breakfast selection looks like this (recipes are included in the appendices):

- Toasted bagels and cream cheese. My local supermarket has a store brand of good bagels with unobjectionable ingredients; I stock up on cream cheese, which stores well, when the price is good.
- Eggs, scrambled or fried, with shredded cheese and any leftover breakfast meat crumbled in; toast with plenty of butter.
- Papa's Special (method in appendix A)
- Pancakes on the weekends, with breakfast meat left over from during the week crumbled into the batter. (This is incredibly easy with my pancake mix.)
- Oatmeal Porridge Like Mother, Like Daughter—filling and yummy. I confess that we don't eat this often, because I'm too spacey to get it ready the night before, but when I do, it's appreciated! Also, leftovers are easily microwaved; make a big pot.
- Cereal. Since mostly we like eggs or bagels, there isn't a lot of cereal consumption around here. But it is handy in a rush, if used cautiously and with guidelines:
  1. Mix the cereal. At first, this concept was not appealing to me. But then I saw that if you insist that a child mix a small amount of sugary cereal with granola, the child is happy and you know he's getting more; it's actually tasty. No eating even whole-grain Cheerios by themselves around here. And by sugary, I mean what most people consider health food. The really sugary ones are not for breakfast or even for anything at all.

2. Make your own granola.
3. Include a piece of hearty toast with lots of butter, some yogurt, or a piece of cheese. Teenagers will get away from you on this, but by that age, they know how they'll feel by ten o'clock — it's up to them. But no six-year-old is having a bowl of cereal and calling it breakfast!

A lot of this can be done by the children themselves. I let them more or less choose, although if someone is feeling wan or acting up, I make him some eggs.

Not all breakfasts must feature hot food. Do you know what Egyptian children eat for breakfast? Pita bread, feta cheese, and olives. Sometimes eggs with dates and fava beans mixed in (the Egyptian version of which is like refried beans).

You decide if you will have everyone eat the same thing or if you will let each choose and make his own. Do track how much chaos ensues if everyone is pulling things out, toasting, scrambling, and so forth, and think through the system so that you aren't left with an exploded kitchen when they've all departed.

Here, we each get what we want during the week, I fix some things for some people, if they want. When the kids were little, I got their breakfast for them. On Sunday, I make one big breakfast for all, often featuring something someone has requested. Do what you want! But do it.

All of this decision making works its way to your grocery list. Try to figure out how many packages of bagels you use in a week. Next week, adjust. Store extras in your big freezer.

Buy more than enough eggs. Eggs are cheap. They last. You want to get many dozens at a time, so that you'll have a good supply for more than a week.

Buy good sharp *shredded* cheddar cheese along with the brick form, if you find that it's no more per pound. Add shredded cheese to scrambled eggs to make them heartier. If the cheese is already shredded, you are more likely to use it than if you have to shred it yourself.

Stock up on oats and other grains for porridge. Buy a few cartons of buttermilk. (I don't hold with dry buttermilk. By my calculations it seems much more expensive, and buttermilk isn't going to spoil around here with all the pancakes and biscuits everyone likes!)

Get extra bacon on sale, cook it on Sunday morning, tuck some away before the family gets at it, and hide it way back in the fridge or in the freezer to use during the week. Same with sausage.)

Don't practice false economy by skimping on breakfast. What you spend in bagels you will reap in snacks: the pricey fruit roll-ups can be foregone if the tummy is anchored.

Process Veggies for the Freezer

Gardening helps a lot with the food bill. Having some of your own home-grown produce stashed away couldn't be more satisfying, and you don't need a lot of room to grow at least some of your food! Here are my issues with putting up veggies in the freezer. Maybe you can relate—probably not if you grew up on a farm, but maybe if you have tried a little garden too.

1. The veggies are not all the same size. The ones you buy at the store are, the ones you pick are not, whether we are talking about beans, peas, broccoli, or asparagus, which are what I'm likely to be dealing with in this manner. This bothers me into paralysis.

2. There are often not enough all at once to process, but too many to eat right away. Stalemate.

3. What exactly is blanching, how is it different from plain old cooking, and no matter how well you define it, I will still feel that I'm doing it wrong. More paralysis.

4. I don't have a vacuum sealer thingy. Wandering around ... looking for a book.

5. Even if I go through it all the way you are supposed to, won't they come out mushy and gross, like regular frozen veggies you buy? (I like frozen corn and peas, but broccoli and beans — sort of unpleasant.) Feeling the energy draining out of me.

I think I've conquered my anxieties.

1. Sort them into sizes. Let's say we're talking about green beans: teeny baby ones, medium ones, sort of leathery ones that might be good in a stew, and ones that need to be shelled.

2. Do this over a few days as things ripen out there; nothing bad will happen. Keep them in a cool place covered with a towel or refrigerate.

3. Before freezing the extra harvest, blanch it. Blanching just means boil quickly — we can do this. It brings the food to the temperature at which the enzymes that cause breakdown will be killed without fully cooking it. The books say boil three minutes but with super little beans or tender snow peas, just cook until they brighten slightly — maybe between one and two minutes. Use your common sense, and you will be okay. See a useful resource, *Putting Food By*, by Ruth Hertzberg, Janet Greene, and Beatrice Vaughan, in the latest version (which will have all safety updates). The book is up my alley, being chatty and also strict about stuff that you should be strict about.

4. Use ziplock freezer bags, and simply press the air out, or suck the air out with a straw. It might be undignified and a little dizzying in the heat, but it works fine.

Five Food Thoughts

I t seems pretty clear that keeping food simple, making (and even growing) our own if possible, and avoiding highly processed food makes a difference to our health and to our finances. And then we venture into the topics of "organic" and "grass fed" and "locally produced," and it all seems so complicated again.

It's funny how even the question of which potatoes to buy relates to our goals and our vision, isn't it? We have to know what our "things" are if we are going to make "first things first." It's paralyzing to contemplate the many facets of a very elemental issue in our lives: food.

One important point: we can't always be throwing out all our resolutions when a new one comes along! Who needs this revolving door of anxiety, I ask you? The prudent thing is to make do with what we have and with our own limitations, staying calm and trying always to learn more.

I care about food; too much so, actually! Once Suzanne and I were laughing together about how we have to remind ourselves to do something other than cook, clean up, and eat!

Branch out a little with some other activities once in a while!

Instead of having crises over food, whether about its production, purchase, preparation, quantity, quality, or any other issues, may I suggest a few key "first things," ordering principles if you will, that help me to stay on the right track?

1. We are committed to living on one income, with my role being to make the home on the day-to-day basis. Being the homemaker isn't drudgery; it's the most creative thing most people will ever do! It's important because it brings peace to your family.

But yes, that means that I put a lot of effort into making good, wholesome, healthy food for a large family, and yes, our budget was always tight when our children were growing up. I've made up my mind to accept these realities.

2. We have to trust that God sees that we are doing our best. Ultimately, our well-being depends on Him. We can't guarantee good health or good fortune merely by our efforts; far less by trusting in our dollars to bring us security. Our priority has been to have good family life for the nurturing of the whole person entrusted to us. Health, as good a gift as it is, isn't something to worship or to lose peace over.

3. This excellent observation from Joel Salatin expresses what I think (not just about food, either): "Now that the high prices [of food labeled "organic"] have attracted unscrupulous growers who enter the movement for the money, people realize that no system can regulate integrity."

No system can regulate integrity.

As parents, we have to use our common sense. Just because something seems to promise purity doesn't mean that it will deliver. Just because it's labeled "organic" doesn't mean it's better for you or even that much different from the one that isn't labeled that way.

There are serious issues with our food production, but I personally am not in much of a position to change things on a large scale. Sometimes I remember my trip to Egypt when I was a girl. I remember the meat hanging out in the market (on a hot day, of course) with flies all over everything. There are always going to be problems.

At some point, we have to trust that if we do our best, we don't have to worry. (We shouldn't be worrying anyway. It's pointless.)

4. I have to accept where I live. If I were to "buy local" all year, I'd be living on kale and parsnips for a good bit of it.

Maybe some of you live somewhere with a desert climate. Maybe you live in California, and I am not bitter about your CSA box being all avocados, blood oranges, and strawberries (although these things also come at a price in water use). Be realistic and thankful that you *can* get food from elsewhere if you need to.

When you are able, get your food from nearby, but don't make this a stress point. I do appreciate that the smallish supermarket (with good prices, for which I'm grateful) where I usually shop often sources things from our area. The reality is that, in our climate, this means that the local produce begins appearing in July, and by the beginning of October, it's all gone, other than the winter squash, which I have a bunch of already, from my garden!

My meat and veggies might not be labeled organic, but they are very good. And my ice cream is amazing and is made right here in New England, so I'm all set! But it's not my first priority for things to be organic *or* local, because I'm not convinced that it ought to be.

We are amazingly blessed in our country to have good food, basically when we need it. If things are otherwise for you, you will have to get clever (and start a little homestead farm). But do it peacefully.

5. If I return to the system I've devised, knowing what's for dinner (and lunch, and breakfast), and Saving a Step as I work, and knowing that my stash will support me in a pinch, I can provide simple, wholesome food for my family (thanks to my dear husband, who works hard and provides so well). My system doesn't wear me out, and I don't think it will wear you out either. You can still nurse the baby, go to the kids' games, and even read a book—most days.

My system will work for your family because you can tailor it according to all your needs. It will help you take into account your schedule; you'll finally figure out how to have the meal you need for a rushing-around day, a leisurely feast day, an ordinary day—whatever you have going on, you will be ready, because you will key your meal planning to your calendar. Your food will be as much from scratch as you hope it will be, but you won't be in the kitchen all day—unless you want to be!

Even with lots of kids and not much money, you can eat well. You must work at it; don't get me wrong. And you won't be able to buy everything at that upscale organic national chain, but as Salatin explains, you probably shouldn't even want to, even if you could afford it.

Thrifty Eating on the Road

When, for one reason or another, you are on the road and need to eat, consider packing food for nutrition and frugality—and also because it will likely be much better than what you can buy, even supposing the option is available. Here are some suggestions:

- A loaf of sliced bread with jars of peanut butter and jelly, plus plastic knives. *Don't* make the sandwiches ahead: avoid the risk of a smooshed, soggy, unappetizing mess.
- Cheese and crackers, especially with a bit of dried fruit on each one. Cheese and crackers might not excite you if you are getting the bland versions of the key ingredients. Try the sharpest cheddar you can find and the nicest crackers. Brand-name crackers have a lot of salt and sugar in them. Try water crackers, pita chips, or any other European-style ones. Usually they are crisper and let the cheese shine through. A little dab of fig jam on each one is so tasty, and kids love it.
- Sandwiches with cold cuts and cheese. Try buttering the bread the way Germans and Hungarians do, with a little brown mustard on one slice.
- Summer sausage, cheese, crackers, baby carrots, and fruit.

- Hard-boiled eggs with a little container of salt (try a seasoned salt of your own making, adding dried parsley, chives, dry mustard, or cumin) for dipping.
- A hot container of refried beans in a cooler, a bag of tortilla chips, and some shredded cheese for spooning on-the-go nachos. Make this your first course, to avoid having the beans cool down to the point at which they are not safe anymore.

For a baseball-game kind of picnic, take a good, heavy, cast-iron pot and fill it with the bean soup of your choice. When the soup is good and boiling, and has been boiling for at least ten minutes, set it in a cooler padded thoroughly with towels or a cheap camping-style "emergency blanket" in case of spills. Some muffins on the side will round it out.

Plain yogurt is easy to flavor with jam, and Greek yogurt doesn't make much of a mess. I make my own by straining a whole batch of yogurt at once with a potato-sack towel set in a colander over a bowl. (I use the whey in my breads and as a substitute for buttermilk in pancake and such-like recipes.)

- Any kind of pocket bread or pastry type of dish: calzones, pasties, empanadas, and so forth
- A container of hummus, or one of guacamole, or both, and pita or tortilla chips
- Chicken salad, along with a loaf of bread, some large lettuce leaves for wrapping, or tortilla chips
- Nuts

For something more along the lines of supper, cold fried chicken is always delicious! You could put it in a cooler, and bring some heated baked beans in a thermos. If everyone has a thermos or if you have one large enough to share, red beans and rice (perhaps with ham or sausage included) works well.

If it's an evening game that is throwing you off, have your big meal at lunchtime and something more snacky at supper.

How about keeping a "picnic bag": pick up plates, cups, bowls, and silverware from yard sales and such. It cuts down on forgetting important items, because you store them in the bag. The bag with the silverware also contains a can opener and a wooden spoon. Wash the items later and return them to the bag for reuse.

Organizing Food:
Refrigerator and Freezer Talk

f you follow my "buy low, sell [eat] high" recommendations, and of course you should, you will soon find that you have to organize your rapidly filling freezer space.

When your family is small, if you have the opportunity to choose, prioritize a refrigerator with a larger freezer area, preferably one large enough to have a shelf. Eventually, you may find that a second fridge is helpful (especially because, if you follow that advice, your fridge area will necessarily be smaller, but your children will be drinking a lot of milk, which takes up so much space). Also prioritize a large freezer in that second appliance.

You can get along for quite a while with these two fridge freezers. Think in terms of what the best cost-space ratio is: you will save more money by freezing meat you've gotten on sale than in freezing bread, which is bulky and not as pricey (though it's not cheap either; I feel your pain). Don't waste precious space on items that don't save you much money when you stockpile them.

Eventually, if your family gets large enough, you will *also* need a deep freezer. I prefer a chest style on the grounds that it is more energy efficient.

The food stays fresher for a longer time, because an upright freezer has to go through a defrost cycle, meaning that the temperature fluctuates, with a negative effect on long-term quality.

Organizing the Chest Freezer

The problem is that a chest freezer is quite the challenge to organize! For the longest time, I had been put off by the thought of a large chest of food with everything all tumbled in there, covered in frost, unidentifiable, trackable only by the use of a clipboard—only how are the inventory and actual items correlated if the latter are all thrown in?

Here's my low-tech solution:

In the produce section of the grocery store, you will be able to catch at certain times the stock boy piling up nice sturdy cardboard boxes that have plenty of holes for ventilation; these often have handle grips punched in the sides. Nab a few of these in various sizes; you can always put them in your own recycling if they don't work.

Broadly and mentally divide up your food into categories, such as big roasts, precut meats, breads, produce, and partially cooked stashed food (which I explain in "Save a Step Cooking"). Use a box for each kind of thing (or miscellaneous smaller items that tend to get lost in the deep freezer).

Stagger the boxes as you pile them up, with the big roasts below or between them. You see that not every single thing goes in a box: the boxes are for organizing anything that is not a large ham or a leg of lamb or a big carton of hamburger patties.

I'm very visual, so I found that the extra step of recording the freezer's inventory on a clipboard did nothing to help me keep track of all the undifferentiated frozen things in that big chest. Instead, every week or so, as I'm making my menus and grocery list, I lift out my boxes to see what's in there. (This is made significantly easier if you remember to label everything, so keep a Sharpie handy in the kitchen. And in case you've forgotten to label something, keep a Sharpie by the freezer as well, along with paper towels to dry off the plastic so you can write on it.) The box method is simpler than keeping up a written inventory, but it's definitely compatible with it if you do want to have a written record.

If you have an upright freezer, arrange the boxes on the shelves. You can pull the boxes out like drawers to remove the items you need so that frozen items aren't constantly in danger of sliding out and burying you or breaking your foot.

I keep bread in the section that the freezer manufacturer helpfully divided off with a rack, over the motor, which you may or may not have. If not, fruit box to the rescue!

The wire basket that perhaps came with your freezer holds the little odds and ends that would otherwise fall to the bottom. If you don't have one, it might be worth scavenging one from the recycling center or online; the basket uses space at the top of the freezer that might otherwise be lost. I might use this basket to hold freezer bags containing small amounts of ham for soup, breakfast sausage rolls, a concentrated broth of some sort in a jar, a bag of frozen fruit that I've already opened, or a small container of ice cream that I'm saving for a treat. A lot fits in this way but it's never just a pig pile. The pig pile is the downfall of the deep freezer, and what makes it so scary: things (often small) are there at the bottom; not only have you forgotten them, but you can never really reach them (if you're short like me, anyway). The boxes solve this problem.

A Handy Surface

You'll need a horizontal surface of some sort next to your freezer—any narrow table or shelf will do; mine was a roadside find. There is no way to avoid frequently moving items around in the freezer, and you need a separate holding place for this activity. When you are putting things away after shopping or simply rummaging, you can set things down on the shelf or table instead of on the garage or basement floor, while you reorganize. Long-term success with freezer organization depends on the boxes and on this staging surface.

You do have to *think* each time you put things in. Sometimes, for instance, bread has to be put near the meat so that it freezes solid before you can fit it into the bread section without crushing it. So there might be a brief period of seeming "disorganization" while newly added items freeze properly, but then, when the meat is well frozen, the bread is safely hard, and so forth, you can apply logical storage by category. You are never quite done with food storage, I find!

The Real Secret to Planning Menus and Having Peace in the Home

We will start with a reader's question, and then I will tell you the secret that will set you on your way to success in homemaking.

Dear Auntie Leila,

I can't get past the step of making a huge list of potential meals. My husband and kids aren't much help. My kids, five years old and under, can't tell me what they want to eat because their likes and dislikes seem to change from day to day! My husband says, "Make what you want!" I feel paralyzed when I sit down to think about it. I don't like being in the kitchen anyway, so the thought of all the time I'll be spending making this stuff and then cleaning it all up is depressing, to say the least.

Then the dilemma of what to make? Should I stick with fun and delicious, but decidedly not-healthy things? Grandma's Jello fluff salad? Chicken-cream cheese pockets made with Pillsbury crescent roll dough? Nigella's pasta? Then there's that diet plan I'd theoretically like to follow, to lose the last little bit of baby weight (or, since I'm newly pregnant, to keep from gaining my usual sixty pounds).

Will my kids even eat what I fix? If I make something they like one day, they'll turn up their noses the next day, or one child will love it and the rest won't touch it, which definitely adds some unpleasantness to our mealtimes. Then there's the health angle to consider: Am I struggling with anxiety, depression, and exhaustion because I'm gluten/dairy/soy/sugar/food-intolerant and don't know it? (Or is it just because I'm a constantly nursing or pregnant mom—sometimes both—and life is hard!) I used to eat anything, all the time, and it didn't make me anxious. In fact, it was rather enjoyable. Should I be drinking kefir and making my own bone broth and fermented sauerkraut? Would that magically make me a new person?

And then don't even get me started on the budget side of groceries. Yes, we are very poor, and the less we spend on food, the better, but since sticking to a tight budget seems impossible, we don't even try! My husband says, "Spend what you need to!" and I take him up on it because why stress myself?—even though it still stresses me because I know we're spending too much! Help!

Love,

Frazzled

———————————————

Dear Frazzled, and all of you out there who *know* you should be making menus, however simple (also known as planning what you will eat for at least a week so that you are not spending all day staring at a package of ground beef and wanting to run away to a circus or a convent or anywhere where they will just plunk a plate in front of *you*); dear reader who needs help overcoming this obstacle to the first step of a life of peace and order, *which is making the menus*: the secret of the French and the Finns and all the other cultures with which we are daily browbeaten, who are so superior to us and never feel overwhelmed by the necessity of feeding their families:

> Every person in the house must be polite and respectful and grateful for the food that is served.

If anyone doesn't like it, that's okay. Lots of people don't like lots of things. They can even let you know what their preferences are. But it must all be done kindly and with courtesy.

Talk to your husband about training your children to speak respectfully to you about the food. It will require both of you to make an effort, but you can do it, and honestly, a requirement is that you—husband and wife—speak to each other kindly and respectfully about everything.

All this won't happen on its own. Training must occur, and you must do the training. It will take time and not happen overnight. But one day you will realize that it's a pleasure and not the burdensome task you imagine to plan your menus (relatively speaking) because it's a pleasure to sit down and eat with your family.

How to bring this impossible state of affairs about? Auntie Leila will take you through the steps.

1. *Talk to your children beforehand about what they are and are not allowed to say.* I grew up being told, "We don't say 'hate' about the food." I wasn't even allowed to say "stuff" as in "What is this stuff?" My stepmother thought it was disrespectful. Begin by saying, "We don't say that about the food." Work up to making it clear that if *one word* that is not polite—"Oh, gross." "Yuck!" "I hate this!" "I'm not eating this!" and so forth—comes out of their mouths, they will leave the room. You will know when enough is enough.

I would not threaten loss of dessert. We are trying to cultivate true enjoyment here (see number 4). Simultaneously, give your children the exact script that you want to hear from them. "This looks delicious." "Thank you, Mama." "I like the [mention something they do like here]." "You are a good cook, Mama." "Don't worry about the burned green beans, Mama; it's okay." (This last one often has to be said to me, for some reason.)

An option: Silence.

2. *Surround your meals with ritual.* Whether, as sometimes happens, you feed the children first or they are sitting with you at supper, and no matter how simple the meal, have the table set beforehand (note I do not say *you* set it beforehand—distribute tasks as necessary and possible). Light a candle.

Teach your children not to eat until Mama has sat down. Daddy has to do this. He must wait for his beloved wife to collect herself. Of course, he has pitched in with the prep (perhaps by distracting hungry children elsewhere) and then sat down to model patient waiting. There is something shocking, in the normal course of things, about a man who begins eating before his wife has collected herself or guests have been served. When Mama sits or otherwise indicates she is ready, he leads grace.

For a ritual to occur, you must be prepared. Rituals are never spontaneous. Great care goes into their maintenance. It's up to you to realize that every single day you will need a drink, glasses, napkins, silverware, serving utensils, salt, pepper—a whole host of things! Instead of getting those items *after* everyone is seated, as if visited by a daily revelation regarding these matters, think it through beforehand. Keep the things close to or on the table, possibly on a tray. Minimize fuss at the table by supplying what

Here is my dear friend Emily's solution to one of the tasks:
a utensil caddy. This honestly never occurred to me, but I think
it's delightful. Later, another one could be added and they can be
kept on a sideboard nearby if the table becomes too crowded.

is necessary with forethought. Try not to be continually surprised by the things you need.

Even the other meals need a bit of ritual, appropriate to their lesser status, but still, this sense of orderly preparation will considerably enhance the experience. If you take care of the details beforehand, you will notice that when you sit down and pray, there is peace. The agitation comes from jumping up, not being ready, and general disorder due to lack of forethought.

3. *Every member of the family should bend over backward to be sure that every other member is well supplied with what he needs and what he prefers.* I have a friend who says that her father would take the sweet part of the watermelon on the grounds that he was the father. Well, this is not my experience of fatherhood, based on how my husband acts. He holds back and makes sure that I have what I like. If left to himself, he takes the least appealing portions. He notices what the quantity of food is and how it will be distributed. I usually have to urge him to take the last bite of something left on a platter or in a bowl.

Actually, I have to watch like a hawk lest all my family members leave at least what amounts to one small serving, no matter what the quantity of food has been, such is their habit of restraint. Sometimes I have been known to insist—with a sense of gratitude for their forbearance, but still, to insist—that ten people surely can manage to relieve us of the burden of putting away a quarter of a cup of chicken potpie or one lone broccoli spear.

But this forebearing attitude comes from habits instilled long ago: to have consideration for others and their needs. Even small children can helpfully pass what is next to them and can notice what other family members especially enjoy.

In volume 1, I told of a priest friend, a monk who hails from a large family, who had mentioned the principle of FHB: "Family Hold Back." This means that when there are guests, the family is already aware that something might run out, and so they hold back to be sure that the guests have enough—a simple guideline for hospitality, but a beautiful one. This kind of courtesy comes with practice! Practice with each other.

Young children can be taught to jump up and get the butter or the marmalade. Rowdy boys can be encouraged to pick up someone's dropped napkin. Older kids who aren't absolutely riveted by the adults' discussion of the latest world crisis can take the baby for a turn.

4. *Enjoy the food, however humble it is.* One issue with grumpy children is that we parents (and mothers in particular) do not feel free to enjoy our meal and to be confident that we did our best, however humble. We are hovering over our children with great anxiety that they (a) eat enough to ward off sudden expiration and (b) affirm and approve of us. We somehow feel that our worth as parents hinges on how they behave at the table, and yet we do not supply them with the proper behavior or even attitude. Thus, grumpiness occurs.

If someone truly does not like something, he can, if asked, answer, "It's not my favorite." That is the extent of the negativity! For instance, if offered more liver and onions (after his one bite which he must eat unless you know it's a real aversion), the child may observe, "No, thank you, I'm full." If pressed, he might say, "It's not my favorite." He can certainly have more of whatever else is offered, especially bread and butter. However, and see number 3, he can't hog the delicacies, because that is rude.

It's possible that a given child is simply too young to be at the supper table. It's fine to feed that child earlier and either let him sit up at the table with some bread and butter or play quietly nearby. Maybe dinner can be scheduled late enough so that he can go to bed early after his own simple meal.

5. *When finished (and for a small child, this might be in ten minutes), each person should thank the cook.* "Thank you, Mama, for this nice meal; may I be excused?" When your husband thanks you, thank *him* for being a good provider. (Remember Ma and Pa Ingalls in the Little House stories? So gracious to each other, while eating corn pone and salt pork or some such starvation meal.)

At least implicitly, we should be thanking God all over again, and there are those who say a little grace after the meal as well. It can be as simple as "Thank you, dear Lord." I remember my own father, who was not Christian, saying this prayer in Arabic after the meal, as is customary in Muslim culture. You can go on sitting there and enjoying the food and conversation with whoever is left. See "Seven Strategies for Dinner with Barbarians" in volume 1 for how children should leave the table and what is expected of them.

Wait, that's one secret?

Yes. Having a culture of kindness and good manners. I'm just telling you how to get that culture.

Once you institute this culture or feed it if you already possess it, you will find that you feel much more free to plan your meals. You won't worry as much about who will or will not like what you decide on. Since with my method you are consulting your family (or observing them if they really aren't forthcoming or are very young) and taking their preferences into account, your fairness *with* them meets with good will *from* them.

Only, you have to teach them that goodwill. I'm giving you a sketch; feel free to do it according to your own family style!

But a warning: do not fall into the trap of thinking that the family style is to have no manners. No way.

Once you plan your meals, you have an amazing amount of time and a lot of confidence quickly to take care of the other tasks that face you, including addressing the issue of getting kids to help. And then your environment, which is the key to educating your children, is orderly and, thus, open to wonder!

Manners (kindness and courtesy) are the secret.

Dear Frazzled, I think you will benefit by reviewing the "Menu Planning" chapter and trying to internalize what I'm saying. You will really get things in order if you try to make some lists. You can probably make all the things you are dreaming of, one at a time. Let's be patient with ourselves, and you know what? We can ask the family to be patient with us too. Kindness and courtesy.

One thing at a time. Worrying about it all at once is a good way not to succeed.

Most of all, let's enjoy one another's company, the good food, and life.

PART 3

On Conquering Laundry

Now that you are serenely sure of what your family will eat in the foreseeable future (or for three days), you are ready to systematize your laundry. Remember, if these two areas are orderly, your days will open up with possibilities for the many activities you *really* want to do. Spending a week scrutinizing and rationalizing your laundry will pay you back a hundredfold.

Laundry Problems
Start with Clothes

So, here it is: the secret. The one thing you have to grapple with to be able at last to emerge from the mountain of dirty clothes blocking your access to the very machines that can help you, and to navigate the ocean of clean clothes piling up in your room. It's not all you have to do, but it's the indispensable first step: *Have fewer clothes*. And I don't mean this just for the shopaholics among us or the victims of the overgenerous grandmas and aunties. I mean it for the frugal, thrifty, "simple living" ones, who have a lot of kids and not much cash.

In some ways, we have it worse, because we're afraid of letting go of something in case it could come in handy later on, what with the little sprouts outgrowing their togs faster than you can find them at the thrift store.

Our family got by for several years when the kids were little entirely on bags left on my porch by kind neighbors. Yet this posed a problem. Anxious to keep anything with any possible use, I made a lot of work for myself and prevented my children from helping me effectively.

The truth is, children tend to wear only a few outfits on a daily basis. They don't like change; they like predictability. Not only is it no use fighting this trait; it's counterproductive. Their drawers and closets are so full of things they don't wear that they live out of their laundry baskets most of the time. They simply can't put things away because there's a clog in the works—namely, the clothes they aren't wearing.

In addition, they function within a paradox: they want to wear only a few things, but the knowledge that they have many things gives them implicit permission to overuse the laundry system. Clothing doesn't fit in drawers, so it ends up on the floor or, if you are lucky, in a hamper. A garment on the floor is by definition dirty! Everyone knows that instantaneous contamination sets in as soon as the item is cast off! Also, how much easier it is to throw it in the hamper than to put it away! Thus, you are overwhelmed with unnecessary laundry.

Here is what your pre-adolescent children need (or at least use this list as a starting point, because of course, we all have to think): a few, five at the most, bottoms (say, two pairs of jeans and two corduroys in winter); a scant week's worth of tops; two light sweaters (for Sunday and other formal wear, girls need a simple but stylish cardigan, and boys can possibly use a vest); and for church: for boys, a good pair of pants and two good shirts; for girls, two nice dresses or two church-worthy skirts and blouses. Much more than this, and you will find that it all sits in a drawer getting stuff heaped on it. If the child has six drawers and they don't close, you have an issue. (My older kids shared dressers and basically had two drawers each—for all their clothes.)

Now, at the same time, each child also needs more underwear than you might think.

First, socks. Please, for the love of all that is good, try to buy socks in a minimum quantity of six to a pack. And buy two identical packs at a time. Why? Because, this way, if you lose a sock, and then you lose another sock, you still have a pair! But with the cute unique socks you are getting your children now, lose one and you are out a pair of socks. I once met a poor lady who had an entire laundry basket full of single socks. You couldn't hope to find the missing one in that pile even if it happened to be there. Or was it just a basket of single socks? Who could tell? I suppose, in a pinch, you could include figuring it out as a particularly challenging intelligence

Laundry Problems Start with Clothes

test for your children in your homeschool curriculum, but maybe there are better ways to spend their time.

Buy the style your children like (but avoid low ankle socks in winter). Never buy tube socks. Don't skimp on quality; get the good kind at your favorite discount store. Get good tights for the girls and one pair of dress socks for each boy.

Try to have at least eight pairs of underpants and at least six undershirts. You will be doing less laundry by the time I'm done with you, so your children will need to have enough underwear to survive the gap, including if you are sick and can't get it done, the power goes out, or some other disaster befalls you.

Go through those drawers with an empty laundry basket, a mending basket, a trash bag, and a donation bag by your side. If something is out of season, throw it in the laundry basket. As you pull each item out, ask yourself (in the case of everyday wear) whether you have seen it on a person in the past two weeks. If the answer is no, give it away or put it aside to try on the next kid. Maybe it's too small, too big, or he just doesn't like it. It's hard to accept that last one, but there it is. Just get it out of your life, at least for now. If it has a hole or tear, it can go in the mending basket; if it makes whoever wears it look pathetic and not a credit to the family name, throw it in the trash bag.

If it's pants or jeans that have holes in the knees, put them in a separate bag. Schedule a day to cut those pants off at the thigh and hem them (pretty easy: just turn under, turn under again, press, and sew). Now you have shorts to store away in the appropriate place for summer. (In the appendix I offer a tutorial for patching jeans if you need them long.)

Fewer outer clothes, more underclothes: that's the beginning of the path of laundry wisdom, according to Auntie Leila.

On the Subject of
Clothing Oversupply

You're sitting at my kitchen table, and you take a sip of iced tea. "I just don't know what to do about my laundry," you say. "Nothing I try seems to work. Sometimes I find folded laundry in the hamper, ready to go through the wash without ever having been worn! I can't get to my washer or even see it over piles of dirty laundry. What am I going to do?"

Laundry problems start with clothes, as I am hoping you are starting to see. You need quality control. Sorting and folding are two tasks I like to do myself most of the time, because they help me with quality control, and I realize I am going against popular opinion here. Some aspects of the laundry can be delegated, and I'll talk about that later, but if you ever want to crawl out from under the crushing weight of your laundry problems, stick with me here.

As I am sorting and folding, going through the clothing in its clean state, I can easily notice whose undies need replacing, and who has been wearing one shirt over and over. I make note of a pair of pants that turns up in the wash without really having been worn (maybe it put in an appearance for an hour or so) — a sure sign of a wardrobe misfit (or possibly a person who doesn't understand the concept of putting a clean article back in its place without having it go through the whole system).

Something not really worn is not worth keeping around. Or it could be a sign of a problem in the storage system. If there's no room in the drawer for a pair of pants, and the rule is "No clothes on the floor," then into the hamper it will go, worn or not. But that gets us right back to where we started: too many clothes.

While you begin to implement the suggestions below, use the laundry process itself as a step in the system to reduce unnecessary items. As you are folding, you can throw away shabby underwear and add replacements to your shopping list; you can remove that blouse you've noticed is just too small for your daughter; you can make note of the kinds of colors your son prefers.

As you put things away, look in the drawers and closets. Yes, usually everyone should put away his own clothes, but once in a while, you have to do it yourself to see what's *really* in there, and I am aware of the horror factor here. First and foremost, are the clothes in season? Why are shorts cluttering the world up if it's winter? Note to self: establish a place (with its own system of shelves and well marked bins) for out-of-season items.

When was the last time you saw the items worn? Encourage everyone to weed out items that don't fit, are the wrong color, or otherwise don't meet personal or family standards. Once a quarter or so, as you get people to do this, grab two big trash bags into which you put those items that can be given away and those that should be thrown away. Then hustle them (the clothes, not the people, regardless of the temptation) out the door.

The number of items each person possesses is a personal decision, but it's clear that some quantities will not to work. Usually people don't need twenty T-shirts, or eight pairs of pants, or ten sweaters. Often when children are wearing hand-me-downs, they accumulate these things, or we accumulate them on their behalf as a hedge against the odds of finding something to wear.

But the hand-me-down system *can* work if you exert quality control. Think of it this way: if you were buying the clothes, you would be more careful about size, color, and suitability. Just because something didn't cost you much or anything at all, it doesn't mean you should keep it. Be just as fussy about bargains as you are about items you pay a lot for. The point isn't how much you paid for it, but how much it's worth to you. A blouse that fits and shows quality workmanship should be cared for no matter how much it cost. Regardless, something suitable will cost a lot to replace, because good clothes are hard to find.

Any clothing you buy will stand you in good stead, both for the person it's purchased for and down the line, if you keep in mind some criteria:

- For children, avoid clothing with pictures or animated characters printed on it. Those things look *instantly* tired and mismatched—how will they look in a year?
- Trends such as unfinished edges, deliberate tears, or pre-distressing are anathema to the thrifty family, not to mention a scam and an insult. One washing (never mind the hundreds we have in mind) will put the article out of commission.
- Fitted clothing is best, but make sure that sleeves and waist are in proportion, with enough length to allow for growth. A sweater with reasonable sleeves but short in the waist is useless for what it's intended for, which is keeping the person warm.
- Some things must be bought new (as opposed to a thrift store) and are worth spending a bit more for (as opposed to getting a cheap version that doesn't last), and here is where you have to think carefully. Underwear falls into this category. Even in our most direly penny-pinching days, I never found a way to avoid buying socks!

The Laundry Process

I f you have a good system going for your laundry, then good for you! I affirm you! And a lot depends on whether you have a dedicated laundry room with plenty of workspace, or whether you have to make do in the basement or the mudroom.

I'm going to tell you about my way. This is a kid-tested, decades-honed, homeschool-proof, flexible system that does not take over your life.

Fair warning: it also does not produce a home free of laundry baskets in various stages of delivery. If you are looking for such a system, one in which a basket of clothes is nowhere to be found, I suggest you take one or more of these steps:

1. Hire a laundress.
2. Give up ever doing anything other than laundry.
3. Go naked.
4. Get rid of almost all of your children.

Otherwise, welcome to my world, where there is always a laundry basket *en route* to somewhere! If you are seeking permission to have clean clothes on a reliable basis *and* laundry baskets wandering around your house, under control but in various stages of the process, consider it given! I don't know any other sane way to go about it.

Everything I tell you is based on a family of at least six. If you have fewer, you may not need so many baskets.

Dig Yourself out of the Piles

In the beginning of this journey to laundry order, you will need to rid your laundry area of the piles of things you have in there. Most likely, you have a lot of stuff that you thought at the time, "That is an unusual load of things. I'll get to it soon." A bedspread you're not sure your machine can handle? Some sweaters you think might shrink? Some very dirty towels?

Whatever it is, get to the bottom of it. Dedicate a day to this project.

Take the bedspread and a couple of other oversized things to the laundromat. Start some loads of towels before you leave—with hot water, detergent, and bleach (1/4 cup per load). Pick out the sweaters for a later "hand washable" or "delicates" cycle or get them to the dry cleaner by putting them in a bag and taking them out to the car (meaning, this is not a mental exercise but a real one!).

On this laundry battle day, pull everything to the middle of the room and plow through all the piles until, one way or another, they are gone. Put all the clean things into a different room to be sorted later. If you don't have extra space, use the dining table and eat in the kitchen until you're done! Motivation!

Now, while the bedspreads are at the laundromat, go to the store and get yourself four plastic hampers. This is what you need: one for lights, one for darks, one quite large one for towels and sheets, and one for "special needs" loads (not large; I'll explain soon). There are also good hampers to be found at those nice discount stores; they look like wicker but are plastic over wire (necessary to avoid mold).

You also need an airy hamper (real wicker is fine) for ironing, and something for the kitchen and mudroom area, where a lot of laundry is generated but might not make it to the laundry area right away.

If you don't have any already, you need four ordinary sturdy plastic laundry baskets, preferably stackable. These should be rectangular with handles on all sides.

Now, find a place not far from the bathroom or bedrooms for the four hampers. They can go in a hallway.

Here is where you have to convince yourself that your children can and will understand what they have to do. And they can and they will! — if you insist. They must, every night upon disrobing, place their dark clothing in one hamper and their light clothing in another.

I am here to tell you that even a two-year-old, if a girl, and definitely a three-year-old, if a boy, can learn this. Usually they interpret it to mean that outer clothes go in the darks and underwear into the lights, and if you firmly explain that a light yellow T-shirt counts as light and black socks count as black, you should make headway. Yes, you will have to remedy the occasionally misfiled object. Sometimes a girl gets it into her head that one of the hampers is for "pretty" things and the other for "not pretty" things; see what you can do.

Insist that your children put *two* socks into the hamper. Spend a week making a point of directing them to put whatever socks they have randomly thrown about into an appropriate hamper. That hamper in the kitchen or mudroom is fine and now you see why, besides kitchen towel management, you need this downstairs (or not bedroom-oriented) landing place for dirty things.

I am death on taking socks off wherever one happens to be. Any perpetrator will be dragged from kingdom come to dispose of them properly. This is why most of my loads come out sock-even. When your children master putting their socks in the hampers, train them to turn the socks right side out first. We're talking brutal efficiency and strict adherence to the norm; there's no mercy in socks.

The reason single socks proliferate is that children take them off in random places. You will thank yourself if you establish early on your clear disapproval of the placing of socks in any receptacle other than the hamper. Children regard a wet sock as a sock they want to forget about. They think nothing of leaving such a thing in the middle of a room. They get hot playing in the den, and off come the socks. If you register disbelief that anyone not inhabiting primordial ooze with the dinosaurs would throw his socks behind a sofa, and immediately require rectification of the error, you will find that these sorts of terrible misadventures rarely trouble you.

Towels and bedding[5] go in that larger hamper.

Laundry Tip

By way of a little drill-sergeanting and cheerleading, let me comment on something I've noticed when people talk about laundry. They seem to think that you must sort, wash, dry, fold, sort again, and put away—all at once! Do you think that? Go back over the info here in this section. If you have more than two children, how about viewing each step as different chores that you cycle through at different times of the day?

Let your children give you a hand with or even completely accomplish the various parts of the process, and let them put away their own clothes. If there are too many to put away, there are too many clothes!

But don't try to do the whole task all at once. Don't consider it a failure that it's never all done; instead, redefine. Otherwise, it all seems like—and is—too darned much!

More on Sorting: Hampers and Towels

Hampers

As I said, and it bears repeating, even the youngest child, if he is able to remove clothing, has the ability to distinguish between at least two kinds of hampers—the lights and the darks! If he can toddle, he can toddle down to the designated spot and place his garments therein. Well, you can tell him what to do until he gets older, but the older children who are doing the laundry will handle it better if they don't have to touch dirty clothing to sort it.

---

[5]   If several beds are being stripped at once, you won't have room in one hamper for all that bedding. This situation is my only relaxation of my "no dirty clothes on the laundry-room floor" rule, as there is not much else to do with them. But the good news is that you can work through them quickly, and they don't disappear behind the appliances the way small items tend to do.

If you have room, deploy four hampers, two of which are approximately laundry-basket-sized; they hold one or two loads: one for lights and one for darks; a large one for sheets and towels; and yet another for items that require special care of some sort (permanent press, delicate, or hand washable; also for lingerie, bras, and pantyhose).

The reason the laundry room gets out of control is that there is no hamper for occasional sheets and towels, so these items get piled up in front of the washer. But clothing gets priority, so the piles of larger items become fixtures; people literally climb over them to do more urgent loads.

But—and this is important—wet things should not go in hampers! They will become a moldy mess! So you need to think through how you will get dirty things *dry* before they are placed there. Bath towels should be kept on a hook or a rack to dry after use and collected frequently for laundering or placement in the hamper, but there is always that one that has been left in a heap or used to dry the dog; it needs to be hung over a railing until it is tossed directly into the washer or is dry (if dirty) and can be put in the hamper.

Any special clothing, such as sweaters, dress shirts, nice delicate cotton knits, dress pants, silk tops, and lingerie go in the smaller permanent press or "special needs" hamper. I have always taken care of those things myself, since a mistake can spell disaster here, where the other categories are more forgiving. You can point out to the little person that his item needs to go there, as needed.

Think about it. If the laundry is presorted, doesn't it make life easier? Do we really enjoy sorting through *dirty* laundry (left in heaps in front of the appliances or jumbled into one big hamper) on washing day, to get it in the right place? Is it necessary to add this dreaded step to an already Sisyphean, thankless task? Yes, no, and no. And this is my secret: *presorted dirty clothing.* It's worth it.

Towels

Some mothers wake up one day with the realization that half their laundry is doing towels. Some never realize it; I have heard of some who do towels every day, and I am all astonishment.

The solution is to get each child his own color of towel, or a monogrammed one, or something (color-coded tag, for instance) for when they are tossed around (the towels, not the kids). Install hooks (or buy the kind that go over the door, if the children are tall enough to reach). This system saves you money: washing those towels constantly and replacing worn ones is costing you! Show the child how to hang up his towel after he uses it.

If the hook is low enough, even a toddler can do this. But it must be done, because bath towels can remain clean and usable for days *if they dry out between uses.* If it has not been hung up, it's easily identifiable, and the offender should be made to hang it up. A week's worth of training and enforcement will yield a habit.

Dirty towels go in the towel hamper, but they must be dry, or the hamper gets smelly and the towels become difficult to get really clean. (An adult has the responsibility to decide when a child's towel is dirty.)

With this system of towel management and hamper sorting, doing a load of laundry shouldn't present a problem for anyone who can lift a full basket. After all, how much finesse does it take to put a load in the washer, measure some detergent, and get it started?

Well, it takes training, but it can be done. And with the grossness factor of sorting dirty laundry removed, even an eight- or nine-year-old can be taught what to do.

Laundry Solutions

If you and I were sitting and talking about what highly intelligent folks talk about ("The problem with you women is that you just want to talk about the price of potatoes!" a male friend once scolded. Hey, we can talk about the stimulus package or the One and the Many if you want to, but we are interested in the price of potatoes as well!) and also about laundry, you will say to yourself, "I can do that, and I can do better than that." Yes, it's as I've been telling you: if I can do it, so can you.

So here are some notes on simplifying the laundry. This part is blah-blah-blah … it just goes on and on. Oh my goodness. I'm so sorry.

Those of you with high-tech nuclear-powered washing machines and dryers are on your own. Read your manual and figure it out. Actually, everyone should read the instructions that come with household appliances. These machines are expensive to replace, and they are not magic!

It's easier to explain to a child how to use an appliance if we really understand it ourselves. Have you completely internalized the fact that if you consistently overload your washer it will fail you long before its time? (I know of one family whose washer failed that one time when their returning college student put *all* her laundry in it at once!) This knowledge will help you explain to your minions how to choose a water level or cycle.

Laundry Detergent

Choose a detergent that doesn't have a scent. Some tend to try to save money by buying off-brand detergent that has an overwhelming scent at the expense of effective cleansing agents. Be sure that you are smelling your clothes, not the detergent.

Really clean laundry has a clean smell of its own. Some people's laundry smells clean from far away, but if you get into it and really smell it (as when they're giving you a hug), you can tell it's not clean deep down. So your scented detergent might be masking this sad truth from you.

To provide deep-down cleanliness, you need a couple of other products and the occasional run-through with warm or hot water, and outdoor line-drying in the sun if the weather allows.

I realize that we are all trying to be frugal and washing in cold water, but permit me to say that refraining from using warm or hot water when you need it is causing you to wash certain things more often than they need to be washed, which is costing you in electricity, water, and wear-and-tear on your machines and your clothing.

What makes things smell, for the most part, is body odor and molds. To handle the former, use warmer water; often presoaking does the trick. As to the latter, towels need bleach and at least warm water. In the summer they need hot water or line drying. One summer, we stayed at a beach house that supplied towels and sheets. I ended up washing all the "clean" linens before we could use them. I had to go buy bleach and proper detergent to do it. They were so musty, yet overpoweringly perfumed with the cheap detergent the owner had on hand that I couldn't bear even to be in the house with them.

Mustiness is that "whiff" of something that's not dirt or sweat, that you get from damp towels, sponges, washcloths, rain gear, old shoes, or anything that has been sitting around in damp. That "whiff" makes me crazy! The only cure is bleach, hot water, a hot dryer, and a good airing in the direct sun.

If you find that laundry in drawers after a few days no longer seems clean and fresh, try doing your wash in warm water for a while and add a little bleach to the whites. The problem may be your "thrifty" homemade laundry soap; commercial detergents have surfactants, which are chemicals that bond with dirt *and* water, making it possible to wash the dirt *away*. Homemade soaps will not be able to do this.

Stains

Here are some of my secrets to add to your usual stain-removing aids:

- *Lestoil* (a cleanser with pine oils, which will remind you of those old-fashioned floor cleaners, plus sodium tallate, a soap) will remove those grease spots on knits and chino pants. (I realize that this is possibly a regional product, which is why I gave you the basic ingredients to check against what you may have where you live.) You know how you always seem to drop a bit of salad on your favorite polo shirt? Or how your husband seems to plunk pizza on his new khakis? How about that ring around the collar of winter jackets? Rub Lestoil into the grease spot, let it sit for a few minutes, and launder in warm water. I've never used a more effective grease spot remover, so I don't buy the others anymore. I pour the Lestoil into a squeeze bottle (for condiments) from the dollar store so I can target stains precisely—better than trying to pour out of the big bottle.
- *Ammonia.* For articles that seem yellowed and for sheets and other vaguely greasy objects, try ammonia according to the directions, and warm or hot water. Your pillowcases won't get really clean with bleach. You need ammonia! (And remember, *never mix the two.* A toxic gas will result that will harm your lungs if it doesn't kill you outright.)
- *Oxygen-type bleaches.* I do like oxygen-type bleaches for some things. You can even use straight hydrogen peroxide. You can make a paste with the powder and warm water and rub it into berry and wine stains. Then wash the item and dry it in the sun if possible.
- *Soaking.* Giving soiled articles a good soak is a time-tested method of removing stains. Unfortunately, many washers today don't

have a soak cycle. If yours doesn't, here's a tip that works with my top-loader (I don't know if it will work with a front loader, but you can puzzle it out): After you treat your stains, fill the washer as usual and let it agitate enough to distribute the water and detergent evenly. Then pause the machine and unplug it. If you just pause it, after a certain (short) time, it will drain, so that won't work. Set a timer so you don't just forget this soaking load; I suspect that one reason manufacturers eliminated the option to soak is that it's not good for the machine to be left a long time this way; it's certainly not good for the clothes to be left with bleach or detergent for days, which sounds unlikely, but people do get distracted. Anyway, when you're ready, simply plug the machine in again and press the start button. Give it a minute to recover its senses. It should just start up where it left off.

- *Bluing.* For whites that have yellowed, try bluing. It works! So old-fashioned!

Drying

In cold weather, I use one-quarter to one-third of a dryer sheet (really all you need) in my regular loads to prevent static (not with towels—fabric softener works by adding a substance that attracts a little moisture; this would defeat the purpose of a towel, which needs to be *dry*). The cheapest, most generic dryer sheets are just fine.

You really need a folding drying rack for lingerie, delicates, spandex, and whatever else shouldn't go in the dryer, but always ends up there just because you don't know what else to do with it, and that will not be good for them; alternatively, your home will be draped with washing.

A line outside is so comforting, and of course there is the bleaching power of the sun. If you can't have a clothesline outside for some reason (or it's winter), perhaps you can put one in your tidy basement or cleaned-out utility closet, where the furnace keeps the air dry. The Irish call this *the airing cupboard*, because they don't have basements, and their climate is so damp. This sounded oxymoronic to me, as a cupboard seems the opposite of airy, but my Irish friend explained it to me, and now I would really love to have one.

Distributing Folded Clothes

Remember those baskets I had you buy? Get the loads out of the dryer (most days it will be two loads) and take them somewhere handy for folding, if you don't have a laundry room with a counter. I use my bed. That way, I have to finish the task—or I won't be able to sleep! If all else fails, bring the baskets to the sofa, make yourself comfortable, put on a show, and get all your laundry folded!

As you fold, place the piles carefully in the baskets by *room*. If, for instance, your four girls share a room, place their clothes together in one basket. I would put the big girls' clothes on the bottom, side by side, and then the littler ones on top of those. They know whose is whose and the older ones can help the younger ones. Ditto the boys. If two girls are in one room and two in another, use two baskets. The point is to get the clean clothes to their destination. When the children have put their laundry away, the baskets get returned to the laundry area near the hampers. Sometimes you have to call a "basket roundup minute" to accomplish this last step.

Some families have the space to have dressers by or in the laundry room, and that is a system that could definitely work, on the principle that things should not travel far from where they are taken care of.

Dish-Towel Talk, an Interlude

Speaking of good and bad and having standards, what is up with dish towels that are coated, impregnated, or otherwise imbued with some substance that prevents them from absorbing moisture? Is it that people generally use paper towels and consider the dish towel an ornament, not called upon for actual use? I use paper towels on occasion. But I need my cloth towels to dry things.

Too much to ask? I think not.

I sometimes find myself with a stash of dish towels that is getting tired. It's a carefully curated stash, purged of anything lacking in absorbency. But I find it's a tired stash. So I go shopping and refrain from the cutesy and the seasonal. I resist. I have criteria.

Waffle-weave dish towels are my favorite. I like potato sacking okay, but I find the fabric thin. The simply flat-woven doesn't measure up. It's damp where I live. I want my hands to feel less moist after a wipe. I want my dishes to be lacking in dampness after contact with a towel.

So I find some towels that seem promising. They are big. They are beefy. Some are waffle weave, albeit only partially; a dubious characteristic that makes me tremble at portents of future distensions. But I spring; I purchase them.

Then, I am boiling—with rage against the unjust treatment of cotton, yes, but also literally, with water on the stove, in an attempt to rid the towels of this bad coating of water resistance and to provide myself with new towels that actually dry.

How to Remove Mildew Stains

Continuing in a dish-towel vein: What if yours is mildewed? It may be that you need to throw that thing away. Other than rust, I don't know of a harder stain. Until recently, that's what I did. Just gave it up for lost.

But I, your friendly laundry consultant, will share this immensely important discovery I have made of removing mildew stains.

The worst has happened. You've somehow left a towel or bib or blouse damp and wadded up. Days later, you find it and—little black spots. Ugh. Nothing will get those spots out, you think. You've tried bleach, OxiClean, vinegar, vinegar and baking soda, magic elven dust, essential oils, and every other laundry remedy, including sunshine, and you know that once you have those spots, that's it—game over.

But a while back I had an aha moment. If I'm going to throw it away, I might as well try the last-ditchest of last-ditch efforts, right? So that's what this is.

A really hard-core solution. Don't be shocked. It works—or it doesn't and you throw the item away, which is what you were going to do anyway.

Where we live, it can be damp, and we do have a problem with mildew. Having used foaming bleach bathroom cleanser to remove mildew from the grout in the shower, I know it works. (It is merely more concentrated bleach, but the foaming aspect makes it adhere, rather than run off.)

So, I thought, why not spray that mildewy towel? The heavy-duty bleach spray will definitely bleach out anything it falls on that is not resistant, so you have to be careful. It's a strong chemical, a solution of last resort, as when you have black in your bathroom and need to get rid of it.

And, if you spray it on the spots on textiles, they will disappear. Most towels are bleach-resistant—they have to be, because people need to bleach them, most cities put a little bleach in their water, and often people take towels to pools, which, of course, have chlorine added to the water. Some articles of clothing are either white or bleach resistant, and you won't know until you try! The fact is, you were going to throw it away, so why not? And for something like a bib, I'd rather have it be bleached out than mildew spotted. A faded bib or towel is no real tragedy.

Wet the item all over, spray the spots, and let it sit for a bit; then rinse it, and wash it with your normal load.

It has worked for me many a time! Just be sure you aren't wearing your favorite jeans or shirt when you do it, and watch what's behind the item when you spray it.

You Can Beat the Laundry

If you struggle with the laundry, suffering from a sense of overall defeat, I hope that I have helped you to think deeply about all the issues raised here and inspired you to make a plan of action. I must speak seriously, based on the overwhelming obstacle laundry presents to mothers attempting to achieve some sort of competence in homemaking: if you have more than three children, and up to seven (after that, you are on your own; Auntie Leila has only seven children), you will be doing an average of two loads of laundry a day, every day. You will fold at least four loads of laundry every other day. A battle indeed! When you have a baby, you will be doing more. If your husband has a dirty job, you will do an extra load of his clothes. And probably at least once a week, you will do many more than two loads, because you will also do the towels, the permanent-press items, and some bedding. That will be your *real* "laundry day": every other day is just "doing laundry" along with everything else.

You need a new paradigm in which you don't think of laundry as a surprisingly immovable obstacle in your way, one that doesn't have much of a solution, but instead as a constant aspect of homemaking, with its own satisfaction, once you accept it and accept that *it does take time*. There will always be laundry to be done, but it will be under control if you follow my plan.

PART 4

The Reasonably Clean House: Its Organization, Upkeep, and Justification

ow can one have anything resembling a clean house when trailed by a pack of expert house wreckers? What is the point? Should we ask the Almighty to "bless this mess" and just forget about it? Is it possible to have a tidy home?

There is a point, and it can be done. Little by little, using my methods, you, dear reader, can have a Reasonably Clean, Fairly Neat, Comfortably Tidy house!

The Reasonably Clean, Fairly Neat, Comfortably Tidy House

I've always written for people more or less like me: people who would rather be reading than cleaning; people with lots of other people around; people who will stop whatever they are doing to hear a good story; people who like children and dogs, at least in theory; people with big ideas who are continually surprised at the intractability of the material world—its propensity toward disorder, for instance.

We would rather make plans for a difficult and complex project than execute it, and we tend to get bogged down in the details. But, I'll say this about us: we do realize that the details matter, and that somehow we must stoop to conquer. We don't scorn cleaning a bathroom even if it doesn't come naturally, because we know we are happier when things are clean. We know they could be *cleaner*. We're good with clean.

In this section, you will find the deepest thoughts I have on the Reasonably Clean, Fairly Neat, Comfortably Tidy House (hereinafter referred to as the "Reasonably Clean House"), and that will take some time. I will give you some secrets on how to maintain a Reasonably Clean House with a passel of kids, because we all know that if we lived alone, we, too, could be just like any paragon of organization featured in magazines—it's just all these *people* who are causing our problems.

For starters, have you ever read the following books? Look for them at the library. They are the ones that helped me the most, and I'll tell you why.

Confessions of an Organized Homemaker, by Deniece Schofield. The author raised five kids and thought things through analytically, in light of the good of the family. When I had no idea how to get started, this book really helped me a lot. Schofield is realistic and practical.

Schofield's book on organizing the kitchen, *Kitchen Organization Tips and Secrets* is just as good. She applies engineering principles to a sector that could well use them. Not every kitchen is the same, but having expressed principles for organizing *your* kitchen is really helpful.

Sidetracked Home Executives, by Pam Young and Peggy Jones: what helped me in this book was the idea of cleaning a room by starting in the same place and working your way around, every time. Thinking about cleaning rooms rather than the whole house works wonders on this easily distracted mind. The authors are genuinely amusing, which is such a blessing when you are contemplating how bad at something you are.

Is There Life after Housework?, by Don Aslett, shows that using the right tools along with time management to reduce housework can be done. Some of Aslett's books descend into product pushing, but his professional outlook can shake us housewives out of our inefficient ways. If it weren't for him, I would have never spent the money on rubber mats for my mudroom, but twenty years later, the same ones are doing the job cutting my housework time. Good investment! An important point for time management: overlap jobs. While you are waiting for water to boil, wipe a counter. Spray your shower, clean the rest of the bathroom, then wipe the shower down—this gives the cleanser time to work on the scum. Use the waiting time in one job to accomplish something in another. Aslett's whole approach has more energy than others I've read about.

Home Comforts, by Cheryl Mendelson: I love the extensive detail in this book as well as the forthright declaration that an orderly home *matters*. As big as *Home Comforts* is, I would have preferred *even more detail* about the author's experiences, and that, dear reader, explains why *my* book is in three volumes! And certainly, for our purposes, the fact that Mendelson had a career and only one child makes her advice nice to shoot for but perhaps not in my "if I can do it" category—not at all! As such, maybe it is a little unrealistic for large-family life. But that's where I come in. And *Home Comforts* does have a huge amount of really good advice for those who love to delve into particulars.

I haven't read every book on this topic, especially lately. When I do read a new one, I am confirmed in my thought that these authors who might seem somewhat out of date are nevertheless the best of the bunch. It's these that I always recommend to anyone who asks.

I'm going to tell you my own way of doing things, and you'll recognize the influence of these writers on my methods. So if, like me, you'd rather read than clean, tackling this book list is the perfect procrastination!

Tidiness Magic

After I wrote this series on the blog, a new book captured everyone's interest: Marie Kondo's *The Life-Changing Magic of Tidying Up*. Kondo captured the truth that tidiness works magic on life — I think the title is really inspired! It's a great read. The core idea, that you can finally declutter by applying Kondo's criteria to your belongings (especially, famously, the one that asks if each one "sparks joy" — and if it doesn't, instructs you to "toss it in the bin"), helps tremendously to cut through the strange hold that *things* have on us. Later in this volume is an anecdote about my experience KonMari'ing some things.

In the meantime, for a detailed analysis for the truly impaired, read on.

How to Start Keeping House

I am convinced, and often assert, that if you have your meals planned and your laundry in process (I say "in process" because laundry is never done), you can handle other parts of your life in a realistic manner.

If you feel you can say "70 percent yes" — in other words, "most of the time, dear Auntie Leila, I have meals and laundry under control" (Auntie Leila would *never* ask you to be more on top of things than she is herself, or she would be going to *your* blog for advice), then you may move on to the next resolution, which is ...

Preparing to Clean

If you are not a good housekeeper, you will have to be patient and do things little by little, just as with menus and laundry. In a bit I will tell you *where* to start. We will talk about how to do more in less time, and even how to make sure you don't do *too much*. Yes, that can be a problem—please tell your loved ones to stop laughing! How rude!

We will talk about how to have the Reasonably Clean House with a nursing baby and a toddler, all while homeschooling. We will talk about how to get your kids to help you and *why* they should. And we will talk about many other things, all of them fascinating and profound.

For now, we aren't going to clean—we are just going to *think* about cleaning. So don't worry.

But I'm going to tell you my biggest secret to getting things done, whether it's organizing a shelf or cleaning the garage. It seems simple. I hope you won't be disappointed. But I can tell you that human nature is such that doing it sort of takes a leap; consequently, one often doesn't, much to the detriment of progress in this area. I have never seen other guides start with this secret. They seem to take it for granted, if they even know about it; sometimes they tell you the opposite, which is a problem. But knowing it makes all the difference.

First, and I apologize for this further delay, I will say this: I really think you should gird your loins for cleaning by going ahead and taking a shower and getting dressed. This is not the secret. This is the pre-secret, explained in detail in volume 1.

Often, I've noticed, persons who stay at home put off the showering and dressing process, perhaps thinking that it doesn't make sense to tackle a dirty house by getting oneself clean first, and sometimes they refrain just because they feel that they can hardly tackle *two* projects—getting dressed *and* cleaning—in a day.

I beg to differ, however. You will work hard, but you really aren't going to get dirty, not for normal cleaning. While it might make sense to clean the bathroom or the garage before taking a shower, for the most part, delaying the shower is counterproductive.

I mean, don't get dressed up. If you think your normal jeans and top will get soiled, you should wear an apron. Not a fancy frilly one—a sturdy work apron made of twill.

If you don't do as I say, what will surely happen is that you will be tired from your exertions and find yourself not all that inclined to shower and dress after all. And then an emergency will arise, and lo! you will find yourself in the doctor's office with a sick baby; tired, not showered, in sweats, and looked upon with scorn by any passing nannies. And that will not help our cause one bit.

Besides, being clean and dressed invigorates you, makes you ready to take on all your tasks, and, to use an annoying word, *empowers* you generally. If you are in your yoga pants, there are all kinds of ways to put off getting up and getting going.

Another thing (also helped by being dressed for action): make up your mind to try to be fast in whatever you do. Right now it's more important to get through a task than to take a lot of time over it.

Some people are in the habit of working so slowly, they really stand no chance against the forces of entropy. They are like those little helpless bunny babies with a great big entropy cat stalking them.

Watch someone lively do her work, and measure your own motions against hers. Could you be faster? Try!

The Secret

All right, here it is—the secret.

When you are cleaning something, particularly for the first time (or for the first time in a long time):

Start by getting everything out and off; *then* sort. Don't try to de-clutter in place.

Put back only what you have determined truly belongs, and not one other thing, even if it means leaving that thing in the middle of the room.

That shelf you are trying to clean? The table you need to locate under the stuff piled on it? Take everything off it. Vacuum it or wipe it down. Then replace only what belongs there, without thinking about how to deal with the rest.

I can't tell you how often I have seen instructions that have you taking things out of a closet, say, one by one, and deciding which bin to sort it into. I'm all for the bin-sorting method of decluttering, don't get me wrong, and we'll get to that. But unless you don't need me anyway, you will likely never be done with the job if you go about it that way.

First, you need the immediate gratification of the gleaming, shining object (shelf or table or whatever it is) carefully arranged with its proper contents. Second, it's all too easy to stop halfway through the task to do something else urgent, and then you might as well not have started! Whereas my way, you will have the newly arranged space and, it's true, the pile of junk to deal with, but that just means there's no turning back.

It's total commitment and instant gratification all rolled up in one step.

So these are the principles or tips, as it were, with which we will start.

- Get dressed.
- Get what you're cleaning cleared off and all the items out.

This Secret in Practice

Here's a little mental exercise that on the blog was a staged tutorial, lavishly illustrated with photos. Here we will just imagine that it's shortly after Christmas, the school year is resuming, and …

Oh my! Look at that sideboard. There's so much junk on it. Looks as if people just walked by and put stuff on there. They probably thought: Oh! A horizontal surface! Let me pile my junk on here. Not permanently, no, why would you accuse us of that?

They thought, "I'll put these things here, just until I do 'this one thing.'"

This sideboard isn't pretty or even orderly, it's just piled with stuff. Should I address each thing in turn, walking it to its rightful place?

Auntie Leila says: no, because this would be tiring. And halfway through, you'd wonder if that Latin curriculum left on there is really the right one for your seventh grader, and you'd go search for reviews, or the phone would ring, you'd be off finding your husband's important papers he forgot, and the sideboard would still be a mess.

You can't even get the offenders together to deal with it, because they are finally studying or off at soccer practice, or the truth is, it was you.

Instead of all these traps, here is how you clean it. Provide yourself with two damp rags, a trash bag, and a basket of some sort; place them near you. Now, get everything off the sideboard. *Everything.*

Some things belong there, such as a cake plate and candles. Should I just leave those things to save time?

No.

What about the wine bottles? They can stay, right?

No.

I wasn't too sure about this gift of Amaretto; such pretty wrapping—or the little apothecary jars I got at a thrift store for twenty-five cents each. What should I do with those?

Stop thinking about it. Take them off the sideboard.

I wish my sideboard were refinished. Other people have refinished sideboards. Maybe I should spray-paint it. Would black be too much?

This is your sideboard. You literally got it out of the trash, thanks to a friend who alerted you that a rectory was being cleaned out and a pile of furniture was out in the driveway! It's a miracle you have a decent sideboard. It even had some linens inside! Maybe it should be painted, but *not now!* This is it, and it needs to be cleaned. Let's clean it today and worry about refinishing it tomorrow. Truth is, you will be a lot more contented with shabby chic when it's all clean.

You obey Auntie Leila and take *every last thing off.* That's what I'm talking about. Completely cleared off. Where is all the stuff? Turn around. It's all on the dining room table! But that's okay, and you'll soon understand why.

I allow you to put some things away right now if their proper place is in that same room you are cleaning. So the box of candles can go in one drawer of the sideboard. (And why, pray, were they not put there in the first place? Literally *right there.*) The linens that were piled on the Latin book—ditto.

Otherwise, just live dangerously with everything else on the dining room table, and get your rag. (I favor flannel rags torn from old flannel sheets and pjs, laundered of course. The rag should be either slightly damp or soaked with furniture oil. Do not dust with a dry rag. (You might as well just not do it, especially in January! You will be merely flinging the dust in the air, and shortly it will settle right back where it was.)

Now wipe off every surface of the sideboard. Start at the top and wipe every inch, including legs and sides. If we were cleaning the inside, you would have taken everything out and you would wipe all the sides of the drawers.

Now start putting things back. Put things back on the sideboard only if

- they belong there
- you really love them there because they are so pretty
- they have a function there
- they are clean

With these thoughts in mind, you may begin replacing certain things, wiping them as you go with your rag, if they are wipeable.

The handmade linen lace from your mother-in-law that goes on top: at least shake it out, or, if it has been a while, launder, starch, and iron it before putting it back.

The candlesticks: wipe them with a clean damp rag. Wash and dry them, if you haven't done so recently.

Here on top is where you "store" your cake stand, because it's so pretty, with the cake dome on top of it. If a cake appears in the kitchen or elsewhere, requiring the stand and the dome, you are ready to go.

The Polish pottery dishes go here; nowhere else to put them, and they are pretty. Think carefully, though. Don't put them back just because you always have. Make a decision about them. It might be that some serving dishes that are taking up room in a kitchen cabinet need to go, and that would free up room in there, while these might stack well in a drawer.

On the other side of the sideboard, you place two of the nicer bottles of wine, to protect them from being drunk willy-nilly on an ordinary day. These pass the pretty test and can stay. The third bottle goes in the wine rack.

You may put on the sideboard the candy dish with the last of the Christmas candy in it, so that someone other than you will be eating it. And a certain little decorative plate will soon go on a wall in the den, so it's okay here too—only because it's pretty!

There. The sideboard is clean, it's pretty, and it feels as if you meant it to be just like this.

What about the table behind you?

Take the apothecary jars to the kitchen. They need to be washed out, and then we'll think of what to do with them (they held Christmas candy when everyone was here; perhaps now they can hold cotton balls in the bathroom). Some of that other junk is Christmas decorating flotsam, so it needs to be stored away or discarded in the trash bag you have provided yourself with. The basket is handy to collect this miscellany so it can be moved to its proper place.

The books obviously go on the child's homeschooling shelf. At this point, it might be worth it to you to put them back yourself, and not wait for the child to do it; put them in the basket as well so you won't risk distraction in that other location.

And now the table looks like this: a couple of gifts received that need a home and a table that needs to be wiped. We can live with this if we need to take someone to an appointment right now or if bread needs to be put in the oven. This is nothing! And the sideboard is pretty and fresh.

If you only had twenty minutes (maybe while talking on the phone to a friend?), you could do this. If you were deep-cleaning the dining room, you'd *use this exact process* in every part of the room and only at the end address the table itself. Dust the room thoroughly (another tutorial for another day) and vacuum. And then the room would be clean.

And it starts with this little secret, which you will apply to all your cleaning tasks, large and small: *Start by getting everything out and off, then sort. Don't try to declutter in place.*

The Heart of Cleaning

Now that the secret is out of the way, we are going to get to the core of this cleaning business.

A little note: some of you are very good housekeepers, and this is all going to seem pointless to you. I'm not one of you, and I don't think you understand those of us who aren't naturally clean, or who would be fabulous at it, if only we didn't have life to distract us. Please understand that we have our issues that can be handled only a certain way. We love you and wish we could be like you.

For the rest, well, I need to give you a quick pep talk on why you should strive to have a Reasonably Clean House.

1. *No one else is going to do it for you.* If someone else does clean your house for you, then lucky you! But it may happen that you go through lean times—at that point, you'll be back relying on yourself. Many have given up the second income (or chosen not to have it in the first place), and a housekeeper is not in their budget.

Don't waste time being bitter about this responsibility. Why would you? Because you're so highly educated? Because you used to be an executive?

Because your mom should help you? Because you could be earning a big salary if, if, if ...? Because your friends don't have to?

Well, if you are home today and your house is dirty and no one is coming to clean it in an hour, then you, and only you, have to deal with it. All that other mental clutter doesn't matter. It's as simple as that. But you'll feel better about it if you know *how* to do it—if you are *competent*.

2. *Order is liberating.* You can think about other things when your home is orderly. You can pray, read, cook, and entertain. You can leave the house without dreading coming home.

By being orderly, you will have taken concrete steps to overcome anxiety and depression if you suffer from those ills, for while a disorderly house might not *cause* mental disturbance (although, then again, it might!), it's a necessary, even if insufficient, step to curing it.

Anyone who has seen my blog knows that my house isn't like one in a magazine. I'm not talking about some unrealistic ideal—just a reasonable standard.

I encourage you, if you're not quite ready to pick up a dust cloth, to train your eye. If all you can manage right now is surfing the Internet, then put that activity to good use by searching for images of *ordinary* tidy rooms that glow with a kempt, cozy light. This will take some search strategy, using the right key words, such as "vintage," "bohemian," "English country style," and other terms that exclude matchy-matchy styles that imply a lot of decorating professionalism and expense.

To become a good housekeeper, you need to have assimilated a lot of visual data so that you can arrange things in a pleasing and effective way. Cleaning is only one part of keeping house! You need to clear your mind of all those perfect magazine pictures and find your own order.

3. *You will be nicer to your children and your husband if you aren't constantly irritated and even depressed by the dirt and "visual background noise" in your house.* You will be able to have a conversation with him or read to them without wanting to scream or cry or run away. You will also be able to offer hospitality with a peaceful soul. You may find that you love making a home for how it frees you to interact with people.

4. *You will be content with your things and finally conquer that vague "if only my house were perfect" nagging feeling that makes you waste time and spiritual energy (and, possibly, money).* You will see the beauty in even the humblest object if it is clean and in the right spot. You will also be more able to handle real problems of household organization and decoration if you have a clean slate (I said clean, not blank) to work with.

5. *You will not mind a temporary mess if your house is reasonably clean.* When the kids make a fort with the living room cushions, or take up finger painting, or pull out every pot and pan from the cabinets, it won't be a disaster. Well, it will be a disaster, but not a fatal one—because those things can be set to rights quickly when things are basically in order. But when their mess adds to an already dire situation, it's hard to recover.

6. *You will be better prepared to make structural decisions if your home is clean and tidy.* I've seen people make costly decorating, renovating, and building mistakes just because what they were living with wasn't bad but only dirty or disorderly, or both. People think they need a big addition, only to find that they virtually abandon the former parts of their home when it's done. Doesn't that imply that they were not using it well in the first place?

If you clean and organize something and still find that it's not working for you, then (and, I'd argue, only then) can you think about renovations in an effective way.

When you really clean, you sometimes find that a room's walls, floors, and windows are not conducive to becoming clean; sometimes these elements need to be replaced with better ones before you can clean them. That takes time, money, and effort, but it's well worth it if you can afford it. I can't say that enough. Even my cheap soft-pine floor in the kitchen, which shows every dent, is a million light-years better than the old broken linoleum.

Paint makes cleaning possible, so it may be that you need some repainting done. Paint woodwork with semigloss or glossy paint (oil based, if possible). Paint walls with an eggshell (not flat) finish so that it will be scrubbable. If the color is dingy with years of dirt, nothing you can do will make it look good. Once you repaint, you will be amazed at how much easier your job will become.

If you can't clean your windows because the wood has dry-rot and the sash weights don't work and the screens are broken, repair or replace the windows. This effort will pay you back in energy savings, and your cleaning job will be significantly lightened. Install wood trim moldings (or paintable resin ones) where the walls meet the floors and the ceilings. Before you paint, caulk edges wherever they meet, using painter's caulk. It's easy, and it makes a huge difference. The caulking may have to be redone every few years. Dust and bugs come through those cracks, making things dirtier; see what you can do to tighten things up.

In the process of repairing, replacing, and painting, you have to move furniture away from walls (if not out of the room) and take draperies and curtains down. Suddenly you will be deep cleaning, despite your reluctance. And then the room will be clean. Remember: don't put back anything you don't need or love, and make sure the thing itself is clean before you return it to its place.

What I Learned from the Cleaning Lady about Deep Cleaning

With me on all this? Well, then, I'll tell you a story.

Once, long ago, when I was recovering from a difficult childbirth, my sixth, and feeling overwhelmed, my dear husband and mother put their resources together to get me a cleaning lady.[6] We really couldn't afford it, but something needed to be done. Part of me was completely opposed to the idea. I did feel as if I should have been able to handle my own problems; I thought that the money was certainly needed elsewhere; I was ashamed of having someone else dealing with my shabby possessions.

But somehow I had lost the ability to keep my own house clean! All I could think to do was vacuum, and that didn't seem to help. This lady

---

[6] This story is in no way to discourage you from getting cleaning help if you can afford it. At the time, we really couldn't. The point is that you need to know how to do these things whether you delegate them or not. And you will be happier doing them if you know how, anyway.

was someone I knew to be kind and helpful, and she needed the money too, so I agreed.

She told me that before she came, I'd have to "pick up," and I did, and that was quite an effort because I still didn't feel well. Then she arrived and proceeded to take two full days to deep clean every single thing in my house—one day for the upstairs and another for the downstairs.

She worked in one room at a time. She opened windows. She pulled every article of furniture out into the middle of the room and wiped down every molding and window frame. She vacuumed or wiped the furniture itself, including under cushions. She cleaned the floors around the perimeter of the room. She washed curtains and towels.

She removed every item from every horizontal surface, cleaned the surface, cleaned the items, then put them back. She took out every book from every shelf, wiped the shelves, and put the books back neatly, rather than in the jumbled way I had stored them. She pushed everything back and cleaned the floors and vacuumed the carpets. She worked her way backward out of each room.

And then my house was clean.

But you know what? Every week after that (for maybe six months?), when she came, she just dusted the wood furniture and vacuumed (of course I had to declutter before she came, and I was getting stronger during this time). For a good long while, that was enough. She never deep cleaned after that first time.

And soon I realized she wasn't going to, and the fact was that with things decluttered anyway, I could do it myself! I knew how! I saw her!

As I got irritated with the fact that she was only dusting and vacuuming (I could do that! I had already done the hard part of putting our clutter away before she got there!), I made the decision to take on all the cleaning myself (and really, we couldn't afford her anymore).

I had known what to do all along, and at one time I had done it, but somehow I also forgot it, but then she helped me remember.

Now, when I get to feeling that things are overwhelming, I remember that it isn't enough to vacuum the middle of the room. You have to declutter (and we will talk about that), pull everything to the middle of the room, clean the edges from top to bottom, pull everything back, and clean the middle. You have to do that in each room, one room at a time.

Then you will be set in that room for at least a few months. If the cleaning lady won't do anything about it, you don't have to either, until you are ready to fire yourself, that is!

Keeping Cleaning in Perspective

Now, just because I talk about cleaning or doing laundry in such a compelling way doesn't mean that those things are the basis of our self-worth.

Even though I think it makes sense from a lot of points of view to get good at what we do in the home, they are important in the grand scheme of things only as *things that we do*, in the "he that is faithful in that which is least is faithful also in much" kind of way (Luke 16:10, KJV), and insofar as they make it possible for us to love others better and be more patient with ourselves.

So making a nice dinner or finally getting a room organized really is worthy of praise, and we can hardly be blamed for seeking praise when we do them. But I think it is good to try to see ourselves as God sees us: needing to accomplish a lot in our corner of the world but not ever being perfect, not in the grand scheme of things. I don't know about you, but everything I do could certainly be done better. That would depress me if I didn't also see that the point will never be to seek perfection here on earth. I don't mean that we should abandon the effort to be better. Imagine saying, "I just won't do it then!"

No. We keep striving, with peace. Trying to keep things orderly allows us to attend more to matters that are beyond, and above, the merely temporal. It's a paradox, but it's true. If we have a reasonably neat and clean house, we will be more able to attend to higher priorities.

Maintaining Your Deep Clean:
Confine and Corral, Part 1

Let's talk about another issue: dirt and kids. Getting your house reasonably clean requires that you *confine and corral your children*.

Don't do anything yet. You are not ready, by any means. We are only thinking about cleaning, not actually cleaning!

But just think about this: pretty much all the dirt in your house comes from two sources: the outside and food. Oh, there are others: wood-burning stove or fireplace, dog, miscellaneous hobbies that involve glitter and glue. But these are the biggies: the outside and food.

And the means of spreading the dirt around your house can be summed up in one word: kids.

I do think that kids can be helpful in cleaning. But without addressing that issue just yet, let me say that even if they aren't actively helpful, you need to focus on keeping them confined when they eat and corralled when they play.

Confine

One of the most important objects in your life is the table. A good, sturdy, easily cleaned kitchen table (if you have room for it). Children need to be taught that they must eat at the table. If you let them run around the house with food, you get what you deserve: a house that smells like old food and has a greasy film over it.

Children are entranced by having their own child-size table and chairs, and if you can fit those in the kitchen, it's a lovely way to help them learn the skill of concentrating on a meal. Of course, having them sit up at the big table, first in a high chair, then perhaps on a booster seat, and eventually on a big chair, works fine.

For some reason, a lot of moms seem to think that they have no right to make their children sit still to eat. They seem to feel that it would be really hard; maybe just impossible. They think it's okay for their kids to graze, eating at all and any times, so it never occurs to them to make them be still to do it. We can blame some of this on the sixties-style parenting advice that has permeated our culture down to this day, for sure, and it has only gotten worse as homemaking has received less respect. Time to do things differently!

Children will do what you ask of them. The proof of this is that when I was a child, no one ever asked a child to sit still in the car, and now no one thinks twice about buckling even the most active toddler tightly in a car seat, every single time.

Yet, somehow, in that same era, a single teacher could enforce perfect silence and order on a class of twenty children for hours at a time (and my husband, who is older and went to Catholic school, had one nun for fifty young children!). Nowadays, twelve children can't be expected to line up without benefit of counsel.

You must teach children to sit at the table, use a napkin, not get food on the outside of their mouths, keep their hands clean, and get up only when they are excused (which they can request, of course). Keep at it; keep it short; don't let them eat unless they are doing what you say, more or less, and stay cheerful. Maybe at first you have to read to them, play a story CD, or bribe them with sailboat sandwiches. It doesn't matter. It must be done!

If they can't manage it, there is a wonderful invention called a high chair, from which no one should ever be released without a good rubdown with a clean, warm washcloth! A one-year-old with greasy, grubby hands can turn your home into a pigsty in about a week. Think about it. The grease doesn't magically disappear. If you are lucky, it gets rubbed off on your jeans, which can go in the washer. But a sofa, a rug, a curtain—it's all fair game, and like the proverbial frog in hot water, you won't even notice until your house is filthy!

Using a clean, warm dishcloth, wash your baby's hands and mouth before he gets down. Then rinse the dishcloth, get it a little soapy, and wipe down his chair and the surroundings. It takes only a minute.

Even a three-year-old can take a plate, scrape off the scraps into the trash, and put the dish in the dishwasher or next to the sink. Then that older child can wash his hands, because of course you have a handy stool for just that purpose and a clean towel that he can reach.

This way, the food residue isn't being spread, inexorably, throughout your home. Indeed, there is simply no way to keep a house clean if its inmates do not follow these simple rules.

Corral

Young children will pull out their toys and strew them all around. The question is, are you letting them have the run of the house, so that nothing is beyond their reach, nothing remains in its place if they choose to pull it out?

Are the little barbarians wreaking havoc in one place as you are cleaning up another?

Even older children have the tendency to seek out a quiet, orderly spot and sort of make a nest there. I am not sure why this is, but I have observed it many times: no sooner have you tidied up a room than there is a child, plunk in the middle of it. You have to make it clear to your children by whatever means—gates, fences with spikes, massed tanks at the border—that there are boundaries they must respect, whether they like it or not.

If a child can show the maturity to be in a kid-free zone without trashing it, then by all means, let him go. I'm all for it. It's a privilege to be earned, and sweet when it is!

But if you know that a mess will result, your sanity demands that the activity take place within the confines of an easily cleaned room designated for the kids. Where toddlers are concerned, the kitchen and the playroom or den are the only areas you should even think about letting them dwell. They are just like puppies in this respect: super cute but completely untrustworthy.

And don't hesitate to take this policy a step further with a nice, spacious playpen in which said small child can spend a half an hour in the morning while you do some necessary things, as well as another half an hour in the evening before supper. It's his little den, and by age six months or so, he can start enjoying it. This blessed time of confinement won't last too long, but it's worth it for those maximum mobility-to-irrationality months. We're talking about an hour a day. Try it!

Something you will notice is that as you train the children to respect their environment and your work, and as you take the time and make the effort to teach them with love and equanimity, everyone enjoys being together more, and after a while, the big payoff isn't just a cleaner house: it's also a more peaceful home. It might take a while, but it will happen.

Maintaining Your Deep Clean: Confine and Corral, Part 2

his lesson is short. In the last chapter, we talked about food and about children. Now let's talk about dirt. You must confine the outside dirt; you must corral it, trap it, halt its spread. And this means *mats*.

If you read Don Aslett's books, you should come away with one key learning: there must be industrial-style, that is, *effective dirt-trapping*, mats at the doors. As Aslett points out, what do stores and other institutions do? They can't ask people to take off their shoes. Instead, they place the proper materials at the door to stop dirt from getting all over. (At home, we really ought also to take off our shoes, but that's not my point here.)

We are not talking about those accursed little rag rugs that seem to be made to keep the emergency room in business. We are not even talking about rubber-backed glorified bathmats that might stay in place but are too small and practically leap up into the beater bar of your vacuum.

We are talking about a large (at least 3.5 by 5 foot) rubber, water-absorbent mat that stays put. You can hose it down; you can vacuum it; you can sweep it. There can be one outside the door where the daily traffic is: a good sturdy coconut or coir mat, or a very decorative Waterhog-type mat (they do come in formal designs and this one can be a bit smaller); but place the large one inside the door.

You will come to see this utilitarian object as beautiful once you realize how much work it saves you! Your children and you can take your shoes off upon entering the house. But guests, workmen, dogs—their dirty tracks stop there, on that awesome mat. Trust me. It's worth every penny.

In the winter, if you live where there is snow, you can also lay down an old blanket or quilt on the floor, beyond the mat, for when a bunch of kids are coming in with their snowy boots and togs. The snow will quickly begin to melt, and there will likely not be enough room on even a big mat for everything. It's not nice to step in a puddle wearing socks, so the old blanket is helpful for all the wet things; after taking off outerwear, one can step onto the dry floor.

So, to sum up, we're going to keep the outside dirt from tracking in, and we are going to keep food from getting all over the house. Confine and corral.

Decluttering with Shelves and the Occasional Well Placed Nail

Iimagine you already know the theory of decluttering. The practice is hard work. Right now might not be the ideal time if you just had a baby and the baby needs to be nursed all the time. Maybe you are sick? Maybe there are pressing things that have to get done.

If it is the right time, you'll have to schedule it in and be ready for a hard day. But don't exhaust yourself needlessly. Think.

You know very well that you need three things:

1. A trash bag, for trash
2. A box, for giveaways
3. A laundry basket, for internal relocation

Now, pick a spot, and keep it limited. Not more than one room, for sure, but possibly even one dresser, one closet, or one shelf in a closet, depending on how dire the situation is.

People are very different. Some people consider one book on a coffee table clutter. Others are festooned with fake ivy garlands and knick-knacks that wish you welcome; love; luck o' the Irish; Boo; harvest; red, white, and blue; and everything else, as if somehow every thought in your heart must be memorialized on a plaque and displayed. And some people have books and kids.

Fact: I personally am not so uncluttered. But when I clean up the bookcases, I do only the bookcases, nothing else. Otherwise it's too tiring. Only you know who you are, how much energy you have, and how much stuff you want around.

Remember my secret, discussed at length above, which boils down to this: if you have clutter, don't try to clean it up where it is. Get it all out into the middle of the room, even though this feels incredibly messy; wipe down, dust, disinfect, and maybe even paint whatever it is you are organizing. (Do you know how delightful a painted closet is? Paint it white so you can see what's in it.) Now and only now, put back what you really want there, using the criterion of Marie Kondo ("Does it spark joy?") or William Morris ("Have nothing in your house that you do not know to be useful, or believe to be beautiful"), depending on what moves you to do what you must. If it's something decorative, for the love of all that is orderly, just make sure you wipe it before you put it back.

One thing I learned from having that cleaning lady was that if I hadn't decluttered enough for her before her arrival, she simply put everything in a pile in the middle of the room, perhaps having cleaned the spot beforehand. After she left, I had to deal with the stuff, and you know what? It's not that hard when it's all in one spot like that, and you know that the room is clean once you just put it all away or throw it out.

Having applied these rules, look at what is left. Whatever it is, *at this moment* it goes into one of four places:

1. In another spot in the room, the room you are working in
2. In the laundry basket if its true place is in another room. Do not leave the room to put it away, or you will become hopelessly sidetracked! You will start cleaning that other room! You will forget that you are in the midst of a hellish nightmare in this room right here! You will then likely end up in *yet another room*, and only after supper, when everyone is exhausted, will you remember what you were doing, and then it will be too late. Your doom will have been deemed: to live, not in clutter, but in utter chaos.

3. In that box you already provided yourself with, for giving away
4. In the trash bag. Just throw it away if it's not worth anything to anyone. Don't overthink this. Don't let stuff keep you from living your life.

Now, I have another secret for you.

Things that you "store" on the floor, be they children's toys, books, pots, brooms, or really just anything, are always going to seem messy. Keeping things (that aren't furniture) on the floor is inherently cluttery and will make vacuuming and wiping down much more of a chore than they need to be.

This is where the shelves come in. And hooks. And nails.

As you are putting things back, or maybe just a moment before, ask yourself if there is any way to get them off the floor. Or the counter. Or whatever horizontal surface they are parking on. Any way at all?

Do you keep the broom in a corner on the floor, propped up against a wall? This is going to sound odd, and you may not believe me, but if you keep the broom on the floor, besides not being good for it (the business end will deform), *you will never feel like a good housekeeper*. But if you put a big nail in the wall and hang the broom on that, you will feel as if you have it all under control. Don't wait for the perfect broom holder. (I had one, and then I got a new broom with a handle too large for it. The nail I am using now is the upgrade!)

Keep the broom, mop, vacuum, dustpan, and other cleaning items out of sight, not near the front or back door or in a corner of a room. They need to be out of view in the living areas. Could they be hung up along the basement stairs? Just outside the door to the garage? Inside the pantry entry? In a closet? Even if closet space is scarce, once you think about *hanging* these items as opposed to having them propped on the floor, storage space will be forthcoming, I am sure.

Don't wait for the perfect container for the other objects lying around. Look around for baskets, which seem to multiply in the house. Pick up some cheap clear plastic bins at the grocery store and put the kids' toys in them for now. You can always use them for something else later. Put the bins on shelves. Look at thrift stores and yard sales for hutches, bookcases, and old cabinets. You might have something in the garage that could be spray-painted.

Metal brackets are inexpensive at the hardware store. I have spray-painted them a pretty color to good effect. Brackets on the wall with a sturdy pine board going across can transform your space.

Get some nails and hooks—and buy yourself your very own hammer so that you can pound a nail in a wall when you need to. Have a stash of those very secure and removable adhesive hooks if the wall won't take a nail (there is a very secure kind that says it's permanent but can be removed with a blow dryer). Look at your favorite household-goods store's clearance section for those handy racks-of-hooks that can go behind any door or on the wall. Shaker peg racks are so pretty and so useful.

The less you have on the floor, the more you will feel that your house is becoming fairly tidy.

Start in Your Bedroom

f you remember, when we started this discussion, I promised that I'd tell you the best place to start—when you are ready to clean, not just think about cleaning.

Did you guess? Do you care? Do you think it matters?

I do!

Whether you are spring cleaning or just going through your normal routine (I know, I know; well, let's work on it!), you should start in your bedroom, and in the process, express your love for your husband in a hidden yet effective way.

Even if your "normal routine" seems less like a line with a starting point and more like an endless circle, I hope you will come to think of the master bedroom as where you begin. When you're a bit paralyzed by all you have to do, start there. When things are going pretty well and you have the cleaning under control, start there anyway.

I mean, when things are going well, you just keep going around and around, doing a little deep cleaning here and a lot of maintenance there, don't you? And no doubt there are problem spots that are always calling out for attention. And then you might lose your bearings. So, although there is one school of thought that has you start with your kitchen sink, and certainly, much has to happen before the sink gets shiny, which makes this idea clever, I wonder: *If you start in the kitchen, will you ever leave?*

The Sidetracked Home Executives (one of the books I recommend) have you start with your entryway, which I do not dismiss. It's about seeing yourself as others see you; we'll get there.

But after about thirty years of reflection, I am having you start in the room you share with your husband. The reason is simple, but profound. Your home has many areas that express family life, but your bedroom expresses the foundational relationship between you and your spouse; the inner sanctum where the sacrament of your marriage is consecrated and continually renewed with the conjugal gift. If it weren't for the intimacy of your commitment, your family would not be. God has ordained it so. It was that way from the very start. It has always been that way. It always will be that way—the family does not outgrow its need for a foundation.

Express this reality by means of your respect for this physical place, for your body, for the body of your husband. Your first steps should be to make the room—the bed and the places for your clothes—truly orderly. From there, it's not far to make it actually beautiful, according to what you both think is beautiful. It will be a sanctuary.

What good does it do to have, as so many families do, a fancy living room, a gleaming kitchen, a curb with appeal, a huge TV and wet bar, but chaos, piles of laundry, dust, and dreariness in the bedroom? Conversely, some people tend toward narcissism in there, but our aim is loving simplicity, not hedonistic luxury.

So it seems fitting to me that the struggle to bring order to the home begins here, where the home has its origin. It seems to me that whatever you do here to improve your sense of service to your husband and the bond you share will redound to the good of your family, joining the grace of your sincere effort with that of the sacrament, bringing "grace upon grace" to all.

When you make your bed, which you should do every morning, offer up the incense of thanksgiving for your husband and a prayer for his sanctification, which depends so much on you!

In difficult times, when you are tempted to let bitterness creep in, try to think of one thing, one quality, that you are truly grateful for in this person God has given you. Remember that God has foreknown, through all eternity, that you would be married to him. Have faith and trust that, in foreknowing, He also ordained it and desired it. In other words, it's no mistake, if that's what you are thinking.

If you're thinking, "Oh, no! I love my husband; he's so good to me!" then this is a good time to tell God you realize His blessing.

And then, maybe go ahead and change the sheets! Even in the leanest times, it's worth having two sets of sheets so that you can accomplish this task with a minimum of effort (that is, without having to wash the one set on the spot; I personally find remaking beds exhausting enough without that pressure.)

So, on to the cleaning. As I told you, you have to ask, "What belongs in here?" A bed, side tables, lamps, dressers, possibly a chair ... an exercise machine, a quilt rack, an extra dresser because the other ones are quite small, a floor lamp, a small laundry hamper—my bedroom is big, and I want you to know that I have realistic standards. For the sake of full disclosure, I will say that it's my clothes that are usually piled on the chair.

If your bedroom is small, consider keeping the dressers in the closet. Sometimes you can put suits and other hanging clothing in another room.

For years, our bedroom had a bassinet coming and going, and a changing area for the baby. That's part of life, if not of magazine pictures. Can you make these things pretty and keep them clean? Don't let dust accumulate under the changing table because you think it's temporary. Don't let your sheets get dirty because the baby will just spit on them as soon as you change them. In fact, you can have a little stash of extra layers, whether a folded twin sheet or a large towel, for spreading out under the baby.

No matter how little it seems to bother him, don't let your husband feel that he's second fiddle to the parade of little ones marching through your room and your bed, or to anything else.

If your problem is that your bedroom is hidden under laundry, review the chapter on solving that lamentable situation ("The Laundry Process"), and make your first move to clear everything out. Even if the piles have to reside in the hallway for a while, that's fine. The important thing is to get *this* room whipped into serene order.

In an ideal world there would never be a laundry basket in sight. In my world, I fold laundry on my bed. That's a given for me. Decide what level of "less than perfect" *you* can live with, and then stick to it (by which I mean don't go beneath it). For me, a couple of laundry baskets in transit is an acceptable level, not to be degraded to the mountains that could be there if I let them. Beware that this danger is especially real if the laundry room is regrettably placed adjacent to the master bathroom. I do think a laundry room *near* the bedrooms makes sense for efficiency's sake, but it's just too tempting to let it pile up if it's "only in my room."

When the changing of the seasons comes for those of us who have to switch wardrobes a couple of times a year, it's inevitable to find a sea of clothes here in the master bedroom. They have to be somewhere! But get them out as soon as you can!

Even making sure we don't throw all the household clutter in the master bedroom when we're entertaining gives us a haven to repair to after the company has gone.

You may be surprised at how devoting some effort and love to your bedroom can make you aware of and resolve some deep noncleaning-related issues in the home. Once you make it a priority to keep your bedroom *reasonably* clean and tidy, you will notice that you've removed the unspoken tension of disorder and gained your husband's gratitude. You will find, too, that you can more reasonably expect your children to clean their own rooms as they are able. They grow to respect your room—and what it represents—more as they grow older. We think they don't notice such things, but, in fact, their whole consciousness of home and family is made up of such details, which they cherish.

Do you see how that consciousness contributes, however humbly, to their understanding of the preciousness of marriage and the home and the reverence that both you and your husband have for your relationship? Do you see how this lesson, an unspoken and even unintended one, will carry its message to a new generation?

Who knew that you were expressing so much by cleaning a room?

No More Boom and Bust: The Moderate Clean and the Blitz

nce you get the idea behind deep cleaning and decluttering, you'll see that these are activities that can't be indulged in very often. It's exhausting and mighty work.

Some books and guides give you a schedule for deep cleaning your house, but as far as I can see, it's just material for an anxiety attack. Having a schedule for power-washing your siding seems a bit overwhelming to me, I must say, not to mention reminders to refold your linens to avoid permanent creases, as in "take out perfectly folded things in order to refold them." I'm pretty sure the people who do things like that don't need to be told to do things like that, or perhaps have a staff whose life mission it is to do them, in which case, that's fine, they can have the schedule with my blessing.

The truth is that once you know how to pull everything away from the walls and clean underneath, wipe wooden trim from the top down, and dust books and shelves before restoring order, and once you know enough to approach a chest of drawers with a couple of bins for sorting, putting back only those things you really want and need, you will start to know *when* it needs to be done.

Do your deep cleaning and decluttering when ordinary methods fail to please. No schedule necessary other than the one imposed by holidays, season changes, and weird odors.

There is more to life than cleaning. But, paradoxically, in order to get to that "more," you have to have order in your daily life; so cleaning is a must.

Enter the Moderate Clean and the Blitz. These are your ordinary methods, habits that are going to keep that Deep Clean working for you so you can do other things. An alternate name for the Moderate Clean that I'm going to describe is "Sparkle and Shine," but the truth is that I never called it that myself. When I heard it called that recently I thought, there goes a better mother than I, a more cheerful, more upbeat mother—a natural sanguine, sunshiny person. I call it "chores" myself.

Master the Moderate Clean and the Blitz to stay out of the dread cycle known as the "Boom and Bust." Do you know what I mean by "Boom and Bust," that syndrome in which things go downhill fast after the Sisyphean burst? You never really enjoy your clean house, because you're always either exhausted from deep cleaning it or living with it dirty. You boom—get mad at yourself, the house, and all the residents, and go on a cleaning binge—and then you bust, because the binge depresses you and leaves you convinced that you can't maintain that level of energy for long—and you can't.

So we'll talk about how to get on a more even keel. Wouldn't that be nice?

The Moderate Clean

If you're booming and busting all the time—if you are either exhausting yourself getting things clean or not able to enjoy a steady state of a *reasonably* clean house, but instead invest a considerable portion of your decorating budget on little plaques plaintively hoping that God will find it in His heart to "Bless this mess" and affirming that a good mom gives kisses, not chores—you, my friend, need the concept of *the Moderate Clean, or Sparkle and Shine*. Throw the plaques out, and let's get serious.

When I read other people's advice (other than the books I've already mentioned), I find that a couple of things aren't taken into account:

1. The person giving advice often doesn't understand what it's like to live with a lot of children, each of whom you are trying to nurture lovingly according to his own interests, resulting in a house full of gravel ("pretty rocks"), drawings (what is it about a stack of paper that cries out for a crayon line? one line per page?), houses (cardboard boxes, by far the best toy, yet somewhat anti-aesthetic, no?) and enough Legos to shake a stick at.

2. The person doesn't homeschool and consequently has no idea that there simply isn't a stretch of time every day when you are alone, able to concentrate on removing fingerprints, and so forth. On the other hand, sending the kids to school could be a snare and a delusion. I found that I no sooner recovered from the morning and got the baby to nap, than they were home and too much in need to decompress to do anything around the house other than play. Plus, all the *paper*—but I digress.

3. The person doesn't take into account that you will be living for years, nay, possibly decades, with at least one nursing baby, and the subsequent feeling of sheer immobility you feel when faced with dirty floors, clutter, piles of dishes, and so on.

This author wants you to have a *perfectly* clean house, whereas you and I know that we want only a *reasonably* clean house; that is, one that has order but doesn't take all day to get that way, and one that we can whip into shape if we really need to, as opposed to booming and busting.

I have this to say: unless you have quadruplets and some kind of higher education that renders you unfit for housework, and *anyway*, aren't really bothered by clutter and dirt, there are two little secrets that, once you internalize them, will make you grow up and take care of your own home.

Schedule an Hour to Clean Every Day

Some of your time each day has to be devoted to certain things: personal hygiene, dressing kids, eating, checking your e-mail, reading to kids and yourself, and other sundry activities. Let's accept that a certain amount of time each day will be devoted to taking care of the home. It's not the same amount of time each day, and yes, there will be days when you aren't able to do one single thing and other days when you will do nothing but clean.

But if you do some deep cleaning as described above, and then get it into your head that you need to clean for a minimum of one hour a day—just one hour, and that includes dishes!—you will have a reasonably clean house.

Does one hour seem like a lot? Can you picture yourself spending that amount of time on such a wretched activity? How about half an hour in the morning and half an hour after naps?

Can you embrace the hour? Or do you feel somewhat offended that cleaning takes any time at all or maybe that it takes any of *your* time? Be honest.

You'll feel better—more responsible, happier—if you schedule it in. Unlike the deep clean (which I told you would announce its necessity to you in various ways), you really do need to know what you are cleaning and when. Consider it a sacred duty. Consider it an intellectual challenge. You are smart! You can do it!

In my own "education of a girl who couldn't sweep," the stages were gradual but inexorable. First, the Holy Spirit came down with little whisperings and made me realize it was immature to wait for my mom to come clean up for me. For one small detail, she lived 182 miles away. I was in denial, all right! But I was also enabled, since my mom *did* come and help me, quite a lot. But after this revelation, I purchased for myself a real vacuum cleaner and a dust cloth and made an effort.

I still just kind of let cleaning happen, sort of in the way young singles approach mealtimes. If you're hungry, eat. If things are dirty, clean them. No forethought, no plan, just react. Pretty soon, I reached deep into my vast stores of reading memories and asked, "What Would Ma Do?" (WWMD) and pulled out that pioneer idea of "Wash on Monday / Iron on Tuesday" ... and that's as far as I got.

It *was* good start, though. I decided I should clean every Monday, as well as do my laundry, because after all, unlike Ma, I had a washer and dryer. I made a commitment not to go out shopping, not to socialize, and not to read on Mondays, but to tidy, dust, vacuum, mop the kitchen floor, and do the laundry from start to finish!

Granted, I think at the time we only had two babies, so there wasn't a lot of laundry —*nothing* like later. But our duplex had two floors and a basement, three bedrooms (one of which I ignored), and the laundry in that basement, so I was really exhausted by Monday night. What a great feeling, though! To have everything done! To embrace, rather than deny, my duty!

Starting out the week with a clean home helped me overcome the depression I was feeling at living somewhere with no friends to share my journey with, everyone else being either still in college or working on their careers. I had no clue where to find friends, and just imagine life with no blogs! But at least I was on my way to feeling a little more optimistic about myself in my new life.

Then I realized that weekends were miserable with things a mess, which, of course they were when I hadn't cleaned since Monday. So—and this was such a stroke of genius, I must say—I decided to clean on Fridays too! That way, I could enjoy the weekend with my husband and children!

It gradually dawned on me that I could even do a little every day, while still keeping the basic "housework" days of Monday and Friday, and my house would be clean and enjoyable most of the time!

The learning curve can be ever so gradual an incline, but eventually you get there. You get over the idea that "staying home" means "not doing work," and you commit to doing some work!

And now my second secret.

Divide Your Home into Cleaning Zones

All of this will be unfolded as we go—remember, we are still thinking about cleaning—but it's really worthwhile to mentally break up the house into separate areas with a promise to yourself that you will almost always tackle only one zone at a time.

The kitchen is one, not to be discussed now. Bathrooms are another. For me, it's upstairs and downstairs, with the downstairs further divided into "hard use" (the den and mudroom, but kitchen separate for these purposes) and "easy use" (living and dining rooms). If you live in a ranch house, you simply think of the "sleeping zone" and the "living zone" and go from there.

Now, when you approach your hour of work, think in these zones. Most of your cleaning time is going to be devoted to one zone only; maybe even part of a zone. The rest get the Blitz, which I'll save for another section, but I'll bet you can figure out that you don't spend much time blitzing.

So your Moderate Clean will consist of approaching your zone with an eye to getting it into shape in less than an hour. You work fast. You have your cleaning tools ready. You have your helpers (also a topic for another section, but you can start thinking about how even a two-year-old comes in pretty handy as a runner). Start in one room and stick to that room until you are done (which is why you need the runner).

Always start at the door and go around in one direction. I'll let you choose whether to go counterclockwise or the reverse; I'm not picky! But do not crisscross the room, whatever you do. Just go in one direction, once around for decluttering and dusting, and once for vacuuming.

Why? Because there is no point in wasting any more thought on this process than you need to! Instead of figuring the process out anew, just do the same thing every time! It's totally liberating! Try it!

Let's suppose that on the first day, you will be found tackling the upstairs (bedrooms and hallway). Don't forget to start in your own room (where you will make the bed and deal with clothes every day!).

For Moderate Clean, you quickly move everything either to its proper place or the middle of the room. Have a laundry basket at the ready for everything from books to laundry that didn't make it into the hamper. Make the beds. Put away clean clothes. Keep in mind that you can get your kids to do a lot of this, but I won't get into that now, and it's a good thing to know what has to be done and how hard it is before you start delegating.

Dust surfaces by wiping them down with a damp (with water) cloth or an anti-static duster. Every couple of weeks, move everything off surfaces to dust and pull things away from the walls, but for a normal, Moderate Clean, you can feather dust in place. Every other time, make yourself do the baseboards and other molding as well as furniture. You can use the brush attachment on your vacuum for this job.

Put the laundry basket (or other container) of random stuff out in the hall. Make the kids claim their stuff and put it away. If any socks were found under the bed, this is the time for a lecture or sweet reminder about the hamper system, discussed in "The Laundry Process." Personally, I would give penalties for every sock found. For instance, they have to clean a window (which most kids love to do, and it's not as if you'll be getting to it anytime soon).

Vacuum only when all is in place and dusted. If your vacuum spews dust, you need a new one! Remember to go in one direction around the room, then do the middle, then go out the door you came in by. Work your way down the hall and from bedroom to bedroom until you've finished that area.

If this sounds monumental and unreasonable, it's because you have too much stuff—you need to go back to decluttering. *The Moderate Clean works only in a decluttered zone.* Without first decluttering, you will never be able to keep your occasional cleaning to an hour.

It may also be that you are working slowly. All that wiping down and scooping up should be done as quickly as possible most of the time. Challenge yourself to make this your workout.

Now, go do other things, knowing that tomorrow is another day!

Remember when we had a little chuckle because I said that my way keeps you from *doing too much*? It's true, though. There are some ladies who never clean. There are others who can't figure out how to do other things they like because they are so focused on keeping the house clean! The problem is that once you start to love a clean house, it sort of consumes you, and of course there is no end, simply no end, to how much you could clean, when, really, you ought to move on.

It's good to know that you'll get to it, whether you are on one end of the tidy scale or the other. Even if things are messy, you have other things to do. If someone drops by, you have the satisfaction of knowing that you are doing your best, even if it doesn't look that way.

We're not talking about how things look to other people but about how things are done to satisfy God, your family, and you. That's what matters, nothing else! It's a different story when people drop by and things are a mess because you've done *nothing* about it, ever, nor do you intend to. That's when you can be a bit embarrassed. But we're fixing that right now.

The next day, move to your downstairs zone, the "hard living" areas: den or family room, eating area, and mudroom. Here you will want to add to your supplies some strong cleanser and a rag for wiping down walls and doorjambs. The basic process is the same. Start in one place—the same place every time. Start where you enter, go around the room clockwise or counterclockwise, end in the middle, where all the stray things will be piled or placed in a laundry basket.

The next day, you can do the "easy living" areas, which might be very quick indeed if you've made sure to confine and corral, as I told you. In fact, you can probably skip this zone every other time.

Many people with young children don't have two separate living areas. I didn't at first. But you can still keep your children from trashing every room in the house by making sure they don't play in the living room *and* their bedrooms, or by allowing them to do crafts on the coffee table *and* the kitchen table. You will be able to figure it out now that you have the basic principles in mind.

One day of the week, Moderately Clean the kitchen and the bathrooms, and make sure your laundry is caught up.

On a busy day, do only the stairs (which I find get lost in the "zones" idea) or quickly triage the house and do the neediest zone.

On Saturdays, if you don't have a million soccer games to go to, you can make everyone clean everything, especially their own rooms. I don't know whose idea it was to make Saturdays "lazy day," but that won't fly in a big family. Up and at 'em! If you do have games or other activities, take an extra hour on Friday for the Moderate Clean. You can also use Family Movie Night, Friday or Saturday, to incentivize a quick cleanup if activities preclude really getting the house in order for the weekend. I will explain that type of cleanup shortly. ·

The most important motivation here is to do what you have to do to go into Sunday with a calm and orderly mind and house, so that the family can worship calmly and have a restful day.

Divide things up and work fast. Do things on the days that work for you; for instance, since grocery shopping with children can be truly exhausting, keep that day's housekeeping light. Look at your schedule and figure out what needs to be clean when. If you are hosting the ladies' tea on Thursday, it makes more sense to do a Moderate Clean in the "easy living" area than the bedrooms on Wednesday.

To summarize:

- Commit to an hour of cleaning a day (usually), and you can break this up into half-hour or twenty-minute segments if necessary.
- Divide your house into zones and work on only one zone (or even part of a zone) at a time.

The Blitz

It's impossible to explain to anyone who hasn't lived through it just how hard it is to keep house with a lot of kids. It *could* be likened to trying to establish order among wild horses, except that I think that wild horses have a limited imagination about what they want to accomplish. I don't know that species well, but it seems to me that they probably just want to run around a lot, and every once in a while, eat.

Whereas kids don't want to do just one thing or two things. Their little minds are firing off in a million directions. They exude dirt and trash. The exponential effect they have on each other means that three kids make nine times as much mess. So really, if you have six kids, they are making thirty-six times more mess than one kid!

This is why I quickly learned that my small-family deep- and moderate-cleaning skills were not enough. Although cleaning on Monday and Friday might work for a family with only one child, it isn't enough for a large family. And, as I told you in my recounting of the time I got a cleaning lady, having a lot of kids made me forget any expertise I had acquired. My brain literally became paralyzed from the necessity of feeding, teaching, and, in fact, defending myself against all my kids, whom, nonetheless, I loved very much; and I really did just forget how to deep-clean a room until another person demonstrated what was required.

Slowly I achieved my new powers of understanding. I grasped the necessity for the Deep Clean; I moved on to the Moderate Clean maintenance theory and practice. Then I identified the self-preservation strategy of the Blitz.

The Blitz is a lightning strike on a room that has been reasonably maintained (in other words, not a room in need of a Deep Clean but simply one that has endured three nanoseconds of kid exposure). The Blitz enables you to live a real life with the sure knowledge that you can whip things into shape in fifteen minutes.

There are two peak times of need for the Blitz.

1. After breakfast and before schooling starts, or you leave the house for the day, or otherwise start your various activities. It's much nicer to know that you have a clean slate and can face the day with a clean conscience.

2. Between 4:00 and 6:00 p.m., or whenever *meltdown* coincides with *Dad's return from work*. I mean, just *before* that point. You will be amazed at how much better you can handle the end of the day if you can rely on your gang to straighten up. (If you don't have a gang yet, train yourself in these techniques because you really want to know that you are up to the job yourself.)

So yes, you will blitz every day. Were you wondering how, if you devoted, let's say, four days a week to the twenty-minute Moderate Clean in one zone (assuming the rest of your hour of cleaning went to everyday chores such as kitchen cleanup and bed making) the rest of your house would stay reasonable? If you are getting the upstairs in order, what happens to the downstairs? What happens is the Blitz.

To implement, you have to have the kids on your side. They have to believe that this is all great fun. They have to understand that we're all in this together and our environment matters. Yet, at the same time, there has to be an undercurrent of real danger. Somewhere in there, they have to believe that if they aren't going to pitch in, bad things will happen to them. Punishment must loom. *So you want an atmosphere of lightheartedness – gaiety even – not uncharged with peril.*

Get a timer or set a deadline. I am bound to say that this worked best in the days when a favorite show came on at a certain time. Those fun episodes of harmless ("mindless," as my father would call them) TV came on at 5:00 p.m., and let me tell you, from 4:45 to 4:59, never was such activity to be seen in my house—and never was half an hour better earned or better timed for maximum predinner efficiency on my part. One little measly half an hour isn't too much to pay for peace and even a kind of cultural literacy, if you look at it in a certain twisted light. I just put them on their honor to mute the commercials, and we were all set.

These days of streaming mean that you must create your own sense of urgency, which is not as easy, I admit. The promise of a chapter of *Little House on the Prairie* works too, but not with that fine sense of finality that TV gave. And you *will* cheat and make them do more than fifteen minutes, which isn't fair. A timer will do, however.

This is bribery, a perfectly useful and acceptable tool in parenting, also known as positive conditioning. Show coming on? Want a snack? Want to play with Legos? Blitz the den. (I use "den" as a handy term for our main living area that has the TV and the toys, but it stands for any room currently in a shambles. By all means, apply to the kitchen, the dining room, the race track, the hall or ninepins alley, or what have you.)

And of course, if you don't participate cheerfully in the Blitz, you can go sit by yourself far away while the rest of us have a great time with *loud music*. Loud, fun, rollicking music.

- Old-time rock 'n' roll: try almost anything from Little Richard
- Fiddling: an upbeat tune from Natalie MacMaster
- Bluegrass: "If Wishes Were Horses" (possibly the best song ever, as heard on the O Sisters CD)
- "Tritsche-Tratshe Polka" with Maurice Andre, trumpet master.
- "Choo Choo Ch'Boogie" by the Manhattan Transfer
- Many Disney songs: the best are from *Beauty and the Beast, The Little Mermaid*, and how about "I Wanna Be Like You" from *The Jungle Book?*

In the true Blitz, you limit yourself to one room (or two if you have enough workers for teams, or whatever you can handle in the fifteen minutes). Your aim is not so much to clean as to give the appearance of clean. And what is the appearance of clean? That things are tidy and even pretty. I will tell you how.

- Go around the edges and from the edges to the center, as always.
- Divide and conquer. Depending on your work force, assign picker-uppers for each category: toys, books, papers, crayons, random socks.
- Assign a runner during the Blitz, but only one person should leave the room in question at a time, lest he find some (untidy) game to play elsewhere. It's all too easy to forget about children who are not underfoot.
- Assign a small person to look under furniture for stuff. Finders can put everything on the coffee table or in the middle of the room. Put-awayers can put away.
- Return any throw pillows to their places (assign a susceptible child to "make things beautiful"—there's always one who understands throw-pillow placement), neaten horizontal surfaces, send dishes into the kitchen (although it's strictly forbidden to eat elsewhere, so it's not clear why crockery is in any other room), make sure things aren't thrown into corners and around the periphery.

Now is not the time for dusting, and anyway there shouldn't be much dust because a hard-use room has to be moderately cleaned at least once a week. But if there seems to be some (imagine!), wipe it with your apron or blow it away. This method is by no means a remedy, but we're going for appearances here.

Lastly, sweep or vacuum the room (a task well within the capabilities of an eight-year-old), but only the parts that you can see—for instance, the rug. And put away or train children to put away the vacuum cleaner! Nothing undermines a tidy room like a vacuum left out. You don't *store it out*, do you? It simply has to have a place to be hidden away, even if it means hanging a curtain from a shelf and sticking it behind there. Children should learn to put the vacuum cleaner away without banging it against the woodwork.

Now, the well trained household can accomplish the Blitz without you (note, *not* the Deep Clean, or even the Moderate Clean — they might be able to do it once, but not twice in a row), *if and only if* everyone is trained in making sure corners are cleared.

Otherwise, they will quickly catch on to the Pseudo-Blitz, shoving everything away from the center of the room *into* the corners — a bona fide housekeeping disaster. Everyone needs to learn that the room can't even pretend to be clean, does not even have the appearance of clean, until the edges at least are clutter-free.

What most militates against internalizing this insight about the edges is that we assume that things will be cleanest when horizontal surfaces, including the coffee table, which is undeniably in the center of the room, display only those things that are meant to be there. But since most of us, living in families as we do, almost always have quite a bit of stuff out, the times we can achieve this desirable state are few — so we tend to give up and unconsciously subscribe to the idea that shoving everything toward the periphery is a good compromise.

But if you can't clean up the clutter or the random things you need right now, try making the piles of stuff neat and tidy, without pushing them to less used parts of the room, where, I can assure you, they will simply become part of the landscape. If all else fails, put your clutter into a laundry basket and put *that* in the middle of another room, one that is out of sight. Later, when you are doing a Moderate Clean, you can and will address the piles, which will be right out there in the open. But during the Blitz, you will have to be satisfied with neatening things in place for the most part, because you are trying to use your time well — not use it all *up* on constant cleaning.

When the Blitz is over, all you have to do is inspect! Don't let them turn on the TV or get out their extra-zowie-tiny-pieces-of-death super construction toys without making them do it right!

What Can Children Do?

ope St. John Paul II tells us this:

P

All members of the family, each according to his or her own gift, have the grace and responsibility of building day by day the communion of persons, making the family "a school of deeper humanity": This happens where there is care and love for the little ones, the sick, the aged; where there is mutual service every day; when there is a sharing of goods, of joys and of sorrows.[7]

My mother was fond of telling this joke:

A woman and her son were visiting a new friend. They arrived in a limo. The chauffeur came around, opened the door, and carried the nine-year-old boy to the house. The friend, who was waiting to welcome them, asked the woman, "Oh my, is something wrong with your little boy? Can't he walk?" The woman replied, "Thank God, we're so rich, he doesn't have to."

---

[7] John Paul II, apostolic exhortation *Familiaris Consortio* (November 22, 1981), no. 21.

You see? We are so prosperous (and preposterous) that we consider it a virtue that our children have nothing to do. Little do we realize the damage we are doing with this attitude — nothing less than sending yet another generation out into the world handicapped by incompetence in daily life. The family is the ideal place for a child to learn to help others, to relate to all sorts of people, and to take responsibility for all sorts of things, because it's impossible for one person to do all that has to be done to keep a home running! Yet we are in the absurd position of simultaneously doing it all and resenting our lonely martyrdom.

How about changing all that?

> A fundamental opportunity for building such a communion is constituted by the educational exchange between parents and children, in which each gives and receives. By means of love, respect and obedience toward their parents, children offer their specific and irreplaceable contribution to the construction of an authentically human and Christian family. They will be aided in this if parents exercise their unrenounceable authority as a true and proper "ministry," that is, as a service to the human and Christian well-being of their children and in particular as a service aimed at helping them acquire a truly responsible freedom, and if parents maintain a living awareness of the "gift" they continually receive from their children.[8]

All very well, beautifully put. Let's talk about what can be done and what to do.

A Child's Contribution

Chorewise, what exactly can a child's contribution be? Let's look at some examples, very roughly by age.

Curtain Climber (Ages 1 to 3)
The curtain climber follows you around and make things much, much worse. He pulls things off shelves, then plows right over them. He grinds

[8] Ibid.

bagels into chairs. He eats kitty litter. (Keep repeating, "My vocation is gestational in nature" and set your sights for the long distance.)

The main thing is to develop a relationship with your baby such that you are responsive to him and he to you. This age is the time for teaching him to do things in order, rather than worrying about chores.

A two-year-old can sometimes put his underwear in the "lights" hamper and his little jeans in the "darks." Your little ones can get up from the table and clear their places. Washing hands after using the toilet, lining up trucks, tucking dolls in their beds, clicking the cap on the toothpaste, putting pajamas in the drawer, getting the puzzles back on their shelf—these are "remote chore preparation" and plenty to work on for now. And then you give them a bowl of water and a rag and set them to washing the deck furniture. Make sure you call it their work.

I Can Do It by MySELF! (Ages 2 to 4)

Do you know why this stage drives you crazy? Because you have nothing for him to do. He feels as if he's not *contributing*. You think of a two-year-old as an eating, pooping machine that has to be taken from point A to point B. Maybe you carry him around all the time, sort of mindlessly pacifying him. You react rather than act, or you keep him buckled in his car seat. You may not respond at all.

He needs to become his own little self, and yes, that's a bit messy. Put your silverware where he can reach it. Get him his own small broom and dustpan and a place to put them. Give him a damp dust cloth and teach him to wipe down the stairs. Let him fill the dog's water bowl. You have a stool he can stand on to reach the sink, right? What's the worst that can happen? Spilled water! If you can't handle that, you need to get out more. Seriously, just keep a stash of demoted towels handy in a nearby cupboard, and let him dry his spill.

Surprisingly Helpful (Ages 3 to 6)

Start making a list of the things you would like to get to, but don't have time for because you have six children under the age of six, or two children and ill health, or other circumstances that keep you from housekeeping perfection. You'd be surprised how many of them your children can do, if you would just grasp, once and for all, that it's better to have it done by a five-year-old than not done at all.

Dusting, Windexing, appliance wiping, deck sweeping, dishwasher unloading, towel folding, dog feeding, egg collecting: these are all things that can be competently if awkwardly done by those approaching the age of reason. Just give them a tutorial, correct them a few times, and let 'em rip.

A pile of shoes at the door is often all that stands between you and a welcoming entry. A totally wonderful, perfectly suitable chore for a four-year-old is straightening out the shoes! You know, a neat row of shoes by the door is a joy. No basket necessary! (Besides, a basket doesn't really work, because the shoes get jumbled, and who has a basket big enough?) A terrible, thankless job for Mom. A great job for someone closer to the floor.

Our William had this job at our house for quite a while. Once I was taking Rosie (who was maybe twelve) to buy new shoes. He really took a stand! "No! I *wefuse*! Wosie has too many shoes aweady!" Turns out that he was struggling to keep up with her supply, which, of course, included soccer cleats, dress shoes, sneakers, and probably one other pair. Poor Will! We took pity on him and made Rosie take a few pairs up to her room.

Indispensable (Ages 6 to 12)

If you've been patient and clever, you will now have an indispensable work force on your hands. Let's remember that Ralph Moody was herding cows solo at the age of eight. That's why you must read *Little Britches*! Nothing your children could possibly do would match *that* for responsibility, danger, and solitude, I'm guessing; so quit making life so easy for them.

Here's what my nine-year-olds could do: process a load of laundry (not their own personal loads, but every step in the process of the family's laundry), clean the bathroom, wash the dishes, vacuum the den, watch their baby sister or brother, get the trash out of the car, make lunch.

Here's what an eleven-year-old can do: mow the lawn (but please, not fill the gas tank: it's really too dangerous because you need height and long arms, and I'm all for kids doing dangerous things, but we have to draw the line at severe burns or death), mop the kitchen floor, head up a car-cleaning team, get a room sparkling from top to bottom. After this, you will know what your kids can do. They will surprise you with their skills.

And of course, once that child's feet reach the floor, he should always be carrying something for you, getting something for you, and generally not being a leech on society. If there is one thing that makes me weep for our times, it's the sight of some poor woman staggering under a load like a packhorse, while her children whine about how they don't want to be there, don't want to leave, or are hungry. Even a kid in a stroller can hold his own sand toy.

If a task demands a safety lesson, make sure it has been given and absorbed. Make sure your children understand that a machine is not magic. I can still hear my engineer father's voice in my head: "Don't force it!" This is the principle of machines: don't force it.

Inspect the job until it's done to your satisfaction.

And occasionally, do it yourself. Two reasons: (1) usually (not always!) you do a better job, and if you don't put yourself in the rotation, your house will suffer for it; and (2) sometimes your children do need a break, and you build trust and model kindness by showing yourself to be understanding when an unexpected opportunity comes up or they are feeling sick or tired. With a young child, just let it go if he has run off to play and some little thing hasn't been taken care of.

It's good to be merciful; you will know when the right moment is to let up on your demands.

Not Every Child Is the Same, and Perfection Isn't the Goal

Now, let's remember a few things. Some astonishingly small children are dexterous and interactive. Their focus is close up. They delight in order and repetition. Some children have large movements and interests. Their horizon seems so very far away, and it's hard to reel them in. *So don't compare one child with another.* Above all, don't read parenting advice and wonder why your kids don't do everything you read about. There's always next year. I'm convinced that there is a much wider margin than we are told for what constitutes appropriate behavior. I once gave the following advice to a friend with two rambunctious boys: stop listening to your friend with one sweet tea-partying, page-coloring girl! I'm sure she's a nice lady, but *she has no idea what she's talking about!*

Oh, and one more thing—and this is what John Paul is saying in the quote below, essentially—the goal is not for everyone to be behaving perfectly! Expect imperfection!

Meltdowns happen, even Mama meltdowns. Yelling isn't the worst thing. You don't want to be yelling constantly, of course, but sometimes your children need you to yell, *because their bad behavior has to do with your excessive talking and misplaced patience.*

(And honestly, sometimes you and I deserve to be yelled at, let's admit it. What could I do that would make my kid want to yell at me? What about this: She's on her way to do what I told her to do, and I tell her to do something else! *I'm* not even listening to *myself!*) No. The worst thing is a tense, overly bright covering up of the sorry fact that no one is helping anyone else.

Family communion can be sought and preserved only through a great spirit of sacrifice. It requires, in fact, a ready and generous openness of each and all to understanding, to forbearance, to pardon, to reconciliation.

> There is no family that does not know how selfishness, discord, tension and conflict violently attack and at times mortally wound its own communion: Hence there arise the many and varied forms of division in family life. But, at the same time, every family is called by the God of peace to have the joyous and renewing experience of "reconciliation," that is, communion re-established, unity restored. In particular, participation in the sacrament of reconciliation and in the banquet of the one body of Christ offers to the Christian family the grace and the responsibility of overcoming every division and of moving toward the fullness of communion willed by God, responding in this way to the ardent desire of the Lord: "that they may be one" (John 17:21).

ASK AUNTIE LEILA

Is It Too Late for Kids to Become Helpful?

Dear Auntie Leila,

In light of "What Can Children Do?," I see the monster of my own making.

My eldest child, a tea-partying, page-coloring girl can practically run the house without me. She's like a well-oiled machine. Loves to please. Very capable. Loves to be a little mama. So cleaning and matronly duties are considered fun by her.

My second child, difficult from day one, has been carried around by me since birth, not because we are so rich, but because this lazy mama would rather baby him than hear him whine, complain, or pitch fits. I know. I can't believe it's like this either! What have I done?

Here is my dilemma. Where do I start in the retraining of him and his mama? Do I start him at stage one until that is mastered? He does have a very small chore list (make bed, clean up toys, feed dog, clear his dishes from the table) that he completes daily, but never without reminders and rarely without grumbling.

I don't blame him. This falls on my shoulders. The worst part is, I know his wife will not appreciate all this. He's eight years old. Tell me this can change! Help me, dear Auntie. Where do I begin? What do I do when he grumbles? What do I do when he doesn't complete his task?

Yours,

Rebekah

Dear Rebekah,

Well, your consolation is that, especially with boys, training in the home (I mean, specific chores) rarely carries through to adulthood! My sons strangely do not seem to regard an empty beer bottle as a blight (I mean, not that they drank beer as children, but they certainly had to clear their dirty dishes). When they are husbands and fathers, it may be that some of it will come back to them. In any case, they are indeed the problem of their spouses, present or future.

I've come to see that, at least for those of us who aren't so neat and tidy that our children just can't *conceive* of dirt, the thoughts here about chore giving and discipline have two goals: (1) to give the children a merely *general* indication that life could be orderly, perhaps in the form of a distant voice in their heads that resembles yours but, apparently, doesn't come through very clearly; and (2) to get *you* through the days, by getting some work out of them.

We just naturally like our children better if they are working and not lolling about. And that's a valid reason to go to all this effort. (We also like them better if they are clean and well groomed, but that's a rant for another time. Nevertheless, take a good look at your son and ask yourself if you just find him … grubby. Then do something about it.)

Begin the rehabilitation as if he has been good all along. An eight-year-old can take out the trash, process the laundry, sweep, vacuum, feed *and* walk the dog, and others things that you will find in "What Can Children

Do?" He should carry things for you, particularly grocery bags in from the car, baskets of laundry, and firewood. (People get wood-burning stoves, chickens, and huge gardens not so much because they love these things but so that their children will have strenuous activity to engage in.)

Tell him that he's strong and big and a big, strong boy and that you need him. Praise his big strong muscles and his ability to carry things and bravely handle stuff that makes you tired or cringy. Big. Strong. Brave.

No toys until the chores are done; no shows, games, sitting down, eating, resting, or any other thing that he would like to do until things are done without whining and to your satisfaction. Make a chore list so everyone's clear.

Tell him that in the Bible it says, "If any would not work, neither should he eat" (2 Thess. 3:10, KJV) and you don't intend to raise a deadbeat for a son. Tell him you'd like to be spared visiting him in jail. Tell him that you've been wrong, but now the iron has entered your soul. Be ruthless, yet affirming.

Talk to his father. Hand your son over to his authority. He has the con (that's nautical for "is in command") when he's home, and his spirit hovers over things when he's gone. This is his son. Undoubtedly the naughty genes come straight from him. Let them get dirty and smelly together. Affirm the punishments your husband chooses to hand out, even though, I warn you, they will appear *so harsh*, due to current levels of enabling.

Meanwhile, read these books to him: *Little Britches, Two Years Before the Mast, Captains Courageous, Hatchet, Hornblower: Beat to Quarters*, and anything by E. Nesbit. I want you to read them *to him* so that you benefit as well; as you read, you will understand just how much adults can ask of children, and just how miserable children can be and still benefit from the experience. Reading time should be after chores.

"Auntie Leila, do you think children should be miserable?" Well, here's the thing. Children do spend a certain amount of time being miserable. You might as well have their misery be about something real. For instance, it's far better for a child to feel a little hungry while he finishes putting the clothes in the dryer or moves the woodpile a foot to the left than to grumble because you forgot to buy him the newest version of his favorite video game. The first problem will result *at least* in his sense of accomplishing something, followed by a meal that he's more likely to appreciate. The second will result in feeding the lazy, disrespectful beast within. Very few things are worse for a child than feeling justified in a grudge against the world, embodied in his parents.

Chore Charts?

Sometimes people ask me if they should make a chore chart. I am all for whatever works for you and makes life easier. There are so many variables: the size of your family, their ages, your ability to focus, the willingness (or lack thereof) of the participants.

At times, we used a chore chart. I put chores on the weekly homeschooling chart. I made lists, posted chores on a board, put chores in a chore jar, wrote the chores on the children's foreheads (not really), and made buddy systems.

I was never very good at following up on rewards, particularly stars. I guess I tend more to punishments, which is silly if rewards work. Just beware: a rewards system easily devolves into endless arguments and comparisons, which indeed make punishments seem simpler. My gut feeling is that if it results in a lot more work for mom, it's not going to succeed as a system.

The Chore Jar

Some years, once we had a preponderance of genuinely useful children, we began each season with a big jar into which I put scraps of paper with jobs written on them. Each job had a level or difficulty number associated with it, based on the time it took, the ickiness factor, and so on. These were not the basic jobs, such as processing laundry or bathroom cleaning, that were assigned by age, but jobs I was pretty sure I wouldn't get to but would definitely be happier if they were to be accomplished by someone else. The kids took turns taking papers out until they were gone. There was a brief exchange or bargaining period, and then the chore lists were written up for future reference. It worked fantastically.

Parents will have to think about the work question in relation to their own circumstances. Ideas are legion, but keep in mind that what looks attractive might be predicated on factors that are not universal. Those with lots of kids have to be more businesslike than those with only one or two. Above all, aim to avoid nagging. Something written down in some form, even graphically illustrated with symbols for the nonreader, really helps.

I'm going to be honest, Rebekah: Your job is harder with only one or two children under that maternal microscope. The two of them are shouldering the whole burden of making you (and the house) shine in the end. But, if this is indeed God's will, then amen, and get them moving.

Schedule your day so that there are certain times when everyone is working. Play fun, upbeat music, and you won't hear any complaining. Make your slacker child miss out on good things if he doesn't comply, but just make sure any punishment is immediate, not remote. Schedule in rests and fun at the park.

Work on the new regime for a week, perhaps easing into it. New habits bring self-control! After a week, set a new goal. Give that a week. In two months, I promise you, things will be better!

You are not failing your child, and you are a good mother! Soon you will like and respect your son again. And he will like and respect you!

A big hug,

Leila

Five Important Strategies for Selling Your Reasonably Clean Home While Homeschooling

I recommend that you read this section even if you aren't planning to sell your house, simply to avoid the trap that has ensnared so many, to their regret; namely, that they applied the energy necessary for organizing their home (and fixing the little things that bothered them) only when they were about to leave it, rather than when they were living in it! I think the ideas here can help a family be more organized even when they aren't selling their house. Maybe reading the following will help you make your house nice enough for a prospective buyer, however imaginary, right now, and hence, more enjoyable for your family.

Selling your home while living in it—especially while homeschooling in it—seems impossible, and if you start to hyperventilate at the very thought of it, I don't blame you. I've been there: homeschooling five children (including two in high school) *and* nursing a baby. It's not peaceful.

The reason people grow old and die in their inadequate and cluttered homes is that they can't face the disruption of moving! But sometimes, face it you must. So here's how.

We will take it as read that you have already searched the Internet thoroughly on the topic of staging your home for buyers. Besides the big things, such as a new roof, that can be negotiated, you know that you need to make a list of little things that need repair or replacement. It's always good to have such a list anyway! It can go in your sticky-note to-do list under a "master household" tab (see the section on note keeping below).

You *know* that you have to declutter, and this Reasonably Clean House section is about helping you do that. You know about renting a storage unit. But chances are that, if you are homeschooling and have lots of kids, you need more stuff than the average advice giver can even imagine. You certainly have more books than the realtors think is appropriate, and that's fine, as long as they are dusted and look neat and tidy (the books, not the realtors). Besides following all my thoughts on how to get a clean (reasonably so) house, there's the issue of these strangers walking in. You can't satisfy their standards, because you don't know them, so the main thing to keep in mind is that whatever you have in your home should be clean and pretty, especially at the front door (this is also known as curb appeal).

I'm going to tell you something that I have learned from looking at thousands of listings. The main reason realtors advise sellers to stage things in the blandest, most "impersonal" way possible—and I say this without judgment in my heart, but it's true—is that most people have trouble making their homes look tasteful. I don't blame them; I blame the mass-marketers who destroyed traditional ways of keeping home and substituted décor that has a built-in dissatisfaction level, to keep people buying.

We can overcome the tension between realtors' desire for us totally to declutter and our need to go on living by striving to fulfill our role as beautifiers of our environment according to principles that you will find scattered throughout this book and in tradition. For a large family with limited resources, it's not possible to render the house personality-free. So please don't worry about it; I believe that the peace and goodness of your home will be attractive to anyone who enters.

To continue with the plan:

You already know that your whole house has to smell good. Now is the time to light that big scented candle you got for Christmas. Put it on your stove, where it won't burn the house down.

You already know that your house has to be warm (if it's cool out) or cool (if otherwise).

Now I am going to tell you how to achieve a sale when your house is not utterly fabulous and high end, your children are numerous, and your school must keep going regardless.

The Blitz

Start at the top and Blitz. (If your house has only one level, start at the furthest point from the door you will ultimately exit.)

Selling your house gets you to deep-clean every zone in your house. Don't try to do it all in one day, but do schedule each zone realistically and get it done. You must be able to declare an area "closed" in the sense of having been deep-cleaned, and then later in the sense of "no one go in there." (It's not a bad idea to have no-go zones for the duration of the selling period if you can swing it.)

Once you have done that, you need to incentivize your children to perfect the Blitz for when prospective buyers come around. Maybe show them the movie *The Hunt for Red October* (if they are older) or take a field trip to the fire station and observe the drill. Once they see that their job needs military precision and a sense of urgency, as for putting out a blaze, they will enter the spirit of the thing and execute.

In the house-selling Blitz, just as with normal living, the goal isn't the Deep Clean or even the Moderate Clean. It's just to make things tidy as quickly as possible so you can get out of the house and have it ready for showing.

You need the Moderate Clean for days you are not showing, or you will end up booming and busting, which is not good when you have so many to take care of; you simply can't do it and maintain your sanity. Sanity comes first, I always say.

The kids need to think this is a fun and exciting process that they do on the run. Besides some sort of model, they probably also need a bribe or a reward waiting for them when they are done. You will end up in the car, so maybe stash some treats there or head out for ice cream.

The Appearance of Clean

Unlike normal cleaning, you are *not* – repeat, *not* – going to clean in your normal fashion according to the areas that need it most or are most used. And you are not going to prioritize actual cleanliness (after you have done that necessary deep cleaning), but instead, *the appearance of cleanliness*.

Thus, pay more attention to wiping surfaces and vacuuming than to getting the area under the sofa cushions crumb free. Windows need to be sparkling more than sheets need to be laundered. (You can do the latter on a non-showing day.) It's more important to get the toys off the lawn than to put your clutter away!

How?

Laundry Baskets

You are not going to put your necessary clutter (as opposed to the unnecessary clutter that you got rid of before this whole process began) away! You would go crazy! You can't do it!

When you get the call, your drill will be to throw any "necessary" clutter that can't *immediately* put in its proper place *into laundry baskets* as you exit the area.

You start to see the importance of starting at the top (or furthest area) of your home and working your way down and out. Besides resolving to do as much eating and playing outside as you can, you must clean yourself out of your house. The children need to go ahead of you, blitzing.

One child (or team) can be in charge of blitzing bathrooms (after you have carefully trained them in the art of making it look clean, which mainly involves wiping everything with the hand towel, putting it in the hamper, and replacing the towel). One team can be in charge of making sure that beds are not only made but that any stray stuffed animals are propped up in front of pillows (which instantly makes the bed look charming). One team wipes down stairs and removes any clutter from them, placing it in a basket.

Put any laundry in hampers or in the dryer. (Identify hiding places for things: bins under beds, the space inside the dryer and inside the washer—but, don't stuff things in the oven or in closets, because people look in there. They won't open the fridge or the deep freezer, though.)

If you are going to stay sane, you can't have everyone running to and fro. No crisscrossing back into no-go zones! No entering areas declared stranger-ready!

I developed this method when I realized that having everyone running around randomly, up and down and around, was giving me panic attacks. My house had three floors and we started at the top (and in the bathrooms, because only so many people fit in one place) and backed our way out.

You are the last to leave a room while your children are tackling the next part—and no one reenters after you have left, as in a fire drill! You are the last to leave a floor.

You give the floor (or zone) you are leaving the critical eye, snatching up personal things as you go, and then attend to the next one.

What do I mean by "necessary clutter"? What you can't face putting away because you know that you just can't. So everyone works their way out of the house, collecting, as they go, toys, books in the process of being read, the ten matchbox cars they were just playing with and can't leave behind, bath towels (and other bathroom detritus), sweaters, shoes, blankets, and the random "personal knickknacks" so deplored by realtors and putting them in the laundry baskets (laundry bags and large trash bags are helpful too). Don't waste time putting every last thing away. Just toss it all in the basket.

Those get put in the back of the undoubtedly large vehicle you use to transport your brood (of course, when you first listed your home, you cleaned out the van too!).

Homeschooling with Backpacks

Consider having your children keep the materials they are using in backpacks or totes that they can grab quickly. Then you can head to the library for the hour or two that it takes to show the house.

If you follow my advice in other chapters, your homeschool will be fairly simple and streamlined, and this won't be too difficult.

Keep in mind two things:

1. If your children were at school, they would have days when schooling didn't go as planned, because of drills and other disruptions. It's not as if every day, every nose is constantly to the grindstone—far from it. So if you use the showing time to run errands or visit a friend, I wouldn't worry about that.

2. Your house has certain basic qualities that make it marketable *if the price is right*. The biggest factor is what other houses recently sold for in your neighborhood. Realtors like to get you whipped up about how important your staging is, but the fact is that most people have decided when they pull up to the door whether they are interested. That your bathrooms and kitchen are functional is more important than whether your furniture doesn't look brand new. That said, if it looks welcoming and tidy, it will appeal to them! So just work on that and don't stress out.

Immediate Homing of Clutter upon Return

This is the key to keeping the system running. When you get home, take everything out of the car and put it, baskets and all, in the middle of the floor in a central place. Spend whatever time it takes to put each and every single item back in its place. Make your children your runners. What you will note immediately is that there are things that you resent having to cart in and out this way, and lo! these things can now easily be donated or discarded because they are right there, probably already in a trash bag!

Thus, the clutter you are dealing with at any point in this house-selling period is what you need right now—not *accumulated* flotsam and jetsam. You start to realize that you can function with much less than you thought. You also notice that this mode is effectively the "post-office system"—collecting things in a central location and then distributing (or discarding) them. As

I say, it's a good method to use even in the times you are not trying to sell your house.

Your children will develop an eye for how things looked when you returned. If you play this period of your life well, you may just end up with higher standards all around!

ASK AUNTIE LEILA

How Do You Prepare for Thanksgiving (or Any Looming Event)?

Dear Auntie Leila,

Could you tell about the things you do to get ready for Thanksgiving?

Love,

Susan

Dear Susan,

You mean the magazines aren't helping you with their advice to set the table the day before? You say you actually use that table at every meal for your impossibly large family? And even if, during those crazy prep days, you could simply hand them food out the dog hatch, telling them that it's normal to eat meals on the porch in November, your nimble toddlers would slip past you and make short work of the china and glassware?

You don't think it would be wise to set the table more than a nanosecond before everyone sits down, even with your linebacker brothers to guard it while you keep the other toddlers from standing on the dishwasher door?

Because you have an infinite supply of toddlers?

I hear you. I don't have any brothers, so it was even worse for me.

Maybe some of these ideas can help. Keeping in mind that this chapter is really for large, busy families with children who aren't old enough to contribute by bringing all the dishes to you, and that I am usually stirring gravy with one hand and forgetting to defrost the pie dough with the other, here are some helpful hints.

General Items to Keep in Mind

Schedule time for your baby. Know that when you have little ones, you are not going to have that one day you can devote to giving the extra turn to your puff pastry, making individual miniature cornucopias as favors, or blanching your almonds.

Remember to sit down and nurse the baby. By the way, this is where I think baby schedules get a bad rap. The schedule is for you—so that you don't push your baby a little past his limit with your busyness but are fully aware that, yes, it has been two hours and he really does need you. Not for a quick sip but for a good, hearty nursing. If you bottle feed your baby, no, you can't just hand him off to others while you run yourself ragged.

The baby is like a big speed bump in the road, but not in a bad way. Slow down; pace yourself. You know for a fact that the baby will need to be held, and, exasperatingly, held more often when your level of frantic activity is up (there is a direct correlation between children desperately needing you and your distractedness—this has been documented by countless women, or would have been if they could have found a pencil).

Even if the baby seems fine as you feverishly work to get the holiday ready (and he's not, because to him it's just a day, not a "special" day, and he wants you), you might get sick if you put him off. At least, if I didn't stay with my babies' rhythms, I would get a breast infection—no fun and no good for anyone.

On the other hand, you have lots of little helpers who can do charmingly naïve approximations of place tags, fashion turkey decorations and garlands, and bring in pine cones. So decorating is taken care of.

Pay your bills and go through your papers before Monday of Thanksgiving week. You will be vexed if you get a late fee because you let yourself lose your concentration.

Do a lot of laundry Monday. Fold it and put it away. Notice today if your family doesn't have enough underwear to get them through Friday. If that's the case, get thee to the store and buy some. You'll still have to do laundry every day (probably including at least processing some on Thanksgiving itself), but give yourself breathing room before the real rush.

No matter how efficient you are, and especially if you're like me and really like to make things from scratch and have them fresh on the day, you will be quite busy on Wednesday and Thursday. You don't want a lot of dirty or wet or jumbled sheets and towels mocking you every time you walk by wherever you stack all your unprocessed laundry.

Clean your room sometime before Tuesday. If you want peace in the few days before Thanksgiving, you need to know that your house is in order. That tense feeling of paralysis comes from the vague sense that you have too much to do, which is, in turn, fed by those little strolls you occasionally take through the house and yard. If you do a big chunk of it—the non-turkey-related chunk—a few days before, you will experience a lightness you never knew you could have.

The fact is that roasting a turkey isn't all that hard. Someone once pointed out, after having fussed over a chipotle turkey with ancho stuffing or whatever, that in the end, Thanksgiving dinner tastes like ... Thanksgiving dinner—no matter what you do!

So keep it simple, and rather than thinking that all will be lost if you don't have five-spice squash, just make good plain squash and do your chores ahead of time.

Complicated Thanksgiving recipes are creatures of magazine editors who sit around all year thinking up stuff for you to stress out about—and then get their own Thanksgiving dinners catered.

Actual Thanksgiving, on the other hand, is about the bounty of nature (among other, loftier things). Put butter on it and it will be lovely.

Let your children help. You know those feelings you have: "I wish I had time to sweep the porch!" "I need to vacuum the stairs!" "Ugh, there are cobwebs in this room!" "Under the trash can the cabinet is so dirty!" "The chairs need to be dusted!" "I can't even think about the car!" Well, those are all things kids could take care of. It won't be worse than it already is. Put your children to work and see if you don't get a bit ahead despite yourself.

When the nether regions of your house are moderately clean, your laundry is put away (I know there's more, but you're on top of it), and your bills are paid, you can take a little breath.

The Details

Now on to more details of how a holiday happens without total collapse:

Make lists. Sit down (with the baby, of course) the week before the holiday and start your lists.

These are the lists you need:

Details of the cleaning that has to be done—guest areas and kitchen. Just before a holiday is not the time for turning mattresses or any of that deep-cleaning fancy stuff. Declutter a little, wipe things down, tidy up—including your messes that you can't deal with right now; just make them as tidy as you can—and vacuum.

By Monday of Thanksgiving week, the unseen regions of your house will at least stop giving you that sinking feeling that you will expire soon. Get the bathrooms in shape. When you wake up next week to the reality of cooking for your crowd, you'll have the satisfaction of knowing that a Blitz will have you in good form.

Nonfood items that you have to purchase: dress shoes for the boys, new kitchen towels (please resist the brown and orange ones, or you'll have to start all over again in a week), a gravy boat (just get one—it's about time—it doesn't have to match), and candles (don't forget the Advent candles—because vexingly for us in the United States, Advent usually begins the Sunday after Thanksgiving).

Extremely specific menu plans for every instant from the moment your guests—including returning children—arrive. You need to try to picture in your mind exactly what you want to be serving for breakfast, lunch, appetizers, dinner, and snacks for the whole weekend. Then throw in a menu for the day before anyone arrives—something simple, refrigerator-emptying, and quick, such as soup or pasta with ham and spinach.

Your menu list should have three parts: the menus, organized by meal; the prep work for each meal, the better to delegate, since even the youngest child can peel a carrot or wash broccoli; and a shopping list. Arrange your shopping list by aisle and department.

The Prep

Armed with your lists, you are ready for actual prep.

Make ahead of time whatever you can: make dessert first; well, make your pie crusts sometime before Wednesday and even weeks before, putting them in the freezer if you are that ahead of things. Once that part is done, the pies are easy and can be baked before you put the turkey in (I really do like mine freshly baked on the day, other than the pecan pie, which can be made the day before—and it does freeze well).

What's really great about this particular dinner is that you can make almost all of it in advance. Since you are likely also having to feed your family on a regular basis until then (why? why do they need to be fed so often?), you probably won't be that housewife who calmly mixes herself a martini an hour before the guests arrive. But here are the things that you can do while you are getting through the preceding non-holiday days:

Turkey: If you can roast a turkey along with your pre-Thanksgiving Sunday dinner, do. That allows you to have already carved meat and gravy, sparing you the last-minute frenzy. You can still roast one on the big day, but it will be mainly for show. One turkey—even a big one, which is mostly bones and cavity—isn't really enough for more than eight people anyway, not if you want the best part of this dinner, which is sandwiches made with leftovers!

Cranberry sauce: Since the sauce has to be cold anyway, make it right now. Homemade is absolutely worth the effort, even if you just follow the directions on the package, leaving out the lemon zest, hand-picked hazelnuts, nori cultivated in special Japanese sea gardens, or varietal red wine reduction.

Canned cranberry sauce tastes like sugar (or, more likely, corn syrup) that met a cranberry sometime in the distant past and can't remember its name. And which one of us hasn't been smacking ourselves on the head on Thanksgiving morning, foreseeing all too clearly the inevitability of warm cranberry sauce, having forgotten about it until then?

While you are at it, make double—it's basically jam, so it keeps and will enhance not only fowl but hams and pork as well.

Stuffing: Any time the oven is on, put a tray of cubed bread in there. Stash it in the freezer after it has cooled.

Vegetables: To give you a peek at how you can prep the vegetables ahead of time, I will tell you about the time I was making pizza and I got the cranberry sauce done while I was already cooking, as well as a nice batch of onion confit, with figs, ginger, and coriander. (Remember, my kids are not underfoot now!) I was slicing onions for the pizza anyway, so I saved a step and sliced extra. If all my dishes are pretty plain (but yummy), the confit will be memorably interesting, and that will be enough variety for an already multifarious meal.

When the oven was still hot from the pizza, I put the sweet potatoes in (be sure to line the pan with foil so you won't end up with a pan of burnt sweet-potato guts to deal with). Those can cool for however long it takes—days, even—to peel them and toss them with butter and salt in a serving dish. And then they are done.

Rolls: When you make your dough for the rolls, make enough for several loaves of bread for the all-important sandwiches afterward. For those, you need some really good bread! Freeze it after it's baked and cooled so no one eats it before the right moment.

Look at your list and try to get a couple of things done each day. Most of the vegetables will keep just fine in the fridge or the freezer—or even, in the case of sweet potatoes, squash, beets, and such, on a cool shelf in the pantry for a day or two as long as they are in a shallow enough dish to cool quickly after they are cooked.

On the Tuesday before the big day you can do your final shopping, knowing that your house is reasonably clean, and if all else fails, you will have pie and stuffing with cranberry sauce.

On Thursday morning, make everyone take a long walk. If they stay inside, they will just get the house dirty. I won't say you'll have that martini, and that's probably just as well, but it's the best it will get until they are old enough to invite you to Thanksgiving dinner!

Seeing Your Home
as Others See It

I can't help thinking that conversation about the role of the woman in the home, including the education of children, is futile without first putting our hands on the tools we need to cope with what happens during the day, at home, with children. On the one hand, there are those who write about the high calling of making a home and give no details. On the other, there are plenty of resources for getting organized, but most don't take into account having a busy household while trying to educate the children.

No one knows as well as I do how hard it is to stay on top of things when you have babies and toddlers and kids running around, because I'm just like you, only with less energy. But keeping a reasonably clean house is part—*not all, but part*, the "necessary if insufficient" basis—of the order in Order and Wonder. A lot of our frustration as women with *life at home*, with implementing all our hopes and dreams, comes from simply not knowing where to start when it comes to housekeeping!

I already gave reasons to start in your very own bedroom. The order we do things in is an order. When we seek order according to the pattern we try to discern in the universe, in human nature, and in God, we find that the wonder increases. Starting with the foundation of the common life in the home—marriage—even in something as seemingly trivial as knowing which room to clean can yield amazing benefits in other less mundane areas.

Once you've conquered your own room, you might find it beneficial to implement the advice I read in the helpful (and amusing) book *Sidetracked Home Executives*. (I fully admit that the books I refer to are mostly from the last millennium. I do read some of the new ones, but I still like these. They are funny and real—and thorough.) The authors suggest something that might not occur to you for housekeeping, although it's often recommended for house *selling*, when it's far too late to reap the benefits for making the home: that you stand outside your house and see it as others see it; then walk in and see what they see.

There's a certain kind of person, self-absorbed, abstract, prone to be found reading novels, for whom this idea is revolutionary! Not only did this advice help me to be more orderly; it transformed my sense of hospitality!

Why is it that we are continually entering others' homes, getting an impression of how they live by what we first encounter, and yet never considering that others are doing the same thing with us? Why is it that we may know some people who never let us have a glimpse of their chaos, if they have any, but we don't feel particularly welcomed in their homes? And others are quite open about having lots of life going on, yet we get an overall sense of peace and contentment?

What's the key to the way those others do things?

We are stuck inside, mentally as well as physically. We are never seeing beyond the dirty dishes. *They* somehow, maybe intuitively, know how to make us comfortable from the moment we walk up to their door. They project something that we need to project! Seeing our home as others see it can be as life changing as that view in the three-way mirror in the dress shop! You will learn a lot about yourself if you do this and do it often (both the home and the mirror, I suppose!).

Take pictures if it helps. My house is just my house. I don't pretend to be any kind of design arbiter. If you come here, you will see lots of flaws. Maybe your house is the same.

A thought, borne out by experience: once a person has an impression, good or bad, of your house, it's hard for that person to shake it. Try to have your friends' first impression of your home be one of tidiness, and they will forevermore excuse messiness as *not you*.

Another thought: everyone has dirty dishes, at least sometimes, but not everyone has stray underwear on the front porch. Don't excuse things because they're *your own special mess*; you know you don't do that with others. If things are basically tidy and clean, a few messes don't register. But if there is a generalized disorder that seems layered by time, *fossilized*, almost, the impression given is of bad housekeeping, and it's really off-putting.

Maybe you always come in the garage but your friends don't. Have you seen your entrance recently? What does it say about you? Possibly it says, "We literally never see this part of our home, but, uh, welcome?"

Maybe your guests enter via the kitchen—here in New England that is often the case due to the way old houses get added on to. Here is the thing: inside, from my point of view, I have a clean kitchen island, only a few things "in transit," and it's relatively neat and clean by at least some standards. But when I enter, I'm tempted to put things on the first surface I encounter. It's not near *my indoor* "center," the sink and the table. It's off to the side, and very handy for stuff that's going out the door as well.

From *my* point of view, things are still pretty tidy this way. But clutter is what greets someone walking *in* via the mudroom, especially because of the narrow entry into the kitchen caused by the brick fireplace hearth which starts to the left with very little room to maneuver. That person may even see an open dishwasher door first thing! It's just the way my kitchen is laid out.

It's all in the point of view. I want someone who is dropping by to sense a welcome, to enter a home that is basically neat and tidy, that is reasonably clean. So I keep that counter nearest the entry to the kitchen clear (which in turn means I need a horizontal surface earlier, in the mudroom, that is expressly for the purpose and won't proclaim untidiness because it's not as high as the counter inside). I try to shut the dishwasher door when I'm not working on dishes.

Instead of making excuses using that false notion that "someday, when it looks like a magazine, it will be nice," we can make others' view of our home attractive *as it is now*. If it's the best it can be, it will reveal itself to be either just fine or in need of something particular that we can realistically plan for; either way, it's good: it's reasonably clean, and its order promotes a sense of peace.

The peace we get when we start outside is not just for guests, by the way; it's for family members too. Kids who are coming home, Papa who has been running errands, even *I* like walking in when the entrance is orderly. Making it so offers me a sense of contentment and happiness.

All these thoughts and efforts come to me after years and years of practice and being patient (or, probably, unaware) as the babies come and grow. I will be honest: *reasonably* clean, neat, and tidy is the best *I* can do, so don't feel too bad or too pressured.

On to Cleaning the Kitchen

I've thought a lot about where *exactly* to start with this mighty topic of cleaning the kitchen, and I've decided that before we get into organization, workflow, and actual *cleaning*, we have to have a little talk about a habit the children must learn.

The Reasonably Clean Kitchen Starts with Rules for the Kids

Although we mothers begin to find meaning in what we do by understanding it as *service*, paradoxically, an important part of that service is teaching the little ones *how to help themselves*; in other words, in *not* serving them—on purpose! Oh, we will still serve them, all right, but, little by little, we will help them learn to do things for themselves and for others.

Some mothers don't teach little ones this important lesson because they don't respect themselves or their God-given authority, and they find that they can't ask someone, even a three-year-old, to do anything. Some don't do it because they truly don't realize it has to be done, and besides, it requires effort. The truth is, we might be tempted to avoid the effort to think about and act on giving the needed training.

Some don't think it can be done; they are unfamiliar with the hidden resources of children or are fooled by the perfect willingness of children to avoid most of the things they don't want to do, even if they thought of them. And, for the most part, how could they? Most children *of course* have no more idea that something needs to be picked up or put away than that there is a man on the moon; any child who does get the inkling can't be blamed for wanting to escape doing something about it. Naturally they have more important things to do!

Many mothers are waiting for someone else or the perfect time to do it. Some are so caught up in serving others—they have such a good heart, in a way—that they feel guilty demanding action.

But sweep all that away, particularly that little voice inside you that keeps whispering, "It's just so much easier to do it myself," as well as the other one that says, "Who cares, I'm too busy [insert description here, e.g., having babies, reading, surfing the Web, talking on the phone, waiting for my mother, and so forth] to exert the energy to do this." It's as if you have two devils, one on each shoulder, and there's no room for the angel who would like to say to you, "Put in the effort for a week, and you will reap the benefits for a lifetime." (Never mind that *other* devil who tries to convince you that you *like* things messy and gross. Please.)

It's not easy, but it is simple. You know how you dread each meal, and when it's done you feel that the cleanup is a sort of particularly sheer mountain you have to climb, only there's also scree that keeps causing you to slip down to the bottom again? You know how your kids spend the whole time running around and then they suddenly are just gone, off to do something fun? And you are left with not only dirty dishes but food everywhere—on the chairs, the floor, the table, the counters. I'm not surprised that you find it hard to keep the kitchen clean.

Sometimes I think that some people really think that their children are no more capable of helping out or acting properly than a bunch of cute little barnyard animals! They regard feeding them with just as much pleasure and derive just as much satisfaction as they would if they were throwing feed into a trough, and they regard the aftermath with the same resignation with which they would clean a stall. I've heard moms say things like "I throw them a bagel."

Auntie Leila doesn't like this way of speaking of your nearest and dearest. I've heard that some moms *always* use paper plates at lunchtime! This astounds me.

If you are one of these ladies, I'm not judging you, but consider. Not only are you depriving your children of an important opportunity to learn how to take care of things, but it's all so self-confirming and dreary. And are you going to be caught off guard when they don't act properly when the table is set? (Also, how wasteful! I mean, once in a while, okay, but every day?)

It's amazing what children can do. Let's try it. Let's tackle just one thing (well, really two), and while you are tackling these two things, keep this in mind: children really like, and respond well, when you make rules! They aren't good at following logic or understanding reasoning (which is why it makes me crazy when parents go on and on, talk, talk, talk!), but a rule is something they can wrap their little minds around. Later the opportunity will arise for you to explain the rule, and that's fine, because Lord knows you have some good arguments backing you up, not least of which is that you don't want them ending up being handed their tray through a slot in lockup, which is where they are going with those table manners of theirs.

Paradoxically, the more you make them behave with good habits, the more time you have for engaging in delightful conversation with them! The more you rely on reasoning (and its evil twin sister, nagging), the fewer enjoyable moments you will have with them. But I wasn't going to get into child psychology. We're cleaning up the kitchen!

Let's make those rules! Rules lead to good habits.

Before the Meal

First rule: the child must come when you call him and do what he is told to help prepare; for instance, set out the napkins, get the cups, and so forth.

You choose what each child should do, but don't let yourself get into a situation where multiple people are grabbing food and plates and shoving food in their mouths and running around while you are still wondering about how to clean up from the last meal. And above all, *never let anyone open the refrigerator without your permission*, at least until they are old enough to clean it as well; and wait to say grace *together* (which means waiting for *you* to sit down) before starting to eat.

You are going to have to tell them that this is coming up. Don't blindside them. Let them know that things are changing around here. It's a good conversation to have at dinner when Dad is there to drive home what you say.

If the kids are really little, just tell them before you get ready for the meal that when you call, you want them to come in right away. To work this point, obviously you will have to be ready with the food and ready to sit down with them and sit still yourself. Don't call them in if you aren't mentally ready or just because calling them makes you feel that you have accomplished something. You will also have to be able to give your full attention to them, interacting with them cheerfully. And yes, I mean this even if "them" is your three-year-old.

These criteria apply to breakfast and lunch as well as dinner. The reason is that, although you might be tempted to think that you ought to have a break by relaxing standards—and certainly, there are different standards for different occasions, within reason—doing well at dinner requires practice! Where will this practice come from, especially if you want to avoid turning dinner (so often the only mealtime the children have with their father) into nagging time? From the other meals, of course—from breakfast and lunch.

A question I have been asked: What if there are two minutes remaining in the game, and when you call everyone into the meal, they can't tear themselves away? Well, I have learned to ask when the game is ending!

After the Meal

Second, the helpful attitude—not to mention the gracious manners—you are instilling require beginning and end points: the ritual and order of the thing. There is grace before the meal, and, of course, each child has to ask to be excused before getting up. He should also thank you for the delicious meal. Some people say grace after the meal as well in thanksgiving, indicating that those who wish to be excused may be.

Second rule: on asking permission, overtly or tacitly, to leave, that child must clear his place!

Tacitly means that you notice the child is done and ready to leave; you say, "All done? Good. Time to put your dish in the dishwasher." I'm not suggesting that you raise a martinet, after all. Later, when there are more of them and you need to rein things in, you can explicitly require asking permission.

By the way, help children understand that they must come in to say grace, not necessarily to eat, if you find they are becoming picky or difficult. They must have only a bite of everything or eat what they can. But the reason for this, and why I tell you to have them thank you before they leave the table is that you want to cultivate gratitude and respect for God; for you, the parents; and for the food.

It might take three trips for the child to clear his place, and in the case of a toddler, you might have to get up and help or ask an older child to help the toddler while you help the baby; but the number-one cause of motherhood burnout (other than failure to establish bedtimes, but that is another topic) is being left to deal with dirty dishes alone. It's too much work for one person! Oh, maybe you are escaping consequences now, but how will it be when you are sick or after you have your third set of twins or when your thirteen-year-old invites all her friends over for pizza? (Note well: it's amazing how, if your child clears her place, all her friends will follow suit; you discover this beautiful reality when a visiting child clears *his* plate and your child follows *his* example, causing you to smack your head with your open hand for never having made this rule, when this other, more clever, mother, has!)

Now, for this rule to prosper you, you must have an empty dishwasher; or at least, if it has things in it, let them be already dirty, with space for the rest. Naturally (with forethought) someone has to have emptied the dishwasher first thing, before breakfast for starters, and before every meal, obviously. And when my kids were growing up, it wasn't I who emptied the dishwasher before breakfast, and it shouldn't be you either if you aren't a good morning riser! If you have older children, assign one to do it. If you have a couple of younger children, assign a rack per kid and one to the silverware, and arrange things so that the place for the clean dishes is within reach for them. (Get sturdy dishes and glasses and teach them to be gentle.)

It's in the Bible: "If any man will not work, neither let him eat" (2 Thess. 3:10, DR). It's okay to ask people to do a little before they get fed. If you need a solid pattern to follow, read *Farmer Boy*. Of course, then you will probably be asked to fry doughnuts.

If you don't have a dishwasher, then the sink area has to be clean, the clean dishes put away, and the sink should have a tub of hot soapy water in it. We'll talk more about the system in a bit.

So, to recap, your children are going to help get set up for the meal in a limited but effective way. Then they are going to stay put and eat it, if only for a short time. And then they will ask to be excused, thanking you politely. Then they get up and put their very own dishes in the dishwasher or gently in the sink or stack them on the counter (you think about it and decide), and also any forks and cups; they will throw away or put away their napkins; they will push in their chairs.

They can take their time doing these things, and they don't have to do it all together. I find it perfectly acceptable and even desirable for two littles to go off while the bigger ones sit longer.

Your part is to get the meal ready for them, even if only to the extent that you know what you want served, and to be attentive during the habit-forming period, which really should be a full week with your older children. This week, repeated as necessary, will help you all to get into the habit of being attentive and present to each other during meals, which is a very good thing indeed. By the time you are on the third or fourth child, the family culture will be firmly established, and you won't remember even thinking about it.

Moms dread eating with their children because they have allowed themselves to hate everything about it or, rather, haven't put in the necessary work to enjoy it. But I ask you: If their own mother doesn't want to eat with them, who will?

Will there be messes? Of course! If you didn't want messes, you should have stayed single! I'm talking about *reasonably clean* here, messes you can handle, recoverable messes. The goal is that you could have company over without needing therapy before or after. A lowish bar, wouldn't you say?

Really, Auntie Leila, is this doable?

I always loved having my kids around even during mealtimes and even as distracted and disorganized as I am, and, in large part, it's because I naturally gravitate toward making rules. (But you knew that.)

You are not alone; you can ask your wonderful husband to join you in modeling all these things for his dear children, but let me caution you against speaking to him in the commanding tone you use for them. Don't treat him like one of them. Don't ruin the good habits you are teaching *them* by getting into the bad, even fatal, habit of acting as if *he's* a naughty child. More women have ruined their marriages by this one fault than you would suspect.

Flow in the Kitchen

Work goes so much better—the house will be so much more reasonably clean—if you think in terms of *flow*. Hence my admonition at the start of this discussion to begin cleaning in a predetermined direction, one you don't have to think through every time. That goes double for the kitchen.

The book *Cheaper by the Dozen* may be familiar to you. The sequel is called *Time Out for Happiness*. Being a person who could never in a million years have done one worthwhile thing at all in engineering school, I nevertheless have time and motion management in my blood, thanks to my engineering professor father, who was, in fact, a recipient of the Frank and Lillian Gilbreth Industrial Engineering Award. Believe me, it was for a reason!

Naturally, I loved this book. For one thing, it's a sweet love story of two remarkable people. Early on we are introduced to the young Frank Gilbreth, who wins a lot of bets from veteran bricklayers that he, a seemingly greenhorn wet-behind-the-ears office guy, can outperform the best of them at their job. He does this simply by analyzing the wasted motion the men have accepted as unquestioned components of what they do. Where they bend and heave, he moves the stack of bricks and bucket of mortar to arm level. Where they backtrack, he moves smoothly from one motion to the next. Over the course of a thousand movements, these little savings add up. His walls are straighter, neater, and more quickly built than theirs. They accuse him of cheating!

Thinking about a task, especially a tedious one that cannot be avoided, is essential, so let's think about the routine in the kitchen and start figuring out where to cheat!

I gave you a head start with the idea of training each child to put his own dish, cup, and utensil in the dishwasher or in the sink (which, of course, means starting with an empty dishwasher or sink; put this important step in the routine) and to throw his own trash away. Even a two-year-old can do a little. Do not end up being the dirty-everything rounder-upper.

Now let's think about *flow*. And time. And motion.

Unfortunately, very few kitchens are designed from the get-go with the proper flow. If they were, at the very least there would be one center with a sink for food preparation and one with a sink for dish cleanup. Since most of us must work with only one sink (even if it's a double sink), establishing flow makes the difference between a smooth system and, well, no system.

By the way, if I had to choose between a double sink and a dishwasher—and I think this is a choice that many have to make because of the size of the cabinets—I would go for the double sink and make sure it has a gooseneck faucet, making filling and washing pots *so* much easier.

Here's a diagram of what we are going to analyze.

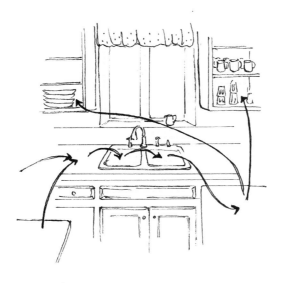

Let's aim for a flow that everyone in your household can understand. It should be simple and should make sense on a basic level of *where things land and where they are headed*. Just as a landscaper takes note of *where the paths already are*, you should see what natural flow already exists.

As with the house in general, it's good to divide the kitchen into zones. There's the food-prep zone, with the subset of a baking zone. If you've never thought about baking in terms of having just about everything you need not more than a step away, you are in for a significant leap in your kitchen's efficiency!

And there's the clean-dishes zone. Even with a dishwasher, you will need a place that is for clean items *only*, and once established, it will be clear to others, including guests, that dirty things don't get placed there. Some hand-washed items will be drying on a rack or cloth. When the dishwasher is unloaded, there are always some plastic containers that are not quite dry. They can't be put away wet and nestled because bacteria will grow in them; these can be placed in the clean-item area to air dry (or, if there is time, shaken out and left on the top rack of the dishwasher until they are completely dry).

Even when you are able to put everything away (an unusual occurrence at my house), removing the drying cloth or hanging up the rack in its spot, keep this area mentally prepared for clean items only by insisting that dirty ones go on the other side of the sink (or in it if it is properly prepared to receive them).

In my kitchen, the zone for food storage — refrigerator and "in-use" pantry cupboard (I have a large pantry off the kitchen for those items not needed immediately) — is to the left of my prep area, as is the bread supply, which is in a drawer below the toaster. I have to keep the pots in the open cupboard on the left, and it's not the best place, since the stove is on the right, but I removed the cabinet doors so I wouldn't have to bend *and* reach behind doors for them. Large, deep drawers would be better than lower cabinets.

As an example of saving motion, suppose that in your kitchen it works to go left to right, dirty to clean; then it makes sense to have clean dishes and pots stored on the right so that you don't have to backtrack through the cleanup area on the left to put things away. For instance, if dirty dishes are being staged on the counter to the left of the sink, then that counter won't be available to place clean dishes on when you are putting away a stack of things, moving them from the dishwasher on the right, because it will likely be soiled with food. (Of course, you can set things up going right to left. The important thing is to have a direction!)

Now let's think about the steps toward establishing the flow.

1. *Think about the flow of clean dishes to the table, dirty dishes from the table to the sink or the dishwasher, and clean dishes back to the cabinets.* Think about how you can establish a routine that makes sense and save steps, even if it's not perfect. You might have to rearrange some things; if you do, wipe out the cabinets before you put things in their new places. Consider putting the dishes in a place that is as accessible to children as possible, both for setting the table and for putting clean dishes away; normally people don't store dishes in lower cabinets, but it might work for you.

My clean dishes should really go in a cabinet closer to the dishwasher, but there isn't a cabinet there. Should I waste my time dreaming about how to renovate the kitchen, or should I work with what I have? Right—work with what I have!

2. *Clean from the periphery in toward the sink.* Don't start at the sink, because it's demoralizing to turn around and realize how much you still have to do. First, clear the table of the meal and the dishes, utensils, cups, and napkins. Then clean it off with a warm, soapy washcloth. Move any cooking items closer to the sink in your "dirty" area, putting warm water into pots and pans for soaking while you wipe down the stove. As food is put away, wipe counters, moving from further away from the sink toward the final task, the washing up.

3. *If you have a dishwasher, fill a basin or large pot or bowl with hot, soapy water;* it will assist you with any handwashing. Clean pots and pans can go back on the stovetop to dry. Now load the dishwasher. If you do dishes by hand: fill one of your sinks (or a basin) with hot, soapy water, place your scraped dishes in it, and as you wash each one, move it to the other sink for rinsing.

While you are thinking this flow question through in your best time-and-motion frame of mind, consider the area above your sink. You probably have a windowsill there, as I do, but whether you do or not, remove everything from the sink area, scrub around the faucet, behind the sink, and the whole windowsill, wall, or shelf. Find a home elsewhere for all the debris that has collected there and put your dish soap into a dispenser, storing the container it comes in under the sink. Then make it pretty, however you would like.

This area above the sink is our own little personal shrine, isn't it? If the bedroom is the altar, so to speak, of our marriage and the dining room table is the altar of our family life, I think the kitchen windowsill is the shrine of a mother's working life. I encourage you to have it reflect that. I think you will find that carefully arranging this one spot will help you organize the rest of the kitchen.

Helping Kids and Yourself to Do the Dishes without Despairing

I t had come to Auntie Leila's attention that some moms with lots of kids find that they can't impose on their children the chore of doing dishes due to the terrible burden of it, and right away I could see the issue (from the pictures posted where I was reading about this).

More on Flow

If you want kitchen cleanup to happen without turmoil, you need to establish flow in your kitchen, as discussed above. Think about it in terms of your kitchen's setup, whatever that may be. My kitchen is far from perfect. What matters is that you do not forge a new path every night. Make the path once and for all.

Why? Because if *you* are tempted to run screaming from your life every single night as you face the dishes, so much so that you post a picture of the disaster on social media to gain sympathy from your audience, just imagine how it looks to a twelve-year-old! No wonder that kid hems and haws and has to psyche himself up. These "recurring problems"—such as doing dishes after every meal—have to be subjected to a process, a system, a set of previously thought-out steps.

Important rule that will improve the situation immediately: don't put the baby's high-chair tray on top of the dirty dishes in the sink. This sort of thing is what is making your young kitchen helper die a little every night, and frankly, you are having trouble too. It's what makes the whole job take so long. The piling is not to be faced. Do one of two things:

1. Get the baby out—deploying what we call "the crack cleanup team": one responsible party to wash his face, hands, and arms with a warm washcloth and another to wipe down the chair (and don't forget to obtain a dog for licking up the floor)—and clean the tray at the sink *before* the general cleanup begins, and return the tray to the high chair, with everything spiffy in that area. This makes sense because usually Baby is done before the meal is over.

2. Leave the tray *at the high chair* until the general cleanup is over, washing it last. Just shove the whole thing to the side. Don't forget it.

But do not put it in the flow. It creates an almost insurmountable barrier to cleanup.

Staging Areas

Figure out where you will stage things. Not every time—once and for all. Then distribute and communicate your plan to all concerned. *You* can't handle a sink full of dirty dishes, and neither can a kid.

You need a place where you can put away food left over from the meal (that could be someone else's chore, by the way, and I recommend it be yours, so that you can manage leftovers). At our house, that place is the island, because there's room there for the serving dishes and the containers for packing leftovers away.

Know beforehand where you will stack dinner plates so that they are scraped and ready for the dishwasher or the soapy basin while the food-storage process happens. Even four dinner plates can cover an entire counter; twenty can stack neatly to the side until ready to be cleaned—if they are able to be prepped.

If your dishwasher can handle it and your children are able to manage the plate-scraping process, have them put their scraped-off plate directly into that appliance. It's up to you and how much activity (that is, how many bodies) you want in the area.

A significant game changer (especially during holidays, but really, at every meal): *have a separate basin or shallow pan (such as a lasagna pan) for utensils.* Getting all the forks, knives, spoons, and serving pieces out of the pile of plates works wonders for streamlining the whole process. Children can be encouraged to clear their places in this manner, putting their plates in one place and their utensils in another, *not* just piling everything on the last persons' items, creating a cleaning bottleneck.

Even separating the utensils to one side of the sink while you scrape and stack plates on the other changes the task from tiresome to the work of a moment. If the utensils *can* soak in their own receptacle, they can be picked up by the bunch and put in the dishwasher, as opposed to loading them one or two at a time as you work your way through a precarious pile of dishware.

Of course, sharp knives stay next to the sink until you're ready to wash them, so no one will get cut by a lurking blade under the suds.

The Art of Washing Dishes

Besides all the prep work mentioned above, there is the matter of actually washing dishes, whether in the dishwasher or by hand. Either way, don't just run hot water continuously while squirting dish detergent endlessly.

For washing in the dishwasher, just put the dishes in after they are scraped. If you have stacked them, you can run a little water in between each one so that nothing will be stuck on them; dishwasher detergent works better if there are some particles on the dishes (and repairmen also insist that you don't need much detergent; they say it gums up the works and a dab the size of a nickel is best in the case of liquid; I suggest you try this minimum—for powder too—and work your way up if you need more).

For handwashing, use your hot, soapy water to wash. Yes, you can put a squirt of detergent on your sponge or dishcloth as you go, but don't run water over your cloth as you wash; you will end up rinsing the detergent off it.

Think about camping. Out in the field, you'd heat up one basin of water, get it soapy, wash everything, and then rinse—because you're hauling water from a distance. Use this as your mental template so that you don't waste water and detergent. Remember, the detergent is formulated to bond with solids (dirt and grease) and rinse away. Even if the water seems dirty, it's working for you. You can dump it out and refill it, but don't wash each item individually with the hot water running!

Know how to do dishes and then teach your child how to do them. Don't just burden him with a problem that you yourself can't solve.

Doing Dishes Helps Kids Open Up and Finally Want to Talk

Here's a bit of a mystery about washing dishes, one that addresses that vexing issue of how, though you are dying to go to bed, your older kids, for some reason, can bring themselves to talk to you after only 10:00 p.m.

Suddenly the deep dark concerns come out—so late, so desperately late.

My friend told me that her mother (of eight children) always "helped" whichever kid was doing the dishes. She didn't want to have a dishwasher (the appliance) because she knew that it was during that time that the conversations would happen. She remembers one sister or another saying to her, "I'll do the dishes with Mom tonight." And that was so they could talk.

You don't have to get rid of your dishwasher, but do realize that much of the time, not only do you need to be in the kitchen during cleanup to direct flow, put away food (so that you can put it to best use later, as a good manager), and oversee this not-exactly-easy chore, you will also have a chance to have a little conversation with your child.

Yes, that moment after supper often finds the baby needing to nurse, and you can send in an older child or Dad to take your place in the kitchen. But as you get good at this game we call parenting, you can also use the time when others are clearing up to nurse the baby and then hand him off to another child for play or a bath—just at the opportune time to be there for the kid who needs you by yourself. Or you may sense that Dad is the one who is needed. He will be better equipped to work in the kitchen if there is an established method (and he may be the one to enforce it with children, in any case).

Some nights, it's not deep consultation, but just singing songs, and suddenly you'll have a lot of help as family members naturally join in. Even if your child is working by himself, he can handle it because it's a doable chore, with you giving an assist. It's not the aloneness that is terrible; it's the impossibility of the thing, and you mitigate that by means of simply having thought it through and then being on hand to facilitate. Well, that's the pretext, but the real reason is that this time is good for talking.

That's family life together. The very things that seem like the worst drudgery create the best memories—when there is someone loving who will put thought into how it will go and be there for the quiet moments.

Cleaning Cast-Iron Pans the Old-Fashioned Way

The information I've seen about cleaning cast-iron pans seems to be written by people who are too young to remember the right way to do it. Not that I am that old, mind you. I blame the sudden onset, back when I was a young bride, of nonstick cookware.

Nonstick brings along with it a set of (plastic and, in my opinion, anti-aesthetic) kitchen utensils that are not really good for anything other than using with nonstick. And those kinds of pans *are* very persnickety about how you take care of them. On top of how high-maintenance nonstick is, there's no way it can be good for you as it burns the coating off right under your nose. If you have nonstick, you begin to look at all your cookware as impossibly delicate, easily scratched, quite volatile as to coating, and doomed to ultimate failure.

Cast iron is ... cast iron. You are not going to harm it. It is not going to harm you.

With cast iron, there are two issues: seasoning and cleaning.

Seasoning

You can't season your pan with cooking oil, no matter what the "experts" say; you can only grease it. To season the pan—that is, to give it a hard coating that will last as you cook—you need to use linseed oil (pure linseed oil, not boiled linseed oil, which contains heavy metals to promote drying). Linseed oil is also known as flax oil. This oil polymerizes—it hardens when it is heated (or over time).[9]

To season your pan, clean it with a stainless-steel scouring pad and remove any rust. Dry the pan completely in a low oven. When it's cool, pour a thin layer of the linseed or flax oil into your pan, rub it in well, and then wipe off the excess. I use a paper towel. Place the pan upside down in the oven (so that any excess oil, which there should not be, can run off and not pool), and heat it to the point that it releases free radicals and the process of hardening begins—at least to 500 degrees, for an hour. Then let it cool and repeat the process. The more layers of polymerized oil you can get, the better.

You can achieve this polymerization with animal fat as well, but it is not as sure a method, as its "drying" contents (alpha-linolenic acid) are lower. If this all sounds too technical, I assure you that many a cast-iron pan has gotten a nice patina just from frying up bacon periodically; I use bacon grease for my pans all the time. However, vegetable oils will not harden—they just get sticky and go rancid. Obviously you can use them—and butter—to cook, but don't leave them in the pan.

Foods that are high in acid (vinegar or tomato, for instance) will strip the seasoning of the pan.

---

[9] I am indebted to Sheryl Canter for a clear explanation on the difference, chemistry-wise, between greasing and seasoning a cast-iron pan. See her clarifying, and informative blog post "Chemistry of Cast Iron Seasoning: A Science-Based How-To," *Sheryl's Blog*, January 28, 2010, http://sherylcanter. com/wordpress/2010/01/a-science-based-technique-for-seasoning-cast -iron/.

Cleaning

You don't need tongs to clean (the recommendations I've seen are to hold paper towels with the tongs), although if you are cleaning a very hot pan, they might come in handy.

You don't need salt. You *could* use salt or even sand because you are trying to abrade, but it's not efficient.

A plastic scrubber will do you no good. Nor will the back of your sponge; you'll only ruin it.

You do need one paper towel (you could use a rag but I strongly feel that paper towels have their uses, and this is one of them).

I'm going to give you the quick tutorial on how to clean those pans, because once you learn it, you will love using them.

Using a flexible straight-bottomed stainless-steel spatula (some call it a pancake turner), and occasionally a stainless-steel spoon for corners, scrape off all the cooked-on bits in your pan while running the water as hot as you can stand it. For this, you might need rubber gloves, but the spatula keeps your hands out of the hot water. It is not easy to find the kind of spatula you really need, due to the proliferation of nonstick, as discussed above, and this fact is a sore grievance to me. For some unknown reason, contemporary metal spatulas are all curved on the business end. You can get lucky at thrift stores, so always have an eagle eye out for a stainless-steel spatula with a *straight* edge.

Now use a stainless-steel scrubbing pad (not Brillo-style ones, which have soap embedded—just a plain stainless scrubber) to scour out whatever grease and drippings there might be. You can't hurt the pan; it can't hurt

you! Just scrub as much as is needed to get bits out; use as much hot water as needed to rinse grease off. And stop there.

Remember, hot water only. No soap. Trust me. That is all you need.

You just have to accept that your pan will be *conceptually* greasy; you will come to see that between the hot water and the subsequent wiping with a paper towel, the pan will be really and truly clean.

Now put it on your stove; it needs to be dry. A burner that has been hot (on an electric stove) or a burner set on low (on a gas one) will do the trick. Leave it there until it is completely dry.

It's clean.

Some old-timers would season the pan by tossing it in a bonfire. The pan would be fine, of course, but I think that you'd have to wipe off soot after the pan cooled.

One grandmother spoke of "firing" her pans to clean them, not just season them. If there got to be a real buildup of gunk (and this does sometimes happen on the outside of the pan), you can put it in the fireplace or what have you to burn it off. Some people also have dedicated pans—for instance, one just for cornbread, to be sure that "off" flavors don't transfer.

Of course, cast-iron cookware can be used in the fire itself—a Dutch oven full of soup can just sit on the grate and be none the worse for wear.

Remember, there are three basic things to clean with:

1. *Soap or detergent.* We know about this one.
2. *Oil or grease.* You would never put soap on a piece of wood furniture; you clean it with oil. Baby's bottom? Clean with baby oil. Hands stained from gardening? Yes, you can wash them with soap and water, but then rub coconut oil, Vaseline, or olive oil on them, and see the dirt come off? What's best of all is to rub your hands with Vaseline before you garden, then put on your gardening gloves; afterward it's not so hard to get them clean.
3. *High heat.* You don't soap down your oven or grill; you fire it up to burn away cooking grease and congealed fats and meat juices. Now you know why I keep telling you to use hot water on your pan, and why you can throw it in the bonfire.

One reader asked about storing the pans, and it's true, the outside can be either greasy or rusty, making cupboards dirty in turn. You can wash the outside — *only* the outside — of your pan with detergent to remove grease. Wipe it with a paper towel so that you'll know that it's really clean. You can hang it on a hook on the wall or a pegboard; that way, the outside will not be touching anything. I always keep my pans on the stovetop, in the oven, or on the woodstove that I have in the kitchen. You can also lay your pan on a paper towel or a paper bag in a drawer or on a shelf.

If the flavor of the food you cook in your cast-iron pan is off, you might need to strip your pan and season it anew, but first check to be sure that your cooking oils or fats are not rancid. Store your bacon grease in a clean jar *in the fridge* so that it doesn't go off.

If the pan smokes when you heat it for cooking, do clean the outside of the pan. Don't overheat your pan on the stove, by the way. Cast iron, unlike other pans, heats up very slowly and then stays hot. Try preheating it at a lower temperature so you won't be tempted to turn it up high at the last minute. For instance, when I am cooking a steak, I preheat the pan on medium high. I sprinkle salt in the pan and turn it to medium. I cook the steak for four minutes on one side (for an inch-thick sirloin), turn it over, and cook it for another four minutes. I usually partially cover the pan for the last two or three minutes of cooking. This method gets me a nice medium-rare steak with a good sear and nice, salty pan drippings. Putting the pan on high always ends with the pan juices burning.

It's so simple to clean your cast iron. The trick and secret is to accept that using soap is *not* the only way to get something clean! And in the case of cast iron, it will just not work. Try this method and see what you think.

Horizontal Surface Management in the Kitchen

The one time I lived (very temporarily) in a development builder–style house with a standard large wrap-around kitchen with lots of counters and cupboards, my counters were always piled high with junk.

These days, I have an oddball kitchen with many doorways, a sliding door, two windows, back stairs, and a fireplace that takes up one wall, and I use the word "wall" loosely. All my walls are abbreviated vertical surfaces for linking openings, but that is another story.

My point is that I have only a little counter space and few cupboards (not compared with some apartments, but for a 5,600-square-foot house and big family). And I am definitely a cluttery person who prefers to have everything in view and takes the short-term view on storage; my thought process is often: "Life is short. Why don't I put this down right here?"

But I aim here to tell you that organization can be had.

I have managed to convince myself that things aren't temporary anymore (and I think I would have been happier overall in the past if I had resisted feeling so temporary about everything and just committed to making where

I was *pretty*). So I've trained myself in a few things that might help you if you share some or all of these characteristics with me. I think I can say that, for the most part, things are *fairly* neat and tidy in these parts, *even taking into consideration* the shortcomings of my personality and surroundings.

I'll never win any awards because I lose concentration at the last minute. My hope has always been, as I've posted pictures on the blog and written about all this, that our readers would look at them and say, "Well, I can do *that!*"

Clear Off and Scrub Your Surface

Start your horizontal surface management with the most important step: clearing every single thing off the counter or table or desk you are working on — every single thing, without exception. Pile all the things on the floor, on another counter, or, preferably, on the kitchen table. Scrub the counter so that, at the end, you could roll out a pie pastry on it with a clear conscience.

One of my girls once complimented me on having counters I could plop bread dough down on! She was about ten and could already sense that it would be inadvisable to do this in many homes she had visited.

Lest you think I am bragging, I certainly wasn't always aware of the possibility of such cleanliness, and the way I came to be a scrubber does make me cringe just a little. I had a friend when I lived in the city, back when I had just two littles. She and her husband had run a lunch place together before her children came, so she was literally a sandwich professional. It was from her that I got the notion that a sandwich had to be accompanied at least by chips and a piece of fruit or a pickle; whereas, before I met her, I just tossed the PB&J on the plate, and that was that. My friend also had a telltale efficiency when preparing lunch for us when we visited her for a play date, a bustling quality that only made sense when she told me how her chef husband had gotten his start.

Anyway, one day, at my house, she was helping me get the children's lunch together as they were playing in the basement — the two of us crowded into my tiny city kitchen. But it did have a butcher-block top on one counter—a butcher block that I never used except to put a sack of groceries on. I simply regarded the thing with utmost suspicion. It wasn't *my* butcher block, and I had no idea how to clean it. I didn't believe it *could* be cleaned. I mean, I suppose I wiped it occasionally, but I would sooner put my food on the floor than directly on that wood. It seemed so insanitary to me—as I'm sure it really was.

Well, whereas I expected her to make the sandwiches on the plates, as I always did, she just turned around and said something like, "Oh, I'll just do these here" and proceeded to suit action to words, working right on the butcher block. I was really horrified, but much more horrified at the thought of stopping her—too embarrassed! Here she *assumed* that my standards of cleanliness were up to hers, and I don't know why! I can tell you that the me of today would not have assumed any such thing about the me of then, given all the evidence to the contrary.

When she was done, she took my no doubt also abominable sponge and really scrubbed after herself. And that's when it dawned on me that *I too could clean the counter, be it butcher block or what have you.*

In fact, the setup of this kitchen was a U—one short wall of butcher block, sink, sink apron, stove, tiny counter; to the right, a window, then on the other wall, the bottom part of a shabby Hoosier cabinet—you know, one of those all-in-one affairs featuring an enameled top at waist height, only the top part was missing. This enameled counter had been painted over, and in my new obsession with bringing my kitchen somewhere in the universe of the standards of my friend, I scrubbed some of the paint off.

That was a discovery! I was able to remove all the paint, and so provided myself with an extra-deep top-notch spot for rolling out pie crusts and bread dough. And thus, in so ignominious a way, I embarked on my quest for clean surfaces!

While you are at the counter-cleaning thing, how about considering how to use the space on top of the fridge? A big tray with tall sides makes the top of my fridge look somewhat tidy. The tray itself is too big to store, yet I do use it to carry meals for families with new babies or with other needs. When it's not in use, it keeps miscellaneous tins and bread baskets corralled.

The cabinet above and behind the fridge is somewhat inaccessible, so I put in there things I use seasonally. I don't even know what's in there. If I haven't seen what I'm looking for in a while, I know it's up there!

Put Everything Back

Now that you've cleared everything off, put things back with these thoughts in mind:

1. Is it in the right zone (see above)?
2. Is this really useful enough or pretty enough to be out in view?
3. Do I need this here, out in view and taking up room on this valuable horizontal surface, or is there a better, more efficient, and more appropriate place for it? How about the cabinet above? Below? How about on a hook that's installed on the bottom of the cabinet above? Or on the wall? What if I could *use* my counter, rather than just store things on it?

This is all very well, and you are getting the idea. But the worst thing about stuff is that more and more of it keeps arriving. What to do about that? Many people put papers, groceries, mail, hardware, and everything else on the counters in the kitchen, because they are entering the house there and it seems vaguely the thing to do. I have a better idea.

Use the Kitchen Table as a Landing Place for Miscellany

The secret to a tidy kitchen with clean countertops and organized horizontal surfaces is to put the incoming items on the kitchen table! Yes! The very thing you feel guilty about doing! Why do I say that? Because by the time you have put the mail in the mail sorter[10] that's by the door, and your bag on its hook next to your coat, and choir binder in its spot—then you must

---

[10] Don't let the mail lie around in random spots. At least by the time you have kids applying to colleges, you simply must have labeled bins for everyone's mail, because I guarantee you that they will not deal with what comes to them, ever. Without something to sort the mail into, you will be forever handling it, and it will overwhelm you.

find a way to get the rest of the miscellany that comes in the kitchen to where it belongs, somewhere else deeper inside the house.

The truth is, you can't do everything at once—and that is how things get put on counters. Once they are on counters, they are out of your consciousness *and* they render the counters unusable. Even one receipt on a counter is an obstacle to efficiency.

Things you or others have brought in—clothes, bathroom supplies, things that belong in bedrooms, anything that doesn't belong in the kitchen, because if it belonged there, it would *already be put away*—put on the kitchen table.

Before the family can eat or do school or homework, all of which take place at that very table, everyone will have to take a minute to put things where they belong. It's all going somewhere else.

If you or your children can eat or do homework right away, sitting down at the table with no issue *because all those things have been shoved on the counters*, the *stuff* will never find its place.

Keep your *counters* clutter free, and make your *table* where you put the clutter. The table doesn't let you get away with it for long. Just don't allow yourself or anyone else to move something from the table to the counter: If you touch it again, it's to put it away, where it belongs.

This kitchen-table thing is so contrary to what you might think that you have to ponder it for a while, but it's how I've kept my kitchen functioning with up to eleven people living here. Always allow a few minutes before meals or studying to put things away. "Come clear off the table!"

Many extremely good housekeepers do not leave their sponge and dishcloth out on the sink at all. But I find that in a busy household, having a little dish on the edge of the sink for those items is a necessary concession. Mine has a drain hole in the bottom; you may be able to find a small, shallow planter that works well. I have the dishcloth hanging over the divider of my double sink.

Putting your dish soap in a pretty pump dispenser is ingenious, I will modestly point out. You can get soap out with one hand, instead of having to hold the ugly plastic bottle with one hand and the sponge in the other. And getting that detergent bottle off your sink is worth a lot in overall aesthetics.

Another Word about Making Things Pretty over the Kitchen Sink

Many women, even after considerable energy devoted to education and career, long to stay home and take care of their family. They feel torn away when they leave home, as if a part of them gets left behind—and that feeling is far stronger for them than the feeling they have when they leave the outside world and feel a little torn about *that*. I think most people understand that you can't have everything, and they make a choice.

But many of these same women do go just a teensy bit insane when they stay home (and I say this because I was sort of this way myself, although I had no outside life I cared anything about at all). And part of that insanity is that it is truly difficult to live somewhere that's probably far from anyone you know or are related to, to have no friends who are willing to do what you are doing, and to spend all your time with small children.

Part of the conflict, though, has to do with not understanding or not being willing to commit yourself *to the little tasks that make up this life*. We talked earlier about seeing things the way others do when they look into your home. The prettiness over the sink is about how, when you finally give in to the reality of your indispensable role, you can allow yourself to be happy; what you see is a little reminder. You are in the heart of your home, looking out.

Just as I suppose a physician or an architect has some little tedious tasks that, when done with finesse and elegance, become pleasurable, so the wife and mother has the ability to turn something that seems like drudgery into a pleasure and even a prayer.

This is not just in the head or the attitude, though, like a kind of mind game. It's very material and palpable. The goodness of little things is visual and appeals to the other senses as well; things have to look nice and smell nice and feel nice and sound nice and taste nice for them to be felt by us to be nice! (Mind that I'm not saying they have to be expensive or nice according to worldly standards, necessarily. Just *fitting*.)

What you see when you stand at the sink could be a confirmation of the respect you have for what you are doing, however humble it may appear to others. So that's why I say to make the area around your sink pretty, according to what you think is pretty! And not just pretty, but maybe even a place where your prayers rise like incense to Heaven even while your hands are in soapy water.

The Things You Clean with Should Be Cleaner Than the Things You Clean!

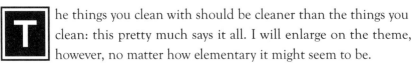

he things you clean with should be cleaner than the things you clean: this pretty much says it all. I will enlarge on the theme, however, no matter how elementary it might seem to be.

It might occur to you, when you are about to wipe that counter that you will then roll a pie crust out on, to wonder if the things you are wiping with (sponges, dishcloths, towels, rags) are clean enough. They sometimes don't look clean. And it makes me remember how things were before I figured this all out at my house, and it further makes me wonder what my lovely friends who were good at housekeeping thought when *they* visited *me*. Honestly, they probably died a thousand deaths. They probably have blogs now, featuring examples of what *not* to do, taken from their visits to me.

I had a couple of dubious dish towels and a sponge. I scrounged for a rag. I can't remember even wondering whether my towels were clean. Once in a while, my mother would delicately buy me a couple of new ones. Some of us are just clueless like that. But we're on a learning curve, and this is it!

It all comes down to this: there is no point in cleaning something with a thing that isn't clean! Think about it! Just because it's *your* dirty sponge, you're used to it, and you are intimately familiar with all the germs that fester there—I mean, they aren't *strange* germs or anything; you know them well—doesn't mean that it isn't gross!

If you use that sponge to wipe something off the floor, even though you know what was on the floor and your sponge is an old friend, you can't use that sponge to wipe a child's face!

Every home magazine and whole shelves of books will tell you how to keep house. I'm not an expert; anyone who really knows me and my house knows I'm not a stellar housekeeper. But I do know this: we need a system so that we can be confident that not only are we cleaning with clean things but other people will be able to step in and take over with confidence as well.

When you are going through hard times and pinching pennies until they beg for mercy, sometimes you don't give yourself permission to buy things you need. Do you buy your feminine products one at a time? Is your toilet paper doled out by the square? Do you run out of soap? Then you know what I'm talking about.

Please get over this. No matter how poor you are, you are going to have to buy those things in some form. Stock up. You can start slowly by using the money you save one month on sale items to buy sale items in bulk the next month, until you have your stash.

Find the lowest price and the quality you like, and go for it. While you're at it, buy a supply of sponges and dishcloths. Not one sponge. Not one dishcloth. Many.

Get the sponges that have a scrubbing side. Everything needs to be scrubbed, honestly, and if it doesn't, turn the thing over and use the sponge side. (For your big pot that you burned potato soup in, you need a stainless-steel or copper pad.) Don't get the kind that are covered with a nylon net. All that happens with those is that the food gets stuck in that netting.

Make sure that the dishcloths are cotton (and *these* can have a mesh side). The microfiber ones will do you no good. They are fine for dusting but don't have the right texture or absorbency for working with dishes and cleaning counters and faces. Under hard use, they pill, which is unaesthetic.

Why dishcloths?

I remember just before we were married, Phil and I were talking about sponges versus dishcloths in kitchen cleanup. (Yes, we were *that* romantic.) He said something like, "I know you'll keep house the way your mother does." It sounded like something he had picked up; you know how you can tell when someone is repeating something they've heard? Let's just say it wasn't the kind of thing he usually said. I thought then I was a sponge person (my mother was a dishcloth person), so I had to laugh, about twenty years later, when I said, "I have to get some dishcloths!" I guess Phil—or whoever told him that—was right!

Dishcloths are useful, I now see, because some things need to be wiped with something that's almost dry, and you can wring out a dishcloth in a way you can't wring out a sponge. As you are wiping something like the counter, you can refold it and have another clean side to work with. With a sponge, after a certain point you are just tracking the mess around unless you stop, walk back to the sink, and wash it out. Too many steps.

Dishcloths have an open texture that helps pick up bits and pieces. And you can throw them in the wash with the towels. Of course, towels should be washed with at least warm water and a bit of bleach. Kitchen towels in particular get quite musty very easily, at least where I live, where it's damp a lot of the time. (This is all discussed in the laundry section.)

I realize that people are passionate sponge or dishcloth partisans. I use both.

Dishcloth people: it's true. How would we clean a floury, sticky counter, egg, or tomato sauce if we had only a sponge, which would simply push those substances around? That said, the dishcloth must look clean as well as be clean. Sponge people: I understand; you want something that holds the soap and feels firm in your hand. Well, the sponge has to be kept clean too! I think we are all familiar with the studies that show that a kitchen sponge is dirtier than the toilet.

That's why I say that you should get a supply, because we all know we hang on to things if we think there's no more left. When your sponge gets a little worn out and not clean enough for kitchen work, let it dry out and then use it in the bathroom to clean the toilet. It's okay to *demote* your cleaning tools! Let them seek their own level, and eventually, *throw them away.*

Always clean the sponge or dishcloth back at the sink before you move on to the next activity. In other words, don't wipe up a bit of sauce and then put the sponge back at the sink. After you use it, rinse it out with hot water and soap, wringing well for next time, and leave it in its dish or, in the case of the cloth, draped over the side. Teach everyone carefully to do the same; the standard operating procedure is that the sponge or dishcloth is ready to go and can be counted on to be clean if it's at its appointed spot.

In an emergency, a sponge or a dishcloth can be left dirty, but then it should be left in the sink to alert the next person (or you yourself, forgetful as you are) of the need to clean it before using it again — because it has to be cleaner than what you are going to clean with it!

And during that sponge's short life span, you can occasionally put it in a bowl and pour boiling water over it or microwave it. Know that very soon, however, even this treatment does not stop the deep-down germs from growing.

Clean the sink itself out well after you finish the dishes. Empty the drain strainers and scrub them. Scrub the sides and bottom of the sink, including the drain opening. Every few days put the strainers in a bowl and pour boiling water over them or throw them in the dishwasher. Clean out the disposal if you have one by running some chopped lemon peel and baking soda through it occasionally.

When we had babies around, we always had a stack of those nice thin baby facecloths for wiping faces and hands. Paper towels are harsh on a baby's face, and it's wasteful to use them for this purpose. At the first sign that Baby was done and about to start clambering out of the high chair, we deployed the "crack cleanup team" — one person removed the tray and the other was ready with a warm clean facecloth to wipe down those greasy fingers and that messy face!

You can also keep a clean facecloth hanging where a child can get it — for instance, on the oven door — and as soon as he has cleared his place, he can wipe his hands and mouth himself. Your whole entire house will stay cleaner if you don't let that little stinker loose to grub things up.

Please understand this: I have no problem with small children getting a bit messy with their food (and babies get very messy!). But commit yourself to cleaning them up when they are done, and you will spare yourself that layer of grime and scent of faintly souring milk that settles on a house where the parents think it's too much trouble to form their own crack cleanup team. When you get down to it, the problem is that they don't have a supply of clean cloths! So the whole house gets dirty. Wouldn't it be a good investment to lay in a supply of washcloths for the baby?

Also, a clean baby is a baby everyone wants to cuddle, whereas a gloppy baby gives babies a bad name!

As for rags, I favor old flannel (sheets, pajamas, shirts) that I've torn into the right sizes for dusting and wiping down. Forget about T-shirts or even the Turkish toweling that Don Aslett recommends; for most applications, I would find that too thick. Flannel is absorbent enough and nicely flexible in your hand. I mainly use rags for dusting, but they certainly come in handy for all sorts of things that you don't want to sacrifice your nice towels to. I have a sizable stack of them, and they are kept *clean*, no matter what they've been used for. If my husband needs one for wiping up hydraulic fluid after testing the plow, I give him a really raggedy rag and then he can throw it away when he's done.

You can wash your rags separately in hot water, although I just throw them in with the towels, also hot water. Don't get into the habit of vaguely designating a rag as "already dirty." You just end up with nasty rags hanging off pipes, draped over otherwise clean sinks, and shoved into corners.

Your life as a housekeeper then becomes trying to assess just how dirty a rag is when you need one, which is too much of a drain on your already overtaxed mind. (And of course, a really greasy toxic rag is a safety hazard, as it could spontaneously combust. In this age of latex paint, people might not talk about not leaving oily, greasy rags around, but maybe they should!)

Keep *all* the rags clean, and that's one less thing to worry about. If it's too dirty to clean, throw it away—this is the beauty of the rag! If it's not that dirty, put it in the hamper (when it's dry)! Knowing you have a stack of clean rags to go to, you'll quickly get into the habit of not letting the dirty ones sit around. You can even iron a few rags and keep them in a special spot for a sort of stop-gap sterile bandage when the need arises.

Now, since your dish towel that's hanging on the hook by the sink is very clean, for wiping *clean* hands, and the dishcloth and sponge are pretty clean, for washing dishes and wiping counters, and the baby cloths, for cleaning baby's faces, are very clean, what do we use to take care of a spill on the floor?

Before I answer that, here's another laundry point: sometimes a towel hanging on the hook *is* clean but doesn't *look* clean, so some people (well, me) are reluctant to use it for their hands (and might grab a paper towel instead, which is wasteful), and some people might use it for something really dirty, like wiping dirty hands on it, or wiping up the floor. When something *looks* dirty, you treat it as if it's dirty. Using a little bleach in the laundry along with hot water, and whatever other methods are necessary, means that your towels will *look* as clean as they *are* and then be used properly.

As I mentioned earlier, before you put anything in the hamper, it should be dry (even though it's dirty!) because it will get moldy in that damp, dark place. Consider attaching a rack to the back of the basement door (if it's handy) or on the wall of the basement stairwell for hanging your kitchen cloths to dry. Don't just throw your used kitchen linens in a heap at the bottom of the stairs or in a corner. Even using a mesh or cotton bag hanging on the back of a door is far preferable.

You can hang clean wet things on your oven door or dishwasher door or what have you, so that they can dry out and be used again, but the dirty wet things should go on a towel rack that you have placed a bit out of the way on your last cabinet side, for just this purpose. I used to have a wooden one, but now I like an old-fashioned metal one just because wood itself can stay damp and get moldy.

Now, back to the spill on the floor. You see that you can grab whatever is drying on the drying rack (preparatory to being put in the hamper) to wipe the floor! The floor isn't that clean, so what you wipe it up with doesn't have to be super clean. A towel that is not clean enough for your hands is fine to mop a spill with. Or get a clean rag for a spill, and once you've used it, hang it on that drying rack so it doesn't get used to wipe a counter.

Things on the drying rack are dirty. Things on a hook or at the sink are clean.

If the towel is hanging on the oven door, we regard it as clean. Sometimes a towel is damp but has been used only to wipe clean plates or something similarly benign; once it has dried on the oven door, it can be rotated back to the hook next to the sink.

I do use paper towels for draining bacon and the occasional wipe-up, especially when the dog barfs (because who wants to use a real towel on that?), but since I know my towels and rags are really clean (are you getting the theme here?) I don't use many paper ones at all.

Sometimes I think that people use a lot of paper towels because they don't understand this gradation, this hierarchy, of cleanliness that I'm discussing here. To them, there's either "spotlessly clean" or "filthy." But just as you should not clean a baby's face with the towel you swiped on the floor, so is it possible to wipe up a spill on the floor with a rag you don't care about much. It's all common sense.

The key here is to make sure the things you clean with are cleaner than the things you clean—by cleaning the things you clean with!

Counting Utensils;
or, Clean as You Go

Apparently, when we were first married, my husband went into work every day and regaled his colleagues with the "utensil count" from the previous night. You see, I had joined the Cooking and Crafts Book-of-the-Month club as a new bride, and new members got four books for a dollar. I got *Joy of Cooking, Mastering the Art of French Cooking*, and another Julia Child cookbook. I can't remember if there was a fourth book or if the two volumes of *Mastering* took up two credits.

We had a small kitchen in an apartment in a neighborhood north of Georgetown University (where I had transferred after getting married) in Washington, D.C. I once shorted out the building. Maybe you can picture the little portable washing machine in this kitchen that did double duty as a counter. This washer and my *exasperating* hastiness were the cause. The washer plugged into an outlet above it on the wall, a little to the side. Of course, we didn't have a dryer—we actually had a little laundry line on a screened-in porch, and a little drying rack. But as to shirts, why, I had the idea of hanging them on hangers and letting them dry like that, only I needed something to hang them from.

For whatever reason, at that moment I couldn't think of any better place to hang the shirts than on the plug, which was large and jutted out of the outlet in that way that large plugs do and was *not quite tightly plugged in*. Immediately, as any sane person would have predicted, the wire hangers slipped off the plug and onto the exposed metal.

I think I knew that could happen, but I thought that (a) they would probably slide down the cord onto the floor, so that wouldn't be so bad and I'd be a little more experienced when I thought up the next place to put them, or (b) there would be not much consequence if they went the other way. However, the electricity shorted out the whole building. There was quite the ominous silence after a hail of sparks.

I had to call the super, and he was not excited, and by "not excited" I mean swearing at me, about going down into the basement (which you accessed from outside), where there was about a foot of water standing at all times. I don't blame him.

Anyway, getting back to the kitchen, I was often hungry, as one is, and I think we can see that when confronted with a question, I tend to choose the complicated, or at least, not practical, answer.

And Julia Child's idea of "mastering"—that one, well, mastered recipes in order to learn technique—appealed to me. I have always been analytical, just not practical. Of course, my husband loved to eat too, and he, always nothing if not affirming of whatever interest I have, amiably insisted on doing the dishes, if I wanted to spend my time whipping up French delicacies for him.

After a full day of classes and extracurriculars, I would come home, take a stab at—not housekeeping (I would not use that word; too exact)—but let's say some sort of chaos containment. There was also a good amount of novel reading and studying. Then I would eventually open the cookbook to see what I would make that night. Then I would go grocery shopping. Need I say, dinner was usually quite late. Quite.

At the time and for many years afterward, my husband got about five hours of sleep by preference (I guess. I have no *idea* when he got up!), so he didn't care how late it was, and hey, I was getting up at 9:00 a.m. anyway, having carefully scheduled no early morning classes. He was quite happy and content to start doing dishes at about 11:00 p.m.; he still says that he was just reveling in the good luck of having found someone to cook for him!

And then there was the hilarity of, as he told me *long* afterward, being able to go into work the next day and simply drop the number: fifty-three. They all knew what *that* meant: I had used fifty-three items in making dinner the night before, all piled up in the sink, all lovingly washed by my sweet husband.

Most things are worth going through *for the story*, we have always firmly believed! Even knowing now that all those people were (rightly) judging me doesn't detract from the contentedness we shared. And guess what: I did learn to cook!

Later, when I realized that it was just unreasonable to expect a man to come home from work and clean up after your gourmet productions late at night, I confronted my inefficiency for myself. And that's when I learned *what* "clean as you go" means, because do you not agree that some people are born knowing what that means and others aren't?

The truth is, people like us think it's dumb and inefficient to put things away and wash up as you are working, because there is working, and there is cleaning. It seems like a waste of energy to mix them up, and it is. We're right!

Well, I will explain it, since it all became clear to me when I had one of those days when, even knowing how I can be, I was astonished at the chaos in the kitchen I had caused. I was working on making dessert bars and also meatballs. For some reason (having to do with things not mixing properly or the bowl I chose not being big enough) I ended up using every appliance, not to mention bowls, I own, just about. And the bars were a little weird. But the meatballs were good.

Since I had put myself in charge of cleanup, something had to change!

Clean-as-you-go can be summarized in these ideas, I think:

Make Time

Think about what time you would normally start your supper prepara-tions—not the fantasy you, the actual you. Start twenty minutes before that.

Before you get going, make sure the counters are cleared off in the manner I have already described above in the kitchen-flow section. Make sure the dishwasher is empty. If you don't have a dishwasher, make sure the clean dishes are put away and the sink is at least empty. Go one step further and fill it (or one side of it if you have a double sink) with hot, soapy water.

Make Use of Stopping Points

As you work, think in terms of stopping points or pauses to clean up rather than clean as you go, which may seem too demanding to you, as I know it did to me. When something needs to simmer or bake or sit, use that time to assess the things you have strewn about. Quickly throw away wrappers and other trash (and try to challenge yourself not to leave such things in an interim spot but instead to put them directly into the trash can when possible; it helps to think through where that receptacle is placed for best efficiency). Can the spices be put away all at once at this point, or do you still need them out? Will the food processor be used again? If not, put its bowl in the dishwasher now.

Soak and Wipe

I ask myself: Can I at least soak these bowls, nesting together and conveniently providing myself with a container of hot soapy water for a quick turnaround of utensils? Can I wipe off a counter while I'm stirring occasionally? Great! That puts me ahead.

Make Things in Hygiene or Taste Order

If you have several things to make, plan them out so that you can use certain utensils in "hygiene or taste order," without washing them in between. Examine your work order. If you are going to use the food processor twice in one session, try to wash it only once. For instance, if I'm making cookies and bread, I can certainly make the bread in the bowl that I've already used for cookies, but not vice versa without washing it out first. If I use the sharp knife first on the tomatoes and then on the chicken, no washing in between is necessary, but the reverse order requires careful washing!

And then clean up in between those several recipes as much as possible. It's hard to have the mess of three courses at the end, but not a big deal to clean up after any one.

Tidy before the Meal

Use the twenty minutes you've spotted yourself at the end of the meal prep to whisk everything into the tub of soapy water or the dishwasher; put ingredients away and wipe off the counters. Your dining self will thank your cooking self, and supper's aftermath will seem a lot less overwhelming. Try to sit down to dinner with the food prep cleaned up. It's amazing the difference to your attitude it can make, to have even a few minutes in between the mess and the eating!

Kitchen Drawer Organization

I have three thoughts that motivate the organization in my kitchen—two are rather self-evident and the third is easy enough: like things belong together, things that are used together belong near each other, and the Pareto principle.

One of the most helpful thoughts ever to dawn upon the person struggling to make sense of things in general is the Pareto principle, originally conceived to explain income distribution among the population, but applicable to almost anything we are trying to observe—in this case, efficiency in the kitchen. I owe my discovery of Pareto's insight to Deniece Schofield, author of *Confessions of an Organized Homemaker*.

This useful analytical tool asserts that things, whether time or steps or actions or features or people, can be divided into 20 and 80 percent, and the 20 percent will account for the usefulness, output, or efficacy of the 80 percent. Twenty percent of the people in an office account for 80 percent of the work accomplished and 80 percent of the people account for 20 percent of the work; 20 percent of your clothing bears the burden of 80 percent of wear, while 80 percent languishes in the closet.

Note two things: First, the principle doesn't say that this means that the 80 percent is useless or can be eliminated. Second, these numbers are just for purposes of making the point about how things work, typically speaking; the actual numbers might vary.

Even so, it's an incredibly helpful idea to remind oneself of when one is falling into the trap of thinking things distribute themselves equally.

For our purposes here, let's consider the kitchen: 20 percent of the things you use will account for 80 percent of the effective things you do. Identify those things, put them where you can reach them immediately, without moving the 80 percent out of the way first, and you will be much more effective in your work.

Most kitchens are not designed to be very efficient, which is fine if you are young and have nothing better to do than run around in there without a plan. But once you hit the part of your life when you are not only having to come up with multiple meals a day for a crowd but are pregnant or nursing while you do it, you need to save your steps.

Obviously, there are many areas to organize in the kitchen, and you almost certainly have more scope than I, who have only a few drawers to work with. But I thought I'd go through the organization of those few (always keeping thrift and probable tiredness or exhaustion in mind) in hopes of leaving you with a basic structure of how to think about setting things up according to *how you work* and *what goes on in your kitchen*.

In one drawer, keep foils, wraps, and plastic bags together; you want a small open container for rubber bands, twist ties, and a few clothespins and binder clips for closing bags of chips and the like. If you have a designated place in a drawer (a plastic container that has lost its lid is perfect) to pop any rubber band you find, including the ones that come on veggies and other goodies, you may never buy another rubber band. (Please don't store your rubber bands on doorknobs or the faucet. It's not attractive either way, and it's too damp and moldy in the latter case.)

I keep a Sharpie in that drawer for marking zip storage bags and jars lest they be lost forever in the freezer with nary an indication of their contents. A marker also helps with keeping people's sandwiches sorted out.

Consider another drawer near your food preparation area (mine is the one right next to the sink) for extra utensils, separate from your normal eating utensils, for cooking, bread buttering, tasting of sauces, and general activities in the kitchen; for all this you need a separate stash, separate even from the container near the stove with your spatulas, rubber and metal, and wooden spoons and whisks for stirring.

One day early on in my organizing life, I was decluttering the kitchen; all my tableware was in one place—matched set and random ones together—and I thought about tossing the unmatched ones. Then I realized how very useful they are if you simply give them their own category closer to where you cook. Using unmatched ones for meal prep saves your place settings for the table (and thus saves you from having to wash some up quickly as people sit down to eat).

I have two drawers that relate to food prep. One drawer includes those miscellaneous spoons, forks, and knives, along with citrus reamers, thermometers, turkey baster, corkscrew—anything that I might reach for as I'm preparing food—and the drawer has dividers to impose a little order. How did I decide what to put in that drawer? Either by *wishing* that I had such a thing in easy reach or by not knowing where else to put something (e.g., medicine cups and spoons, as one does dole out the random dose standing there by the sink).

In the second drawer, in a separate compartment goes *anything* "knifey," including butter knives, spreaders, can opener, and so forth. When I'm making a peanut-butter sandwich, my spreaders are right there by the cutting board that sits on the counter above that drawer and in front of the toaster.

Sharp knives could be kept in a block on the counter (if you have enough counter space—I do not) or on a magnetic holder on the wall (same thing—I don't have a place for that!). I like keeping mine in a wooden insert (so they stay sharp and safe, not jumbled together, which is terrible in so many ways) in that "knifey" drawer.

Near the table but not too far from the dishwasher, you want your silverware and serving utensils. Those things don't need to be near the food preparation areas, which is freeing.

Every kitchen has a junk drawer. Rather than fight the "catch-all" aspect, organize it, and put it on the periphery of the food prep area. I had a real mental block about accepting this drawer, simply because the random nature of the contents—wire, string, extra felt chair pads, hair elastics, comb—made it impossible for me to know whether to ban it completely or to commit to drawer dividers. But how would I function if I always had to go to a different room for the things in that drawer; on the other hand, how to commit to dividers?

Then I hit on the idea of using plastic containers that had lost their lids (or honestly, it's worth even using cheap ones and sacrificing their lids) to customize this drawer for my own needs with a minimum of expenditure. You can even stack clear shallow containers on top of each other, sliding them as needed. In my drawer, I keep my own stash of tools: my hammer, screwdriver with interchangeable bits, needle-nose pliers, and tape measure; picture hangers and attractive nails (nice brass ones!) for hanging the odd picture.

Cleaning the Bathroom

The bathroom needs to be clean. And it needs to *look* clean and *smell* clean. Here are a few little thoughts having to do with cleaning bathrooms *while* nursing babies, homeschooling, being eight months pregnant and not bendable, and in short, just having lots of kids. It's the reality factor that's missing from the books (less in *Confessions of an Organized Housewife*, as the author raised five children; more in *Home Comforts*, the author of which had one child, and I truly believe you can do anything with one child, including have a clean house all the time!).

Cleanable Substances

First, do everything in your power to get a bathroom made of cleanable substances. When comparing toilets, for example, steer clear of the ones with many nooks and crannies and inaccessible places. Once, when we were remodeling a bathroom, I asked the plumber to move my toilet six inches further away from the side wall, because there was simply no way *to see* to clean in that corner as it was.

Why, oh why, did anyone ever invent the cursed shower door? What's so wrong with a bathtub and shower combo? At least if a shower curtain gets gross, you can throw it out and get a new one. And don't get me started on hot-tub-style tubs. You can't bathe a baby in one for the same reason it's very difficult to clean: too deep. No one can afford to fill one. And no one has time for one. Please just get me an old-fashioned bathtub. Please.

An easy fix, not at all expensive, is to replace a normal shower head with one that has a flexible hose and handheld head (or two heads, one fixed and one on the coiled hose) so that you can take it down to rinse walls and corners efficiently—not to mention soapy kids or one's own feet!

Scrape out old caulking with a putty knife and replace it with silicone caulking, very thinly applied so that it fills the gap but doesn't create a ridge on the tile. Use your finger—you can wipe it off on paper towel later. This task is much easier than it looks if you realize that it all hinges on first getting out every bit of old caulk and then using your finger, firmly pressing that bead where it goes, to finish the new.

Use washable paint (mildew-resistant on the ceiling) and avoid wallpaper. Wallpaper plus steam equals drooping, peeling wallpaper.

Living in old houses, we've always had issues with other people's bad construction choices. I'm dreaming of the day when everything will be tightly sealed, mildew-free, and wipeable! Obviously it's easier to clean a good bathroom than a bad one, so get a good one if you can.

Cleaning What You've Got

Moving on to cleaning what you've got. Personally—and maybe I'm revealing even more of my inadequacy than I intended to—I don't see the need for a bucket unless you are mopping the floor. The bucket idea seems to reach back into the mists of time when the bathroom didn't have running water in it. But lo! it does now. Don Aslett says (in one of his helpful books) to use the water in the sink or tub and then clean those last. I concur.

And there are two levels of bathroom cleaning, just like the other rooms: the Blitz and the Moderate Clean (deep clean about once a month, scrubbing every surface). Here's where having lots of kids works in your favor.

The key to your life with them, obviously, is multitasking. No one multitasks like mother. So, you know how all those kids are always needing a bath? And even when they aren't particularly dirty, it's just a lifesaver to get them in there splashing away?

Well, that time is your chance to get the bathroom into shape with a daily Blitz. You have to be with them because they need supervision so that they don't drown or grab razors and medicine and cleanser and what have you. Yet, most of the time when you *are* in there, they are playing happily and you are doing nothing! So clean the bathroom!

Listen. Don't let them drown on account of me. Use your common sense. You know the difference between a baby who truly has to be watched every second and one who is okay in there because there are so many others in that tub that they are all like sardines, propping each other up, don't you? So you, also on the spot, can scrub down the toilet and sink. If anyone expires, don't blame *moi*.

But this is what I did, and my bathroom was cleaner then than it is now that my kids are grown: I used that playing time (and you really need only five minutes) to get the toilet scrubbed and wiped down. Then, since I've used the sink for my water supply, I clean that, using a different sponge (cut off a corner of the toilet sponge so you'll know which one it is), and rinse and dry it off. Wipe off the mirror. Using the towel you are about to change, give the mirror a final shine, dry the sink, and dry the toilet. Replace the hand towel with a clean one (please do this at least once a day with many kids around).

Maybe you'll try, and your child won't be thrilled that you're not right there to attend to him. No fear! Keep working on it. Some fun things to have in the bath are plastic measuring cups, an old colander, anything that pours, a bulb baster, toy boats, high-quality plastic animals, and fun washcloths that can double as hand puppets. Children also enjoy a "cleaning cloth" and a small spray bottle so that they can help clean along with Mama. Finally, get a bin with holes in the bottom or a small dishrack to put all those toys in; hang it up over the shower rod to drain when bath time is done. (Don't hang things on the shower head, which will stress at the point where it joins the main pipe behind the shower wall; eventually it breaks back there, and that is no fun.)

When the kids are drying off and in various stages of getting dressed, running around naked, screaming, and laughing, wash out the tub, gather up your dirty towels along with the children's various items, and back yourself out of your blitzed bathroom.

It follows as the night the day that your supplies need to be right there under the sink or in a handy cabinet. No running down the hall to a distant closet for Windex. Stock up with the following:

- Two sponges of distinct styling (that have been demoted from kitchen use): one for the toilet, the other for everything else (cut off a corner of the toilet one so you'll know which one it is)
- Comet (it's cheap and is fine on porcelain as long as you don't go nuts scrubbing)
- Scrubbing Bubbles–type spray for the accursed shower
- Foaming mildew spray for the accursed shower
- Toilet brush
- Glass cleaner (store brand is fine)
- Paper towels or rags for the mirror (should your dirty hand towel be just too dirty)
- Squeegee, if you are saddled with an accursed shower door (never mind sprays—you need to wipe that water off with a rubber tool)
- Rubber gloves that don't have holes in them—treat yourself to a new pair
- A basin to contain these supplies neatly under the sink
- A pitcher for rinsing dogs, children, and tubs
- Clean towels and washcloths

Once or twice a week, shake out and wash the rugs, dust the light fixtures, wipe the moldings, vacuum and mop the floor, change the bath towels, and you're good to go.

How do you manage to replace bath towels only once a week? *How, Auntie Leila?*

Color-code the towels. A towel that has dried a clean child will be reusable for many days *if it dries out completely between uses* (this is why you need hooks for each child to hang his towel on). To keep track of which towel belongs to which child, *give each his own color towel*—unless you have it together enough to have your towels monogrammed! Do not rely on the placement of the towels (i.e., hooks or racks). All it takes is for two children to toss their towels on the floor, and you will be sunk.

You know the hygiene protocol that you go through with your children, teaching them to wipe themselves and wash their hands? Let me advise you to revisit that training every year or two, asking them to visualize what will happen to their towels if they do not use warm water and soap to wash their hands.

As you leave, ask yourself if your bathroom *looks and smells* clean. Imagine that you are taking a guest around your house. (This happens often, I find. Sometimes they are looking for their child; sometimes they want a tour.) What would you change right now if a non-family member were there? Do it!

Don't boom and bust in your bathroom; you can keep it reasonably clean by multitasking at bath time.

How to Keep a Closet
Neat and Tidy

I wrote about this topic on the blog after we painted and reorganized a fantastically deep and useful closet in my house that stores all the toys and games of a lifetime (not to mention our record and DVD collection). A reader asked how we would keep it in its newfound organized state.

The problem was never with the stuff itself. When we started pulling it apart to paint, it was remarkably not in a jumble, despite years of neglect on my part. (I mean, don't get me wrong: it was scary. But at the same time, there were few puzzles with missing pieces, because I have learned the hard lesson that such a thing is worse than useless; I kept only the most-loved games; I had early on put toys with many pieces in their own stackable bins, and so on.)

No, the problem was with the closet itself, and I think that if we talk about it a little, you will see how it is that anyone can keep the toy area *reasonably* neat and tidy, with normal fluctuations brought on by life, of course.

Before we painted, I, the household manager, did not ever, *ever* want to go in there. It was too dismal, uncleanable, and neglected. I mean, sometimes I did go in and tidy up, but I hated it. The children occasionally did some organizing or throwing away of superannuated or defunct items.

The proper way to clean something, as I have told you when we went on our Reasonably Clean House journey together, is to pull everything out, clean the space, sort and clean the things, and put back what truly belongs there. This is true for everything. Even things that clean other things—such as dishwashers and washing machines—occasionally have to be pulled out, scoured out, and put back the way you want them! So, how much more a toy closet!

But that assumes that the space *can* be cleaned and that you want to try. Thus, unlike me in this instance, make sure you get the closets repaired and painted before you put anything in them, even if it means having its contents out for a while.

People might be frustrated with where they keep their games and toys and skeptical that my closet will remain fabulous, and I will address their assumptions one by one. Not yours, dear reader, because no doubt you are actually a good housekeeper yourself, but *others'* assumptions.

Wrong assumptions:

1. *The space doesn't matter—it's only for storing things.* No. The space matters. Whether it's a part of the room or an actual closet or under the beds, it needs to be something that you can clean when it's empty. The surfaces have to be free of gaping holes or torn carpet or what have you. They have to be finished in a way that they look clean when they are wiped down. This is something to work on. Having mostly lived in old houses, I know the issues. Just be prepared to consider that it's not your *cleaning* that's at fault; it's the space itself! I learned this when I was in my neighbors' basement and saw how neat and tidy all the little spaces were. Their basement was exactly the same as mine; we shared a duplex. But they had made theirs like a ship's hold. Every inch of space was painted and tidy and held only what it was intended to hold. Ever since then, this has been my (rarely realized) dream.

2. *Shelves don't matter.* They do matter. You can't pile things on the floor and then continue piling. Maybe one thing that I did appreciate a lot about this

closet was the shelves—to the point that I thought the space would work without my immediate attention (see number 1), especially in light of all the other projects in the house that had priority. Shelves make a huge difference in how you can organize stuff. Metal brackets and wooden boards don't cost much in the grand scheme of things. Make sure you find the studs when you are installing the brackets.

3. *If everyone puts things back into the proper place, I will never have to clean.* Well, yes, they need to put things back—we're all in this together, after all!— but no, it's still the manager's responsibility in the end (not that you can't delegate most of that responsibility—but not all).

Are things arranged so that there is a good chance that items would get back in their spots? For instance, the bins on the floor, tucked under the lowest shelf, hold various toys with many—a million—little moving, snapping, or fitting parts. Each bin is large enough to hold its contents, the lids fit, and the bins stack. These are the toys that are most likely to be pulled out, and it's not hard to get the bins back. Things with fiddly (but not a million) pieces are stored higher—in ascending order of likelihood that they (a) would make a terrible mess if spilled and (b) are difficult to put away.

Don't put the thousand-piece puzzles within reach of even a six-year-old. Don't put the dominoes or playing cards within reach of toddlers. Some sort of thought process (or maybe fail-safe button or key arrangement like those on nuclear launching systems) must occur before these many-pieced games get taken down. And maybe a stool- and permission-getting process as well.

So the solution rests partly on how clever you are at arranging in the first place. Low-down things shouldn't be stacked more than two items high. They should be spaced out on the self. If this is a problem, do some trimming of your inventory, because it just won't work to expect young children to cope with piles and stacks of toys. Try rotating toys and storing some in bins under beds. Children certainly don't need all their things all the time.

In considering which items should go on higher shelves, you should consider how annoyed you would be if a box or a container of something were spilled out. I can cope with two containers of plastic army guys being spilled out. But I have an anxiety attack if the bingo game is spilled out without forethought, and that's mainly because if one number is lost, the whole thing is ruined. So the bingo game goes on the top shelf.

The exception to my two-item stack rule is board games that go on the highest shelf and are light enough to move around by a responsible person.

Toy-closet tidiness is also a question of inspection and training. Even a three-year-old will put (simple) things back if you spend some time asking him to, helping him, and making sure he does. It takes a while, but it pays off in the end. Some children will consider putting things back part of the process of playing with it, and *simply cannot understand a child who doesn't do that.* Try to get these children if you can!

But—sometimes you need to rush out of the house, and sometimes the three-year-old has a meltdown, and sometimes ten three-year-olds are over to play, and sometimes everyone was just having a lot of fun and a lot of things got taken out, rules or no rules. So just limit how much they can reach in the worst-case scenario.

Every day there has to be a time (the Blitz) when playthings are sorted through and someone makes sure that, in fact, things got put away properly.

4. *So if they don't put things back where they found them, it's their fault, not mine, if the closet is messy.* Well, no. Not that it would even help to think this!

Occasionally this area needs real attention, and the only person with the big picture is you. You have to notice that a toy placed in front of all the others makes things messy and isn't even enjoyed. You have to get bigger bins or multiple bins for a growing collection of train tracks. You have to throw away broken games and puzzles with missing pieces. So, every once in a while (probably during your once-a-week cleaning of the room—the Moderate Clean, or at least once a month), you need to straighten things up. Rearrange, dust, and tidy. A large child (somewhere over the age of reason) could be given this job with you just coming in to inspect. Certain children really get offended if things aren't kept neat—identify and promote.

5. *Then that should do it—just the Moderate Clean?* Sadly, no. The Deep Clean is still a necessity. I always feel that the thing that needs to be deep cleaned

will let you know it. You just won't be able to take the disorder anymore. And really, only you can do it. Pull every single thing out, vacuum from top to bottom, wash down if necessary, air out, and then put things back.

Be critical. Only what belongs there gets to go there.

The reason things were a jumble in my toy closet was that I couldn't face the closet itself. But now it's a joy even to open the door! So who wouldn't want to make sure that only puzzles are on the puzzle shelf, and only board games on the board game shelf!

By the way, children are perfectly happy being given the job of making sure that only Legos are in the Lego bin and Playmobil in the Playmobil bin. To them, that's as good as playing.

Surfing Your Day, or, You Can Do a Lot in an Hour

Sometimes when life feels a little overwhelming to me, and I don't believe that I can tackle all the jobs that are waiting for me—or, truthfully, I feel as if the jobs would take days or weeks to accomplish, so why bother even starting?—I try to remember that I can do a lot in an hour.

We can waste an hour very easily, so we tend to forget how much can be accomplished in that time. An hour is valuable to the busy householder, but the only way to prove it to yourself is to challenge yourself to see how much you can do with it.

You know that thing we do, most of us—clicking around the Internet? You keep clicking, and there are more and more interesting, fun, distracting, or maddening things to read, listen to, and watch, and soon an hour is gone. I'm not going to tell you not to do that, because that's what the Internet is for, I suppose.

But one day, something occurred to me about this quest for a reasonably clean house. As I was working outside, I kept seeing more and more that I wanted to do; I kept going from weeding one area to raking another. And if I went inside, I kept seeing so many things that needed my attention in there, from sweeping the kitchen to folding laundry.

Most of the tasks were pretty small—just like posts online that promise you "Six Things to Know about Your Car!" that can be read in under a minute. As I moved around the garden, there were "Just Six Weeds Sticking Out of This Low Planting!" Or just as your eye is caught by "The Most Amazing Journalist Interviews the World's Greatest Philosopher," I was tempted by real "clickbait": "Move This Pile of Mulch and Accomplish Two Tasks at Once!" These little jobs didn't take me long but kept me running around: "If I Put This Chair Where It Belongs, I Will Experience Satisfaction with This Room."

To see how quickly things can get done, try timing how long it takes you to tidy up the bathroom or even mop a floor. I think you will be surprised that the time most things take is much less than the time and energy we waste in dreading doing them and allowing ourselves to be distracted by stupid things instead.

You can't flit all day among the little tasks that could use attention, just as you can't surf the Internet all day (you can, but you would hate yourself). But for an hour or so, it's a fine way to get things done.

You can do a lot in an hour. And what do you know: it keeps you off the computer!

The Day I Rolled Up
My Kitchen Towels

O ne day my husband mentioned that a camera crew would be arriving to interview him for some news show. Usually they go into his study, and that works fine; it's book-lined and oak-desked and generally has the air of respectability, enough for head shots with blurry backgrounds, anyway. But this particular day, he felt that his office was not up to snuff. And believe me when I tell you, that means it was not up to snuff. (I remediated later.)

So naturally, realizing that a news reporter and a man with a technologically advanced apparatus of digital moving photography would likely be in the *living room*, I was suddenly seized with the need to apply what I knew of Marie Kondo's principles (as found in her book *The Life-Changing Magic of Tidying Up*, which at the time I had not read but had read articles about) to our dressers in the bedroom and to the kitchen island, going through all our linens according to her organization guidelines.

Yes. Yes, I did. Two areas of my home that were definitely not going to be featured or broadcast anywhere at all became the intense focus of my laser concentration.

Suddenly, all that really mattered to me, impending interview or not, was this video I had seen somewhere detailing Marie Kondo's recommendations for rolling items of clothing that are stored in drawers, rather than laying them flat and stacking them.

Skipping lightly over what transpired in my dresser drawers, I will reveal that I had, all piled up in the kitchen island, the following:

- nice kitchen towels
- okay kitchen towels but really excellent for covering rising bread, as they are the right size and tightly woven, which prevents their sticking to the dough (I suddenly realized—the camera crew was about an hour away—that I wanted these particular towels not to be in the towel stack, but elsewhere, because they really just aren't that great for drying your hands—certainly not as good as the others—but I'm not the only person grabbing a towel here.)
- not as nice kitchen towels and dishcloths, very clean of course (I also have a supply in the pantry; they get demoted and are for sloppy messes.)
- dishcloths
- real rags (These are not to be confused with sloppy towels or old dishcloths, because if you use those as rags, they will inevitably get cycled back into the good towels or dishcloth piles, and then a guest will suddenly be washing dishes and drying hands with something embarrassing. As I have told you before, I use old flannel PJs, shirts, and sheets torn up into rag-size pieces, which would never be confused with a kitchen towel by even the most distracted guest.)
- cloth napkins, which we use every day, so I have a good supply

Usually all of these are folded and stacked. The stacks, up until this moment, had been separate and approximately sorted. But now I found it necessary to roll them all up, even the rags. Why not? We are going full-crazy-Japanese-tidiness-guru, and the crew is still forty-five minutes away. I also rolled up my secret dough towels, which I put on the other side of the island, away from the carefully rolled good kitchen towels, so that only I will grab them, sparing my family from having to memorize my towel preferences.

After much soul-searching and conscience-questioning, with the camera crew a scant ten minutes away by my fevered calculations, I failed to roll up the cloth napkins. I like them stacked.

Here are my thoughts on Marie Kondo's method: it's one thing to take everything out of its place and roll it up and put away what you want to keep. It's another to do the laundry this way; that is, to take a basket of clothes, sort and roll, and then transfer to drawers.

Rolled things roll. They roll while you are rolling them (I normally do this on the sofa or on my bed), while you are stacking and sorting them in the basket, and while you are putting them away. Thus, the work motions are greatly, *greatly* increased because there is a lot of retrieving and rerolling, or am I just a klutz? Yes, even though I've been told it's not so much a roll as a sort of triangular wrapping, I find that the resulting item and subsequent pile is not stable.

I am having trouble thinking that children will not get frustrated with this method, although I could see eight- to twelve-year-old girls getting obsessed as well. Personally, when I was rolling all those things (which included all the things in the dressers as well), I was getting frustrated. Things kept unrolling.

See what you think, because in the drawers and on the shelves, this is very nice.

I did manage, thanks to some *intense* blitzing, to make the living room quite presentable.

And the interview took place outside, on the deck.

Building the Creative Environment—and the Culture—with Furniture

I am not a decorator, but like you, I certainly am in charge of making my house pretty. I haven't always succeeded, but I have been in charge. This aspect of my life as a mother makes me think of how spiritual things are affected by the material things that might or might not be taken care of.

This entire section has been devoted to keeping what you have clean, neat, and tidy in a reasonable way. Let's also look at other aspects of making your home pretty and inviting. These are practical ideas for implementing the vague wish of gathering with your family and have comfortable, happy family time.

Cleaning is fine, but you also need to acquire (probably buy, but do consult the thrifting section below for ideas) and arrange furniture to make this happen. I avoided the need for furniture when I first set up housekeeping; I see that some people also have this difficulty of committing to furnishings.

This discussion is not a worldly one or focused on things that don't really count; on the contrary, it's essential to building the culture—the culture of your family and thus of your hospitality; by extension, the culture. The whole world might be affected for better or for worse by whether people can have a nice chat in your home!

Lighting

You need lots of lighting, but not one glaring fixture up above. Overhead lights are fine (not that we have many in my old house), but lamps are a necessity. You need one for every area where someone will sit and read or knit and chat companionably. Every corner. The minimum in a living area is three. In ours, we have three table lamps and two wall sconces.

Most children won't settle down to read if there aren't lamps. A lamp provides not only light but also that pool of cozy warmth that you have to have for the *desire* to sit and read in the evening.

And please, consider it money well spent to have incandescent lights in your family-area lamps. Those compact fluorescents are never going to give you the ambiance you are looking for (and they are made with mercury, which is poison). People will always feel cold, dreary, and slightly alienated. It's just not worth the "savings" to use them. Even LEDs, which can approximate the *color* of incandescents, are cold, and the light they emit is actually jagged—emitted in quantum, discrete sharp waves—and is potentially harmful to eyesight. This is true on the level of physics—luminescence is a low-temperature result of the excitation of atoms; incandescence produces warmth as well as light, which is *relatively* inefficient, yet necessary. I like to point out that it would be more efficient to cook everything in the microwave, but I doubt we are going to do it, because efficiency isn't the only criterion.

To anyone arguing about these hard facts, I quote St. Bernard: "It is vain merely to give light, and it is but little to burn; but to burn and give light together is perfection."[11] He is speaking of St. John the Baptist ("he was a burning and a shining light" [John 5:35, KJV]), but I think we can apply what he says here as well.

---

[11] See Pius XII, encyclical on St. Bernard of Clairvaux *Doctor Mellifluus* (May 24, 1953), no. 5.

If you want your home to feel warm in the cozy, welcoming sense, keep the cool forms of light out of the living areas (they work well in closets and out in the garage or in the basement storage area). Obviously, the kind of light we live in has a tremendous effect on our well being.

Furniture

The furniture in your living area needs to be sturdy and welcoming. Children will gravitate to their rooms (and thus not be "gathered" with you of a cozy evening) if the only place for them to relax is their bed.

The furniture also needs to be *close together*. You can't have three people sitting in a line on a sofa, attempting to hold a conversation with someone on a chair across the room. In my family, we enjoy watching games and movies together in comfort, not craned over a computer or squinting at a little set. We don't go out to movies very often. Viewing them together in our home is part of our entertainment. Thus, I am not averse to a large screen and comfortable seating where we do that. Having the seating in a conversation circle rather than all facing the screen gives the right impression about our priorities.

Throw pillows express personality and offer comfort; quilts and afghans are pretty and help keep us warm in cold weather. To keep things simple, I like the big furniture to be neutral so that the other textiles can express design style and be changed without too much expense. But the upholstery can't be too light, obviously, or it will show the dirt, and it can't be too dark, or every dog hair and bit of lint will show up. I know that some say that white slipcovers are great, because you can wash and even bleach them. I can't help but wonder if the ones recommending this option have children who are home all the time! If you are looking to redo well made furniture, the truth is that slipcovers (custom-made) can be pricier than reupholstering!

Once when I was reupholstering my sturdy sofas, I found some dark chocolate velvet that I loved and seriously considered, but I realized that it was just too dangerously dark for our den lifestyle. A fabric that has worked for me (and took a long time to find) is a taupe (medium grayed brown) linen-like fabric that can withstand plenty of "rubs" (the industry standard to express longevity, so you don't get pilling or shininess). Full-grain leather would be a practical choice if the exchequer could take the hit, and I was thrilled to find a beautiful leather armchair secondhand, going for a song. I *almost* couldn't fit it into my car, but I made it happen! It's the sort of chair that just gets better with age, and the newer ones I've seen don't have anything like the classic styling of mine.

Leather might seem to be too cold in winter, but lovely knit afghans and quilted throws solve that issue. (Consider that fabric such as crushed velvet can seem too sticky and even dirty in summer; nothing is perfect.)

If your rooms seem small or you are working with a lot of windows and doorways, or both, focus on the floor: Several big, comfy floor pillows with washable covers can expand your seating. Those could all be stacked in a corner when not in use to keep the pathways clear and then pulled out whenever needed. These days, stores have really elegant floor pillows for animals. Why not stock up on those? They always have washable covers and are made for hard use; I doubt anyone would be able to tell they are not for people. Children seem to prefer the floor to couches anyway, and there is a lot of play potential with floor pillows. Upholstered ottomans can be pushed around when needed, and sturdy wooden stools can be stowed under the piano or a desk, to be pulled out when needed.

Position some chairs or sofas with your wide doorways behind them—liberate yourself from the idea that every piece of furniture needs a wall behind it. If you place a couple of chairs with a table with a lamp between them, so the chairs are slightly turned toward each other, it creates a "conversation area." One of the chairs venturing out in the path just defines the space. Or put a couple of extra chairs on either side of a large doorway. Experiment with putting furniture diagonally in corners or putting a sofa in the middle of the room, facing another sofa or a pair of chairs; this works especially well if they can be perpendicular to a fireplace. Or put the pair of chairs in the middle of the room facing the sofa. Try making these "conversation areas" appear; avoid having all the furniture just shoved up against the walls.

When your home is arranged pleasingly for all the activities that go on in it, and especially for conversation, reading, play, and comfort, it becomes easier to care for. The work that goes into making it clean and tidy has a tangible goal that makes all the difference: your life together as a family.

PART 5

Handling Money

In this section I will give you solid tips on how to stay out of debt and to get out if you are in. I've been in debt, and I've gotten out. But before we get into the details, I have to tell you that being in debt is not the worst thing that can happen to you. So bear with me here. I wrote the following chapter ten years ago. Since then, our financial situation has improved, and I'll be honest, having my kids grow up and move away has helped—turns out that people are right when they say that having a ton of kids is costly! I need not say, however, that it's worth it.

The point is simply this: you live your life, and you do your best. In my opinion, trading a life with the kids God sends you for financial security (not that you can guarantee that, since bad things happen to even the most careful people) is a terrible idea that I could never endorse. In this section, I will try to relieve guilt about being in debt and offer a few practical ways to be more financially secure.

Five Things That Are Worse Than Being in Debt

When I got married, I had never heard of saving money, being frugal (although I did know about finding old furniture and fixing it up), or in any way living within one's means. Or, if I had, I certainly wasn't paying attention. And I married someone who basically couldn't say no to his little spoiled brat of a wife, and anyway, I'm not all that sure he knew anything either.

So it's not surprising that we got into debt. For many years, we struggled. I won't say it's over. Along the way, I learned some lessons the tough way; for instance, being so deep in debt that the issue is no longer about a budget, it's about not having any money at all to buy anything. Sometimes it wasn't too bad, but sometimes it was bad, such as eighteen months of no steady job, starting the day after our sixth baby was born.

So yes, I've regretted every dumb meal out (not the fun ones, though), every shopping spree, every stupid purchase we've ever made. I've wept over some big choices too, even though at the time they might have seemed like good ideas.

I've read a lot of books, articles, and blog posts about getting out of debt, and they have been very helpful. Sometimes, though, they veer into a strange land, theologically. They make it sound something like this: you'll never be happy if you are in debt; you aren't doing God's will if you are in debt; even—and not in so many words, mind you—your salvation can be gauged by whether you are solvent.

But I have to say there are worse things than being in debt. Here are a few (addressed to you, wife and mother):

1. *Worse than being in debt is losing your peace.* Now, some might say that you lose your peace *because* you are in debt, and the good Lord knows I have been there. But today, this very moment, the situation I'm in is God's will for me when I'm doing my best and am sorry for my bad choices, as the mommies at the playground say. Every moment is God's will for each one of us.

Everyone experiences adversity. It's called being human. For some people, that adversity takes the form of being in debt—even if the debt is your fault. The main thing is to keep your peace, to know that God is taking care of each of us, and to remember to trust Him to provide—at least to provide a way out, in His good time.

Do you use being in debt as an excuse not to trust God? That would be worse even than being in debt!

2. *Worse than being in debt is not realizing how much good comes out of a real struggle.* We all know that St. Paul said, "My strength is made perfect in weakness" (2 Cor. 12:9, KJV), but we don't like to think that it will work if the weakness—or, for that matter, whatever the present challenge is—is of our own making. If God sees fit to try us by the adversity of being in debt, we can't wriggle out of meeting the test by thinking that it's our own fault we're in the fight at all. Whatever the fight is, external, internal, our own making, a bolt from heaven—we should see all the good things that come from it. Good things can come from mistakes that we repent of.

What real benefits do we obtain from not having enough money? I bet if we really thought about it, we would see many benefits, including, possibly, learning patience with ourselves for being idiots.

3. *Worse than being in debt is not having a baby because you think you don't have enough money.* See number 1, and trust in God.

There might be reasons for not getting pregnant—I used to think there are more than I now do. But not having money is not one of them. If you are reading this, you have enough money.

There is only a limited amount of time in which you can have a child, no matter what you might think now that you are in the midst of financial difficulty. Thirty years from now, you won't be thinking about the bills you had to pay.

Do you know what the Bible calls riches? Children.

In thirty years, you will be telling yourself that you should have been willing to live in a tent and eat roots and berries to have had more children. Using debt as an excuse to postpone having a baby would be what the world calls prudent and what I would say is a lack of confidence.

I know, this makes me very bossy. But what I want to convey is that you can get money later, but maybe not children.

4. *Worse than being in debt is getting a job to make ends meet.* I'm speaking to the wife here. Let's be real. Let's take all the exceptions as read:

If you can do a few heart surgeries and rescue your family from bankruptcy, do it.

If your husband is bedridden or one semester away from a doctorate in moneymaking, I get it.

If you are so used to working while keeping house (and your mother and maiden aunt live with you, contributing their own retirement funds to your household) that no one really notices when you are not there, go for it.

But the rest of us are needed at home with our heads in our game.

Don't fool yourself into thinking that you can contribute more by leaving for work, or, if you have more than one napping baby, even working at home. The chaos, confusion, stress, childcare, carpools, and taxes are not worth it. No, literally, the actual cost outweighs the benefits.

All that happens is that you are so frustrated with home that the center is lost, sometimes forever. In other words, you start frustrated about money and end up feeling like no one values family life as you once envisioned it because you can't find your way to pulling it together.

It can seem like medium-age children can be fine with this state of chaos, and for a while they will be. But older children need very much to have order at home. By the time the need is felt, it can be too late. The habit of homemaking is gone, and it's often too hard to recover while coping with the demands of older children. Their locus then becomes their peer group, with all that that entails.

Don't make the mistake of putting *getting out of debt* in a higher category than *keeping the home*. Don't make the mistake of having a vague idea that things will run themselves without you; that's rating yourself too low, my friend.

5. *Worse than being in debt is having your husband think he's not a good provider.* Sometimes he's the one saying you should get a job. I'm telling you that, in the end, he will feel like he's not doing a good job protecting his family, which is the very worst thing a man can feel—*much* worse than being in debt—and leading to worse problems than money.

Tell him that you will do your part to be frugal and work with the money you have (and there is so much you can do!), and that you know he will figure out a way. Tell him you know he is working as hard as he can, that you admire him for it, and that you will back him up, no matter what. Tell him you don't mind being in debt for longer if it seems there is no alternative.

It's not the worst thing in the world to be in debt.

ASK AUNTIE LEILA

Ten Reasons Not to Have Separate Finances; or, Marriage Is about Wholehearted Trust

---

Dear Auntie Leila,

I'm getting married soon, and I will be bringing to the marriage my debt and salary, both of which are moderately large. We're thinking of keeping our finances separate until I at least pay off my debt (at least, my mom says I should do this), but the priest has told us it's not a good idea. But it just makes me so nervous not to have mine separate! I have my own credit cards too. What do you think?

Love your blog and thank you!

Maddie

Dear Maddie,

I know. It seems so old-fashioned or just not an issue whether your finances are separate or not. What's the big deal, right? You've been on your own, and so has he. It seems normal to continue this way.

Well, can I tell you something different? About trust? About the "second decade" of your marriage, that you can't see, but I can; when things change?

People talk about later on in your marriage as "losing the romance" or warn that marriage isn't a bed of roses. Sometimes they blame the children, and for that reason, many couples are afraid to have children! But that isn't quite it.

It's more this: you don't just come to a marriage fully formed and then proceed to experience things in a static way. No. You are in the process of changing, he is in the process of changing, and you also change each other. It's calculus, not addition.

It has to do with things interacting in the dimension of time—the way your car doesn't get the same gas mileage at every moment because you have to factor in the effect of the weight of the gas you're hauling, which obviously lessens as you use it. It's only shorthand to express what's happening as miles per gallon, just as it's shorthand to say, "I'm like this, and he's like that." You're the way you are because he does certain things, and vice versa, and time (together) is a factor.

We hear a lot about how a mother bonds with her child, even on a hormonal level. What we don't hear as much about is how the married couple bond, not only by means of their physical relationship but even more by how they meet each challenge that comes their way. (You might even say that the physical relationship is God's gift for smoothing the path of all those challenges!)

In the first decade, every little and big thing is not only something to talk about and solve but also a way to bond—or fail to bond. If you want to worry about something, know that the scary thing is that it's not apparent how or whether this process has worked until your second decade together. Then, the stresses of dealing with the demands and personalities of your growing children, as well as the difficulties of approaching middle age, will break you if you aren't strong.

So I am warning you now of ten issues you will face, if you are thinking of going into marriage with your finances separate, that maybe your mother hasn't taken into account and your priest doesn't think you'll listen to if he tells you.

1. *Marriage is about unity for the sake of making a family.* Money is the means by which you live. If you are not united in the means, it just stands to reason you won't be united in the ends. Do you really want to risk the whole journey to find out that you are actually on two separate journeys? Marriage is about being "all in" — including debt. When a man and a woman don't act as if they are taking on each other's debt, I wonder if they know what marriage is really all about!

If you are really not ready to marry on account of debt, and obviously it would be better not to have debt, separate finances aren't the answer. Waiting to marry until things are paid off or down is the answer. And usually, very-much-in-love couples will find a way to deal with the debt without waiting too long.

2. *Money represents your plans and goals for your life together.* Money isn't a goal, but you won't reach your goal without money. If your finances are separate, you will find that you end up with different goals. The problem is that this won't be apparent right away; it will be revealed only in the second decade, when stress is high and your bonds haven't formed. By then, it will be very hard to fix. Do you want to take this very real risk?

In addition, having two distinct finances makes the goal of having a family more difficult. Even well-off couples get trapped into thinking that they can't do without the wife's income, simply because of the habits they went into the marriage with. For welcoming children, it's better to be used to thinking in terms of one income stream. Remember, having children is the purpose of marriage! (I heartily recommend using *your* income to pay down any debt or to save until babies come.) Taking care of the home and children is its own contribution, but not one with any kind of dollar sign attached. Seeing that value takes real unity.

What will you do when God blesses you with a child? Start negotiations over who buys what? Please. That's no way to live.

3. *Money represents freedom, but dependence is better in marriage.* We like to think of ourselves as far above having secret thoughts about important things—thoughts we keep from our loved ones. But the truth is that we are only as good as the thoughts we have when the going gets tough. If one line of thinking during a tough time is something like, "Well, I have my own money, I'm free to do what I want," then that is what will define you—not what you think in your best moments.

Just as you don't enter marriage thinking that you can still date others, you shouldn't enter thinking you can always spend your own money. It's the wrong kind of freedom. The secret thought that if things don't work out, you will have your own finances is a stake in the heart of your marriage. Better to face that you can't commit now.

Every choice you make based on the thought that you are really free from your spouse is a choice that will weaken trust. Having one set of finances is not only challenging to the woman's sense of independence; it's also challenging to the man's fear of being depended on. Yet, to have a family, these challenges must be faced; the sooner, the better.

4. *Money represents power, but there is no room for power in a marriage.* Marriage is about serving each other. That is why all the money should be shared. Then all the decisions will be shared (including the decision to leave some decisions up to one of you—that's fine! Who wants to have to go over every little thing? Trust!)

It's not that you set out to use money as a weapon against each other, but when things are tough, every weapon seems handy at the time. Just put this very powerful weapon out of reach from the get-go.

5. *Dealing with money makes you confront your demons: how you handle money, debt, priorities, and children.* This is another way of saying that the process of making your choices, not just the choices themselves, strengthen or weaken your bond.

When you have separate money, you remove some of those processes—the opportunities to decide things together with all the conflict that entails. Hashing things out given your resources is how you become a strong citadel, tested for battle against the enemy. If you don't test your abilities to make tough choices when you are first setting out, with lots at stake and nowhere (i.e., another bank account) to go, you essentially build weaknesses into the walls, only to be discovered later.

Now, for instance, having debt seems overwhelming, but you have no idea how complicated things get later. In about fifteen years, this obstacle will seem like nothing compared with what you face, hopefully together, hopefully with trust. Don't think, "Oh, we'll solve our problems later" if you are also keeping separate accounts. That *is* the problem!

6. *Men's worst fear as time goes on is that their wives will leave them, taking their children.* Ordinary men, men who married with cheerful goodwill, become either violent or utterly defeated, depending on their temperament, when faced with this possibility. For some reason, this psychological fact is a subject for mockery or a reason to belittle a man. I can't understand that. Start now, in this concrete way, to show him that you will never leave him (which is what you are about to vow).

7. *Women's worst fear is that they can't trust their husbands to love them in a mature way.* Sweet ordinary women who married with stars in their eyes fear the betrayal of finding out they are married to a selfish jerk. If a woman's husband is in the habit of living a part of his life separate from hers, with his own credit cards and so on, she will start to feel bitter about his lack of responsibility.

8. *Marriage is about growing together and growing up together; how you handle money is part of the process.* Having unified finances encourages maturity, because you have to communicate. Separate finances encourage immaturity, because you can do things, even irresponsible things, without being accountable. Why enable this pitfall from the outset? What purpose could having one's own money serve other than selfish needs, by definition?

9. *Communication, including communication about the details of handling money, is the lifeblood of marriage.* When finances are separate, communication suffers; even little things can't be discussed because a wall has been set up with the money. Even if you think you can contain money in its own category, you will be surprised to find, too late, that you can't talk about little things

that are seemingly unrelated. Everything ends up being about who spent what, even when it's something like too many beer cans in the recycling or the child's copay at the doctor's office. Instead of loving discussion, it will be all arguing.

10. *Children get the wrong idea about marriage when money is separate.* It isn't just about you. It's about how your children ultimately approach building their own families. If we really want our children to be able to make healthy relationships of their own, unified and generous, we have to be living that way ourselves from the start. Go for it—go the whole distance, together. Go all in. Make it about trust. You won't be sorry.

Maddie hasn't yet begun her life with her husband. Maybe you started on the wrong foot. It isn't too late to change things. Once you realize how much shared finances can enhance your relationship, you can start to have a good conversation about where you would like to go from here. Know that you can start over! Beginning again is better than rushing in the wrong direction.

ASK AUNTIE LEILA

Life Insurance Eases the Risk of Living on One Income

Dear Auntie Leila,

I was and I still am stay-at-home mom. But I always wonder: How people deal with fear? What if something happens to my husband, our only breadwinner? I don't have the qualifications to go right back to work and support myself and my kids.

All the best,

Justyna

D ear Justyna,

Yes, what if something happens?

Very often, it's the husband who has difficulty accepting the burden of being the one income earner; it feels too risky.

Of course, this fear, beaten into us as society pushes for all women to work outside the home, begs the question of what if something happens *to both of you*, and perhaps that highlights the indispensable role of *trust* and the need to accept uncertainty, since we really don't know what the future holds.

We should also think about *how even more precarious* things would be at home if our lifestyle were based on two incomes plus all the outside help needed to sustain two working parents — and one parent dies. Living simply does help when disaster strikes.

Nevertheless, as the old joke goes, "Swim, Johnny, swim!"[12] That is, in addition to reminding you to trust and accept uncertainty, I am also going to fix this worry. It's simple.

We live in a modern age in which, thankfully, you can buy life insurance, the purpose of which is to alleviate this fear as far as possible. God put us in a certain time, in a certain place. In the past, some people did suffer financial doom when the income earner died or was incapacitated. Communities worked to help; my husband's great-great-(great?)-grandfather implemented a forerunner to today's Knights of Columbus insurance provision with a fund to help widows bury their husbands. Such were the works of mercy at the time (and still are very necessary).

Your husband needs life insurance. Some experts recommend that the policy be for seven to ten times the amount of his income. Often, his work covers this need. If not, get it on your own. Make room in your budget for this item.

The couple should also insure the wife who doesn't earn an income but whose contribution is difficult and expensive to replace.

I found it interesting, when I read the arguments for insuring the stay-at-home spouse, that when imagining what a full-time worker would do to manage a home with children in it without his wife, financial planners get serious about the difficulty and stress he would face. This shows you just how vital being the manager of the home really is. It's

---

[12] Have you heard that joke? The little boy's rowboat is sinking out on the lake. His mother, standing on the shore, wrings her hands and calls out, "Pray, Johnny, pray!" His dad, also on the shore, also worried, shouts, "Swim, Johnny, swim!"

impossible to put a dollar value on it, yet when we try, we find out that it would be high.

The enterprise of making a family takes a lot of skill and time! Because we women by nature tend to do our work without boasting and beating our chests, we end up accepting the man's view that what men do is worth more and that what we do is worthless and can be done by anyone.

It all depends on how you look at it. When we speak in terms of the woman's contribution, we think income. But as this discussion of life insurance shows, as soon as we think about the cost of not having the wife there, running things, educating children, saving money, and providing breathing room, suddenly we see the value of this manager. One analyst talks about the husband's having time to be with his kids after his wife dies, versus having to use his free time to figure out food, clothing, cleaning, sick care, and so on. Get your insurance as soon as you can, while you are still young. This advice should be part of every marriage preparation course!

This whole book is essentially about the hidden but indispensable role of homemaker. Perhaps you are convinced, but still worried. Thus I recommend: get life insurance!

Two Practical Money Tips

I'm a fan of money-saving tips, but too much advice dispensed at once often overwhelms me. I also find that important advice is mixed in with silly stuff, like "refinance your mortgage" with "use your coffee grounds twice"! Furthermore, I have read that men get advice that's global and involves managing the whole budget, whereas women get advice that's very detailed and targeted at saving a few pennies here and there. I don't know if that's true, and I'm no financial expert. But I'm going to tell you two things that definitely fall in the category of "learn from my mistakes," and hopefully won't overwhelm you.

I like to start with where you are this moment, as you open the month's bills. But before I even start with my two tips, I recommend that you put a prayer card of St. Joseph on your desk where you pay your bills, or in the bill basket, or wherever he can watch over your attempts to be a steward of your affairs. St. Joseph will help you; he is the patron saint of the family and of the household; he is the greatest protector and provider who ever lived.

On to my two things:

First, do everything you can, whatever it takes, to pay on time the bills that charge you a late fee. Are you clipping coupons that will save you a few bucks and then forgetting your cell phone bill? Do you realize that a late charge of thirty-six dollars on a bill of a hundred dollars represents a 36 percent interest rate? Would you take out a loan that charged you 36 percent interest? You'd be mighty foolish to do so, and yet that is what is happening when you forget to pay this bill.

So, if you are like me, and have several cards because of the benefits you get (free shipping from L.L. Bean, points at Amazon, frequent flier miles, etc.), your chances of missing a due date are pretty good, and then all your benefits are wiped out. It would have been better to pay eleven dollars in shipping that sweater than thirty-nine dollars in a late fee! If you don't keep your checking account balance up to date, you risk bounced-check or automatic payment fees, which amount to a very expensive loan from the bank.

Solution: get into the habit of touching base with your bills every Monday morning. Make a list of when your bills are due and place it next to your computer. Enter the dates in your tickler file (online calendar, for instance) so that you get an e-mail reminding yourself to pay on time. Do what it takes to stop getting smacked down by these fees! The obvious answer is to enroll in an auto-pay service, but perhaps sometimes you have to juggle accounts and can't manage that. Above all, do not be late with your payment. If you make a mistake but you're normally prompt, the company will waive the fee, and it's definitely worth the call.

This talk of interest rates brings me to my second tip for saving money: take advantage of a good offer to transfer your credit-card balances to a lower-rate card. Get out your bills and check the interest rate; it's printed on the statement.

Get the best rate you can (you can even call the company and ask them to lower your rate; sometimes that works). Just make sure that it's for the life of the balance, not just a few months. If not, transfer to a lower-rate card. It's worth paying a little up front to get out from under a usurious rate.

Then do not use that card for purchases, ever. That's where the company makes money on interest. Keep only your transferred balance and pay it off as you are able. Use a different card for new purchases (and be sure to pay it off completely every month).

So those are two tips from a sadder but wiser budget balancer. I'm no expert, but even I can tell that you will save more money doing these two things than hunting down a cheaper can of beans.

PART 6

Thriftiness, Frugality, and Prosperity, and Ways of Doing

A secret that I wish more people knew—doing my best here—is that you can live on one income—even a modest one—and prosper. Even more, as every boy marooned on a creek or every girl faced with a tree house to furnish knows, thrift, or the necessity of *making do with what you've got*, is the true creative impulse in life, and even, dare I say it, where the real fun begins.

G. K. Chesterton, in his book *What's Wrong with the World*, wrote:

Thrift is the really romantic thing; economy is more romantic than extravagance. Heaven knows I for one speak disinterestedly in the matter; for I cannot clearly remember saving a half-penny ever since I was born. But the thing is true; economy, properly understood, is the more poetic. Thrift is poetic because it is creative; waste is unpoetic because it is waste. It is prosaic to throw money away, because it is prosaic to throw anything away; it is negative; it is a confession of indifference, that is, it is a confession of failure. The most prosaic thing about the house is the dustbin, and the one great objection to the new fastidious and aesthetic homestead is simply that in such a moral menage the dustbin must be bigger than the house. If a man could undertake to make use of all things in his dustbin he would be a broader genius than Shakespeare. When science began to use by-products; when science found that colors could be made out of coaltar, she made her greatest and perhaps her only claim on the real respect of the human soul. Now the aim of the good woman is to use the by-products, or, in other words, to rummage in the dustbin.

There are a few reasons I started writing, and one of them is my frustration with the idea that families today simply must have two incomes just to scrape by—as if people in the past didn't have far more insecurity and relative poverty than we do now. And I'm not talking about the normal things that a wife did occasionally in the past to drum up a little petty cash; I'm talking about the notion that she must have a separate career with its own full-time salary and benefits if they are to survive.

The problem is that such an attitude undermines family life and orients it toward acquisition and security rather than toward the more important nonmaterial goods that the family must have to be what it is called to be, day to day, year in and year out. And it takes away the real adventure of life together, to be honest.

Those who have figured these things out—frugal people—might not reveal their ways at first glance. It takes a lot of work and cleverness, and often all the energy is directed at the doing and none at the telling. But as with anything else, deciding what your priorities will be determines how you go about the challenge, and then, soon enough, you see who your companions on the journey are. The goal is to raise the family with what one has (that is, with one income), even if it means going without and making do for years and years—because it's worth it.

This section is practical. Even if you have the means to afford a comfortable life (because, say, your husband has quite a good salary), you might learn something about *spiritual* detachment—about not spending *just because you can*. Of course, sometimes it's better to spend than to drive yourself crazy finding the absolute thriftiest way to go about doing something; sometimes your time needs to be spent somewhere else. But even the richest person must always be checking to be sure that he isn't giving in to comfort but is using his money wisely.

Anyway, here I'll talk about the little things that make living on one smallish income possible. It's about detachment from material things, but also about how to get what you need in unconventional ways. I know that the temptation is to assume that, because other people are sailing off to buy brand-new things at retail prices, there can be no other way. But there is another way!

A lot of our possessions come from yard sales or were even free.

We use a lot of spray paint.

We put off buying new things—just put it off. We wash dishes by hand if we need a new dishwasher and can't afford one (and sometimes discover that family time is quite precious, cleaning up the kitchen together); we go to the laundromat if the washer is broken and a new one isn't possible (and some mothers swear by the efficiency of doing all the laundry at once, and some shopping to boot); we hang clothes in the furnace room if the dryer isn't working (and the electric bill is a lot less at the end of the month as well).

And very often we find what we need secondhand; we just have to be patient. Despite all this sacrifice, we prosper. I don't mean we get rich and have a lot of stuff. I mean we have the prosperity of love and creative satisfaction.

Frugal for Beginners

ou can live on one income and start your journey to frugality. Here are five tips on how to change your habits and discover the romance of thrift.

1. *Stop buying things because it makes you happy simply to spend money.* This is very much like a similar syndrome regarding food. You know, the one where you eat an entire package of Oreos? Why? Because you're hungry? No. It's because for a little while, not while you are actually eating them, but just before you eat them, you think it will make you happy.

In the same way, just walking into a store can make you feel elated, at one with yourself, on the verge of becoming someone completely different. (Ever read anything by Walker Percy? He describes this state with great wit and insight. I highly recommend his book *Lost in the Cosmos* for insight into this phenomenon of seeking ways to feel more *real.*)

Instead, face squarely exactly how you feel during and after you shop (and during and after you eat a bunch of cookies). It's like really smelling your house when you first walk in. It's not what you think it is.

2. *Stop treating shopping as entertainment.* This is a little like tip 1, but different. When you shop for entertainment, you aren't getting your thrill from

spending money, but rather from going out somewhere that seems bright, new, and fun. However, spend money you will.

Instead, find other forms of entertainment! Have you ever spent real time in the library, wandering through the stacks, enjoying the magazines? Gone to a museum (the library has passes, you know), gone for a hike? Instead of shopping, go to the playground, take a picnic on a walk, have a tea for your friends, or take some muffins to a friend at assisted living.

Better yet, stop looking to be entertained and start creating! Each one of those projects that you think you will get to "someday" is simply waiting to happen at the very moment you disappear out the door to wander the shops mindlessly.

3. *Stop reading lowbrow decorating magazines. Stop looking at lowbrow decorating blogs. But also stop getting your ideas from perfectionists who have taste but also know how to ratchet up the anxiety level—and, of course, drum up business and sales.* The problem is that certain magazines and blogs work hand in hand with certain stores to create and then "satisfy" desires. You see a conventionally decorated room in a magazine, and then you go to the store to get it, for a hefty price. Everything in these magazines is new, is slick, and makes what you have look shabby. What you don't realize is that very little of it lasts or is truly aesthetic.

Instead, get your ideas from truly classy magazines, sites, and books. They will feature one of two kinds of homes: (1) ridiculously over-the-top professionally decorated environments (they are creating and meeting their own kinds of desires too, of course) that will hone your taste and help you recognize quality when you see it at the yard sale (2) and truly tasteful examples of people using objects and living in homes that show history, that reflect culture, and that are anchored in real living.

I'm always amazed at how a certain class of rich folks don't care if their leather sofas are cracking or their books are piled up and dusty. Their art is often something they invest their money in, true. But just as often, it reflects just what they like, and we non-rich can do that too!

The more you immerse yourself in this "old money" aesthetic, the happier you will be with your own personal history that's all around you— and you will feel rich!

4. *Stop paying retail for everything.* Having grown up poking around in junk shops, I guess it never occurred to me that some people are uncomfortable with this form of acquisition. I was a bit surprised to find that some regard it as, well, unhygienic, I suppose!

But once hooked, you will never look back. Once you realize that you can find a dresser for ten dollars, a food dehydrator for five dollars, or beekeeping equipment for free, you will kick yourself for paying retail for everything.

So, ask an experienced friend take you to a secondhand store, or challenge another newbie to keep you company. Don't be overwhelmed by a place like the local Goodwill. Start slow. Look only at the handbags or dishes at first. Go back another time to check out the skirts.

5. *Stay home and make home beautiful.* The stores seem, well, arranged. They are clean. They are not grubby. You enjoy being where it's like that.

So, clean everything in your home. You will like it all better when it's really clean.

Make tidy piles of your messes as best you can; arrange what you have as nicely as you can. This step is really key for learning to kick the buying habit. Very often we neglect it, thinking that *because it's mine* it must not be officially great, and what I need is something new, which by definition isn't mine (until that moment I get it home—and then of course, I need to shop again!).

After neatening for a while, get a little critical and simply toss that which you don't feel like neatening any more. Clean again.

Enjoy what you have and be grateful. Stop comparing yourself with others!

You might even come across some things in your very own home that you thought you needed to buy. This has happened to me on more than one occasion!

If you must go shopping—and this might seem odd to some—pray. Ask your guardian angel to help you to be a good steward and to lead you quickly to the things you need so you can get them and get out of the store before you spend what you shouldn't!

Use What You Have,
Buy What You Can Afford

I love beautiful things, and it kind of makes my head spin to open a decorating magazine or check someone's site and see yet another thing or look that I could go for in a second! My house can't be all white (which I love—you know, the fresh and simple Scandinavian style) and *at the same time* bursting with color (which I also love—a bohemian and lively style).

The Internet has provided a resource that most print media never could, just by virtue of the hurdles of real-world publication—namely, ready access to people's visuals of what they do. If you know where to look, you can find affirmation in, of all things, imperfection, which is the most helpful of all. This is not a rationalization of disorder and messiness but the really beautiful inspiration for reconciling the imperfect circumstances of our lives with a harmonious vision of something that we know we can never really attain. Instead of a discontented feeling for what we don't have, this affirmation gives a sense of contentment.

But sometimes, an overload on decorating, a sort of glut of images, does create that unsettled feeling. So how to figure things out?

Here's my answer: *Don't think of what you are doing in your home as decorating.* Think of it as creating an environment for your family that is beautiful (or pretty, if that helps you feel less anxious) in a practical, humble way; that helps you keep order and that makes others comfortable. And try as much as possible to use what you already have.

Take some time before buying something new. Ask yourself, "Do I already have something that I could use for this? Does my mother have it, or do I spy my next-door neighbor putting it out by the curb? [The latter happened to me with what is now, after I painted it, my very pretty bed frame.] Could I clean something up, paint something, or fix something to fit this purpose in a pleasing way? What solutions have others found?" This last question could mean doing a search with your query, which is a good, healthy use of the Internet—and you may be surprised at how clever someone else has been.

For example, I'm not a huge fan of my white Formica countertops or standard wooden cabinets, but they are what I have. After getting some inspiration from magazines (and input from my creative children, who guided me and did the work), I tried to use paint and accents to make them beautiful for us. And do you know what? My kitchen is fine.

I know one thing: if we had gone deep into debt to get something all gleaming, matching, and perfect, and then I had come across something "make-do" but still pleasing in a magazine or on a blog, I would be mad at myself. I would really regret not having tried to solve our problems within our means.

Of course, if what you have is gleaming, then you'll just have to go with that! And if you can afford and need a real makeover, then enjoy!

When you *are* ready to shop and upgrade, ask your guardian angel to help you find the right thing; something that fits your purpose and your budget and is pleasing to the senses, not necessarily something that would be right in a magazine shoot. You will be surprised at what you find!

Always try to buy the best quality that you can, given your budget. A full-grain leather sofa will last a lifetime; a fake-leather sofa will last a few years. But even a cheap sofa is expensive. So it does make sense to buy a good one if you can.

Getting Used to Being Thrifty

Don't think that I consider myself a particularly good example. I am not always the most thrifty person in the room. So you know that anything you read here (and especially any photos that you see on my blog, which are included only because I like a post with photos) is offered in the spirit of "If I can do it, so can you!"

At this moment, the "it" I'm talking about is living on one income. I'm talking about having lots of kids if they come to you, sending them to college, feeding your ice cream habit, and in general living with what the world would consider some sort of crazy risk-taking; but, once you get used to it, it just seems normal and actually gratitude-inducing for how much plenty we encounter all around us!

I have some great friends, and along the way I have been edified and often rescued from some fairly silly pity parties by their resourcefulness and can-do attitude. I think everyone needs a friend, someone who will encourage you and tell you that you can do it.

Take, for instance, when you need a rug. You know that I firmly believe that if you make up your mind that you need something, it will turn up. "Something is bound to turn up." (Mr. Micawber in *David Copperfield*, of course; in a slightly different and not altogether apt context for the present discussion, as he was referring to longed-for relief from his pecuniary entanglements. Well, in a way, that works.) Either you will get the money you need to go out and buy the rug, or, more likely, somehow the right thing will surface at a yard sale or even free from someone who considers it a castoff. You must be patient, and thereby you often have the surprise of discovering a better solution after all, one that wouldn't have occurred if you had been able instantly to gratify your desires.

Don't get me wrong. I am all for the more well-to-do spending their money on top-quality things! If they didn't do that, there would be nothing for those of more modest means to thrift! I shudder when I read stories in the newspaper about the well heeled dabbling in secondhand shopping. Such a bad idea. Thrifty finds don't drop from Mars.

But the rest of us have to be committed to spending very little for the sake of a higher good (in this case, so that you can be free to make your home and educate your children by providing a beautiful environment for them). To make things work, you have to be willing to look everywhere, and you have to tell everyone what you need.

A Thrifting Tale

Want to hear the whole thought-and-action process?

In the back of my mind, I had a rug for the third-floor bedroom in mind, something to go under that iron bed from which Suki had the habit of letting her book drop as she fell asleep! (My room is directly beneath.) I don't know what I wanted, but I thought that a rectangular rug of some sort, big enough, would be nice. I checked all the usual places, but anything remotely to my taste was too expensive, even on clearance. We were planning two weddings! And it was not yard-sale season; the junk shops had yielded nothing.

I also had on my mind where I would put all the other returning (grown) children. I decided that what we needed to increase our capacity was a sleeper sofa in the rec room (on the second floor), and suddenly, a deadline loomed when friends who really needed to be near the bathroom were visiting. In our house, rooms near the bathroom are few. My own room is a good solid sprint as far from the bathroom as you can get.

I found (actually, Rosie, doing a search from California, found for me here in Massachusetts) on Craigslist the ideal used sleeper sofa: never even used as a *sofa*, with the mattress still sealed in plastic. Because we can all imagine the issues with buying furniture this way.

As we were picking it up, ever willing to put my needs out there, I asked the seller (a used furniture dealer stockpiling things in a barn) what else he had. Any rugs? Well, among a rather stunning number of dining sets and crazy stacks of chairs from some sort of institution, he had one, and one only, rug.

At first, I wasn't sure. I hadn't thought of a braided rug at all. What if the colors didn't go? It was certainly big enough and in very good, nay, perfect, condition. He hadn't priced it yet. I waited (the sofa, which I paid his very reasonable asking price for, as it was well worth it, was safely in the Suburban) while he mulled the question (and in my own mind, I decided how much I wanted him to say: $30). He said $50. I offered $40. And that was that! In retrospect, I believe he could have asked $250 and gotten it if he had listed it, but I was on the spot and my guardian angel was on the job.

Home we hauled it, and it waited on our truly herculean efforts to get the sofa in the (I now fully acknowledge) inaccessible rec room. (And a big tip of the hat to our neighbor Ben who rescued us from divorce, destruction, and despair by figuring out how to get around the last bend of our small back hallway!)

So Bridget and I deep-cleaned the rec room, got the sofa bed in place, and then headed for the third floor. I was still not sure!

By dint of inching that large rug under the bed, in a display of hilariously exhausting and inefficient and incompetent making do (I think my husband was on a deadline and unavailable for what was clearly a three-man job), we got it deployed. And, voilà! It's perfect!

All this is to say, don't let things out there in the world, where people claim that a family simply can't live on one income, and that it's a luxury for the wife to stay home,[13] prevent you from identifying and homing in on your goal. If you are motivated by what you know to be good, you can do it.

---

[13] The wife's vocation is to make the home, even though I don't describe her as being a "stay-at-home mom" just because, in the course of history, wives

Remember that it's not fair to compare the probably now-prosperous home of your parents with your own; they've lived through their shabby times (if they had them). You may have even been there, but you don't remember it. These more well-to-do homes and lifestyles might indeed be the result of two incomes, in which case it takes a dose of humility and realism to recognize that you have other, less visible priorities — and that's just how it is.

Instead of comparing yourself with rich people, compare yourself with genuinely poor people. Doing so never fails to restore the proper perspective! You will soon realize the abundance that is all around; how blessed we are to have loved ones to sacrifice for and how energizing the challenge can be.

---

and mothers have done a lot of things while making their homes. Making a home means that the family lives on the husband's income, as it's his vocation to be the provider. In our economy, which is based on raising one or two children on two incomes, devoting oneself to creating a beautiful environment for one's family will require hard work and dedication and is well worth the effort. If I can help, even just by cheerleading, I will.

ASK AUNTIE LEILA

Thrifting Advice

Dear Auntie Leila,

Some advice, please. I would love to make our home more beautiful. It sounds, though, that it would take a lot of time to go to thrift shops and so forth. When I do go, I usually don't find anything worth buying. I usually buy things we really need (e.g., furniture) on Craigslist, which can take a lot of time too. With two young kids to rear (who don't want to go shopping!), and not being a crafty person who can make pillows, curtains, and so on, am I consigned to live in a bland, boring house until the kids are older? Please help! Thanks!

Frugal Dreamer

Dear FD,

Yes, things in this world take time or money or both! Usually when you don't have money, things take more time.

My biggest tip to you would be to use your Internet time to poke around at the sites of those who are really good at taking castoffs and making them useful and beautiful. Train your eye! Once you do, you will see things everywhere. I have high standards and take it for granted that any given trip to the thrift shop will yield nothing. Just make a lightning strike and get out. When you find something, it will be worth it. Many couples make a pact that, due to the necessity of thrifting for this lifestyle we've chosen, if we can glorify it with the term "lifestyle," the husband will watch kids and get chores started on Saturday mornings so that the wife can go out unencumbered. It may be that a couple likes doing this together, in which case it can be a family outing or a reason to get a mother's helper in to watch the kids.

Beauty in your home starts simply and can be the result of just keeping your eye out wherever you go. Many things in my house have literally come out of the trash or from the side of the road. Ask your guardian angel to help you make your house lovely, and you will see the opportunities pop up. Also, the two things you named, pillows and curtains, are by far the easiest possible things to make, accessible to the least crafty person, due to the mainly straight lines used in their production. Many books from the library will show you just how to do it, not to mention video tutorials online.

The other possibility is to scour clearances at stores that carry the things you like. Again, it takes longer, but eventually you will find things you like.

Focus on a real need: a rug, a sofa, kitchen chairs, plates, a kid's bed. Get ideas online and then go on a mission. You will be surprised at what turns up!

Another question has to do with how to account for the fluid cash needed for thrifting in a budget. Your budget might be very detailed, which is great for keeping down extra spending. But trouble starts when you see a perfect bed or set of chairs or bedside table for forty dollars somewhere, because you can't anticipate that. If you know you need a new couch, we can save up for it, but how to make sure you have the cash on hand when you see at a yard sale something unexpected but important—or even just something that you know will make your home more beautiful?

The answer is to put in your very detailed budget a category for yard sales and bargain shopping. If yard sales are seasonal where you live, withdraw the money and keep the cash on hand at that time. Thrifting saves money on clothes, shoes, coats, household items, and even birthday and Christmas presents for a large family!

If nothing else, start the fund with twenty dollars. If you don't find anything, roll that dough into the next month's budget of twenty dollars, giving you forty dollars to work with. If it's something you know you simply have to have (every family simply has to have a table and chairs, for instance) and you know the prices and you see something special, then eat beans to buy it (meaning, find the money somehow!). Why? Because unlike something in stock in a store, it won't be there next time.

If you don't have twenty dollars, then clearly God doesn't want you out there thrifting, He wants you to make do with what you have. You can always put a board on sawhorses! You won't be the first struggling couple to do it! There is no way surer to know God's will than to see what it is that we can afford! So we can be peaceful about that.

Getting Good at Thrifting

I come from a long line of ladies who like to wander through dusty barns, find old broken-down things, wipe them off, and put them into service. While my friends' parents were going on shopping trips to Bloomingdale's, I was with my mom, poking around junk shops. I didn't necessarily know it at the time (in fact, I disliked the dirty atmosphere and resented being dragged away from play time, just like any other kid would), but I was getting an education in form, line, and construction. I could spot a beveled mirror at twenty feet. I knew a dovetail joint before I could name it. A gummy finish couldn't hide nice wood grain from me. I was wordlessly trained to spot patina.

Getting this expertise is easier when you are committed to not spending much. Ever. On almost anything. It sharpens your eye. If you can't just buy what you want when you want it, you learn to be patient and snap up what you like when you see it hidden under a table in a Goodwill, or out behind the recycling center's dumpsters.

Here are my general tips:

1. *"Have nothing in your house that you do not know to be useful, or believe to be beautiful,"* advises the British Arts and Crafts Movement designer and

poet William Morris. In other words, make standards for yourself. Start to learn what your own likes and needs are. Arrange things accordingly, as far as you are able.

2. *Train your eye.* Examine every photo that claims to feature "flea-market style" or "shabby chic" or "upcycling"; notice the things that you yourself would have passed up but look fabulous or useful. Notice colors and shapes. Notice when the DIY style has resulted in something worse than the original, for that is part of training your eye. Be critical and take note of what you don't like at all. Then look around you.

3. *Avoid the temptation to think that you can restore everything.* If I can spray-paint it, I probably will. But I've learned that I don't have time for real, professional refinishing, much less heavy-duty upholstering or slipcovering, other than the most basic square-of-fabric-stapled-onto-an-ottoman. The best find is one you can clean off and put in its place right away. Second best is a fix that you can do. Worst is a pile of things in the basement that you'll never get to.

4. *See things separately.* Look at a picture; look at its frame. Those are two different things, and even if one of them is not right, the other might be. The same with sheets. It's the pillowcases that go first, so it makes sense to buy those when you can find newish ones on clearance. The truth is that when the bed is made, the pillowcases are all you really see. Vintage ones look really cheerful and often that old percale wears the best.

5. *If it's unique, get it.* I've never regretted passing up someone's Target cast-off, but there was an antique blue hand-painted bed once ... Sigh. Here is incentive to create a "discretionary fund" even if it means having two soup nights a week! If you squirrel away twenty dollars a month into this fund, you will soon be able to dip into this account when the opportunity presents itself.

Realize that doing so is the opposite of spontaneous or unplanned spending. It's more like "planning for the unexpected," and the truth is that you can't live the frugal life without being ready and poised to seize the chance for an inexpensive way to get the things you need and would love.

6. *Know the trash days in your area.* People put good items out with their trash, hoping someone will pick it up. The law, by the way, is on your side, as trash left out on the curb is fair game. If it's not obviously trash, however, you should ask before taking it. Some people who live near me have a nice white bench out by their curb where they also put their trash. I don't think they want anyone taking it (although I do always look twice).

7. *Know that learning to be thrifty is a process.* You won't learn everything at once, and that's okay. Don't wait for anyone's permission. Just plunge in.

Regions differ, making it hard for me to give a lot of specifics. Find out where people in your area get rid of their castoffs and go there. Are there church rummage sales? Yard sales? Thrift stores? Resale and consignment shops? A "shop" in your recycling center or dump where people take and leave things? A neighborhood list-serve site where people post their curb pickups?

Be patient and vigilant. If you love something and it's cheap, go for it. After a while, you will learn from your mistakes. Just remember to get rid of *your* junk if you don't like it. The great thing about thrifting is that things didn't cost you much, so you can let go of them if they turn out to be a mistakes.

Remind yourself on occasion *why* you're being thrifty. People who are trying to live frugally so that their families can prosper without a lot of income are doing a good thing. This is how Mama can stay home with the children. It's how Papa can go to work without a lot of stress. Go at it with energy, look around, and be picky.

How to Feed Your Kids Fruit the Frugal Way

I am all astonishment when I see moms handing their young children a whole apple, peach, or other fruit.

And then I am further mystified when I read "tips" on how to rescue half-eaten apples to be made into something in the name of frugality. Even the venerable Amy Dacyczyn, author of *The Tightwad Gazette*, a person who would rather make a diaper cover out of old bread bags than buy real ones, advises her readers to save chewed-on apples to make a dessert with later. Yuck (residual saliva will be doing its number on that fruit) — and also, a waste of sugar, flour, and other expensive ingredients. Have you priced butter lately? And I don't know about you, but my time for making extra desserts is limited; certainly, it doesn't keep up with the demand for fresh fruit in a busy family.

Now, I am going to tell you just what to do, but I realize that it will go against a strong American trait, which is precisely an aversion to cutting up fruit. Perhaps this is because, in America, fruit is plentiful, or perhaps we Americans don't have a love affair with our food the way other people do; but for some reason, I find that most of us laugh at the idea of cutting fruit up into bite-size pieces. However, your typical European or, say, Egyptian (and I get this trait from my Egyptian side) is shocked at the offhand treatment of comestibles because in these cultures, one makes a ritual of even the smallest snack.

It takes less than a minute to cut up an apple and put it on a plate or a cutting board. It's also something an older child could do for a younger one.

You can find a nice, sharp paring knife for a few dollars anywhere. (I'll bet your mother has an extra one you could take!) Cut the fruit in half or in quarters or what have you. Deftly slice out the core or toss the pit. Remove the skin if it's objectionable (sometimes it is), or convince your children that it's tasty and the best part. Arrange the pieces (further sliced if you like) on a plate or in a bowl. Put the bowl anywhere at all, and watch the pieces disappear.

Alternatively, you can make what we call in our family a bird's nest, using a melon baller to remove the core of an apple that has been sliced in half—somehow very appealing to a child, and usually, half an apple is all anyone wants and it's more portable than slices.

I'm afraid that, other than while apple picking, or maybe with the smallest fruits, your average four-year-old is not going to (a) have the appetite for a whole apple or (b) stay interested long enough to finish it. Most children seem to take delight in abandoning a half-eaten apple (it sort of does get unappetizing, you know?), whereas few can resist just one more crisp untouched slice. Any pieces that *are* left over will be mercifully free of taint, and so can be tucked away for next time or gratefully consumed by you.

My way (and the way of most of the world) has the advantage not only of saving on fruit and those expensive ingredients subsequently employed to rectify its waste *and* of being more aesthetic, but it also relieves you of ever again finding a mushy, yet dusty brown substance behind your sofa.

Cutting up the fruit has the side benefit of putting your random sweet thrifted dishes into play.

Living without Air Conditioning

When we moved back to New England after a long exile in other lands (nowhere too far, just not *home*), I walked into my husband's childhood house on a hot, humid day and gasped with relief. It was at least twenty degrees cooler in there, and I knew that his parents, Grandma and Grandpa Make-Do-Use-Up-Wear-Out, didn't have air conditioning!

One clue to their attitude was that, when we lived in the swamps (literal and figurative) of Washington, D.C., they gave us the one AC unit *they* had been given by a concerned relative for their own bedroom, "because the robins had nested on it and we couldn't disturb them by using it, and we'd rather have the window open." (Obviously this was after the robins left and the heat had started in earnest, so you get the picture of how detached they were from the AC.)

I know that not everyone agrees on this, but I'm with Grandma and Grandpa. I detest air conditioning. I am writing here for those who also have the possibility of doing without it.

My mother-in-law was really the genius at keeping things cool, simply because she had learned from her forebears, and I learned a lot from her, much of which, admittedly, would not work *as well* in a place like D.C., although with the right architecture (such as was found in the South long ago), I think it would go a long way.

Here's what she taught me:

Early in the day, close up the house on the sides that face the rising heat.

Shut the windows. This seems counterintuitive, but if hot air is coming in, the window needs to be shut and the curtain or shade drawn until things cool down.

Lower the blinds, draw the curtains, turn off the lights. Start loving the cool darkness in the heat of the day.

Open doors and windows on the cool sides of the house. A bush on the northwest corner will do amazing things to cool the air coming in a window on that side. You want to catch that coolness in the morning.

Later in the day, that western side is the one that gets closed. The eastern windows can be opened as the sun recedes.

Any north-facing windows can be left open all day except on the hottest days. You can feel the air. If it's cooler than what you've got, let it in! If it's hotter, keep it out.

Open the top of a warmer-side window and the bottom of a cooler side to get a flow going through your house. Try opening them a small amount at first to see if you can set up an air current.

A fan placed near a north-facing window will do wonders. A standing fan is great; Grandma always had one by the window behind the piano, and another in the kitchen (which also faced north).

Best of all is a ceiling fan, and if I had the money for it, I would not get AC, I would put a ceiling fan in every room. Even with AC, you should have ceiling fans. Turn the light off, and get the ceiling fan cranked up (in winter, reverse the direction and set it on low; you will be amazed at how much warmer the room feels). Yet, there is still peace and quiet.

If you are lucky enough to have a screened-in porch, keep it shaded with your landscaping or bamboo blinds during the hot hours. The air that goes through it will cool your whole house on all but the hottest days.

I don't have a screened-in porch but I do have a shady deck, onto which open the slider in my kitchen and a window that lets out to a shady nook at the back of the deck on the shared wall. I can leave the window open even during a storm, because it's protected by the little alcove, and it's always cool.

I was thrilled *finally to* replace the less-than-pleasing light over our kitchen table with the fan. I know it paid for itself the first year in heat savings, and it makes the kitchen pleasant in the hot weather.

At night, once you are used to it, a fan is just as cooling as AC and a lot quieter. On the very hottest nights have the children sponge bathe with cold water or take a quick dip in a cold tub right before bed. An indirectly placed fan (or that wonderful ceiling fan) will have them sleeping better than the frigid, unrefreshed air of the AC.

In short, keep in mind that your body experiences cooling as a "zone" and not a temperature point. What matters most is the sensation of air flowing over your body, and that is why air current and, of course, fans help a lot. If you live where you must have AC, make it a priority to install ceiling fans as well; you can set your cooling higher and be more comfortable.[14]

Pace your activity. The hottest hours are a good time for quiet reading. Keep your lemonade cold and take the hot days a bit slower, rather than trying to obliterate them.

In regions where you simply *must* use AC, you will save on your bill with my methods. Yes, you can open a window while the AC is on if the air coming in is *cooler* than your setting. How many houses have I been in with the sun pouring in the south-facing, uncovered windows *and* the AC cranked up? This is madness.

Try not to bake or turn on the oven during the day; use your mornings or evenings and bake enough for several days. Use the grill to keep the heat of cooking outside. Set up a simple outdoor or garage kitchen using a hose in an old sink and an outlet for your slow cooker and hotplate alongside your grill. But for the most part, use the least-intense method of cooking you can, and go for cold food when possible.

---

[14] Lloyd Alter, "Why Are We So Reliant on Air Conditioning? (It's Not Just Climate Change, It's Bad Design)," Treehugger, updated June 5, 2017, https://www.treehugger.com/why-are-we-so-reliant-on-air-conditioning-its-not-just-climate-4861463.

Shading your house with deciduous trees helps. Sleep with open windows if you can. Use an attic fan to pull the hot air up and out, while the cooler night air comes in your windows. In the morning, shut it off and draw your blinds and curtains. You can tint your southern windows! And an overhang that lets in the slanting winter, but not the high summer, sun will be a lifesaver.

If you have forced-air heat, you can turn on the fan (leaving the heat off, of course!) and open interior doors. This draws cooler air up from the basement, circulating it through the house. Box fans pointed outward in the windows help discharge the hotter air upstairs.

Builders aren't required to design for airflow, so they don't. If you have the chance to build your own house, research on natural cooling and heating would pay off. For one thing, what about when the power fails? Look up evaporative coolers if you live in a place with relatively low humidity.

You feel much cooler in appropriate clothing. Jeans are not good for hot weather. Try light cotton skirts, and don't forget that linen is an amazing fabric that keeps you feeling cool.

Living frugally, we become committed to family life without too many needs. Some grew up that way; some learn later. Thriftiness enriches life, because who isn't better off with a screen door slamming, the outdoors not hermetically sealed off, the chirp of the crickets audible, the sounds of the children playing outside wafting in and out of our consciousness?

A life enclosed indoors all the time isn't a good one, I can't help thinking. I know that in some places there is a stretch when nothing can be done because of the heat. Certainly, here in northern climes, there are times when nothing can be done because of the cold and the ice. That's part of the rhythm of life. But when a breeze comes up, you want to catch it, not be oblivious to it because the stale air circulating around you prevents you from noticing. And, you know, kids are impervious to heat that slays adults, as long as they are given a respite. There is no reason to keep them inside when they could be out playing (rather than carting them to organized sports, season in and season out). Even if it's only a whiffle-ball game well before noon or a pickup basketball game in the evening with a kiddie pool in between, that's where memories are made.

ASK AUNTIE LEILA

Keeping the House Warm in Winter, Frugally

Dear Auntie Leila,

I'm hoping you can offer some wisdom on prepping the home (both house and people) for the winter months.

We are familiar with life in the cold, but it was before kids. I've never experienced a winter while running a household or with children. My boys are eight and one. My parents run a very efficient household but have trouble articulating exactly what it is they do and why.

Adding to my confusion is the fact that our new home is older (1940s). It is heated with steam radiators and has all the original windows. I was able to use some of your "keeping a home cool in the summer" tips and am hoping you may have similar tips for winter.

We have steam radiators, and I hadn't planned to install radiator covers. However, a neighbor mentioned that steam radiators get quite a bit hotter than water ones. Should I be concerned?

When is a good time to transition window screens to storm windows? I'd like to do a thorough cleaning while I'm switching them, but what if the weather turns warm again and I miss the screens? I'm thinking late October.

I've heard that large coats aren't supposed to be worn if a child is in a car seat. Assuming that a little one cannot yet take his coat off unassisted, do I put the coat on, walk out the door, get into the car, take his coat off, buckle him up and repeat in reverse order when getting out? Should I invest in a good-quality fleece coat for quick trips from the house to car and use the coat only when my son is outside?

Finally, I'm trying to slowly acquire the outerwear we will need this year. Any tips on brands or items that are a good investment?

Thank you!

McKenna

---

hat I am trying to do in these pages is gently help you know how to "live differently" — for instance, living on one income, knowing that perhaps you, like us, do not have the money to spend on luxuries like cranking up the heat.

I'm well aware that readers live in different parts of the country, of course. Some can't imagine temperatures lower than, say, the forties, but I'm not addressing their climate here. I also write with the idea that your children will not be climate controlled at all times but will want to play outside most of the time, regardless of how cold it gets.

Even those who live in the deep South can be hit with a cold snap in the teens or lower. Would you know how to cope? How about if the power goes out (often the case when the weather is extreme)? These are survival skills every mother needs to know. At least you will know which chapter to turn to here!

A lot depends on your circumstances. There's no question, for instance, that schools are overheated, so it really is folly to send a child all bundled up.

Yet, it's also strange to think that even as we collectively feel pretty guilty for using up the world's resources this way, we seem incapable of just turning down the heat in a public building and relying on people to know how to dress.

When this subject comes up, many will respond with a resistance that suggests that they think the heat will always be on, that the car will always be gassed up and working great (and that no crazy person will crash into it, that it will never run over a nail and get a flat tire), that the power will never go out. I get it that even in very cold conditions, the usual thing in our day and age is to go from one warm spot to another. But my point is that we have the luxury to do so.

If we don't, or if circumstances intervene, I myself like to know what to do—how to keep from dissolving into a helpless puddle of anxiety and neediness! So that's what I'm getting at here. I'm assuming that you, dear reader, actually want to know how people cope with, in this case, the cold, when the optimal conditions do not obtain.

With that explanation out of the way, on to the question!

Dear McKenna,

Here is what you need to know! You should install the storm windows in early fall, before absolute necessity sets in, while the weather is nice during the day. That way, it's not a problem for you to get them out, clean them, and make the necessary repairs. It's still warm enough for you to caulk around frames, which will really help keep things warm.

If your house is like my husband's parents' house (built in the 1920s), you also have screens to put away, and you want to be sure you do that in an orderly way (labeling carefully), saving yourself grief in the spring.

The days are still not so short that you would have to rush when you are cleaning windows, and the leaves haven't started blowing around and making things hard to clean.

You will probably find that the storm windows have a mechanism so that you can prop them open. Thus, if the weather is nice during the day, open them up at the bottom and push them out. You don't have to worry much about screens since the bugs are gone. (You can always get a few of those little adjustable half-window screens, but a stray wasp isn't really such a big deal; it will be too drowsy to be a problem.) Even if your windows don't have this feature, you can leave off one or two of your storms on the sunny side of the house and pop them on when things really get cold. You won't need much more than that.

This way, you can set your heat at a reasonable level and enjoy having it on in the chilly nights but still open a few windows during the warm days. It can get cold! Our heat will come on once or twice before the daytime temperatures go down as well, but I have replacement windows, so it didn't take long to close them up. (By the way, the old-fashioned windows work just as well with their storms, so don't worry; just keep them in good repair.)

The radiators probably will need covers. My parents-in-law had them (we have hot water heat, so only a few covers here). Covers give you a little more horizontal space on which to park a couple of kids or a stack of books; there is nothing wrong with them aesthetically (and a nice paint job will spruce them up if they are, in themselves, not presentable).

Figure out a way to make some sort of airlock arrangement where you enter the house, at least for the door you will use most. That is, your house will stay significantly more comfortable if your outside door doesn't open directly into your living area. If you can shut it before you open an interior door to get in, you prevent direct contact with frigid outside air! In my house, the door from the kitchen to the mudroom stays open until the heat goes on, and then I am very strict about keeping it shut! Yes, the mudroom is cold, but at least the whole kitchen isn't cold.

As you move through the year, consider, if you don't have this sort of arrangement, enclosing the porch and installing a door at the entry to the porch, which will then act as the winter "outside door." Or it might be that you need to build such a porch. Such are the joys (and expenses) of figuring out how to keep warm.

Now, you want to notice this year how the heat flow works in your house. Do you have zones for the system? If so, you want to set your upstairs to a lower temperature than the downstairs. The bedrooms really don't need to be as warm as the living areas, and of course, heat rises. When you have good bedding—flannel sheets, down comforters, duvet covers, wool blankets for in between the layers—you find it's preferable to sleep in air that is not too stuffy. When the heat is high, everyone wakes up with stuffed noses and headaches, and the rooms get very dusty.

Babies should wear cotton pajamas with fleece blanket sleepers zipped over them. The cotton is to wick moisture, because they will sweat. I had an eczema sufferer, and that salty sweat really aggravated his rashes. With the cotton, all was well. If it's really cold, put cotton socks on under the footies of the blanket sleeper as well.

Blanket sleepers can have feet or be sacks—the best kind of sacks are sleeveless. That way, Baby can be warm but not overheated, and if it's really cold, you can add a layer underneath the sack.

The children should wear flannel pjs with undershirts underneath. Undershirts are the key to feeling cozy but not overheated.

Here is the purpose of the undershirt, my dear readers: it's so that you have a layer that you do not remove, keeping your body heat close. A child can put his undershirt in the wash before his bath. After his bath, he puts a clean one on, tucked into his underpants. The PJs get put away and the clothes go on, but never is the poor bare skin exposed to that lower temperature in the bedrooms.

That's the old-fashioned way. Maybe today people just pay no attention to that sort of thing (I know I had to figure it out), but it's good to remember it in case, for some reason, it's much colder than you expected—for instance, when the power goes out and you aren't able to check into a hotel for the duration.

Slippers make a huge difference to how we feel about the cold. They should be easy to get on and off, but enclosed and comfortable. Wool socks work well too, but a leather sole helps with slipping. For a full treatment of how to dress warmly in winter, see "On Dressing Children in Cold Weather," in volume 1.

Anyway, back to the house. Even if you only have one zone, you can keep the different areas warm if you have doors to shut. Your challenge will be keeping the warm air downstairs. Yes, you can go on heating the first level continuously all day, or you can keep the heated air downstairs.

You may notice one area where the heat really escapes and there isn't a door. You can install a heavy curtain there. Use a strong rod (conduit pipe works well and is inexpensive) and nice matelessé quilts or heavy velvet curtains (these often turn up at thrift stores). You can even block off a stairway this way, using curtains or quilts and as many rods as you need, attaching them to the ceiling with the appropriate plumber's strap if you need to (just be sure you attach anything like this to a stud).

Just as, in the summer, you kept the strong sun out of your rooms, in the winter, you want to let that sun in. A really well designed house takes advantage of the sun's angles in the different seasons. The overhangs on the eaves of the house can allow the low winter sun in, while shading the rooms in the summer, when the sun is higher in the sky. Even modern glass in the window itself can filter the light, or not, according to its angle.

As evening falls, close your shades or curtains (or preferably both) to keep the heat in. Wooden or insulated blinds, Roman shades, and heavy curtains really help with what are basically holes in your shelter.

That ceiling fan that cools you off in the summer can really help move the warm air down from the top of the room; simply reverse the direction by means of the little switch on the base.

If you have a fireplace, you can see how well it works this winter. Usually fireplaces, unless they are of the Rumford design, actually lose more heat than they provide, which is rather depressing! For more on Rumford fireplaces, read the little book called *The Forgotten Art of Building a Good Fireplace.*

Depending on how it goes this year, you might want to install an efficient woodburning stove in the fireplace, if yours is not one of the good kind. Combined with a ceiling fan and depending on how big and open your house is, you might find that you can use your central heat just to keep your pipes in the basement warm, using the stove as your main source. Just be sure to set the thermostat at the *right* low temperature, lest the woodstove prevent the heat from cycling on, exposing your pipes to freezing and possibly bursting.

In any case, an important part of just *feeling* warm is to have a source for the heat around which you can gather; radiant warmth makes you feel much warmer, as long as it's not whooshing past you on its way higher up, bringing cooler air in its wake; it's the same principle as feeling cooler when air is fanned. Convection heat is moving, so it does not feel as warm; it also tends to get trapped at the ceiling. Radiant heat reduces allergens for the same reason: the air isn't moving as much. (Of course, this advantage is offset by allergens produced by a woodstove.) For this reason, if you have to replace floors, you might want to consider radiant heat under the floor you replace.

Get in the habit of feeling around with your hands as you do things near your walls. It may be that cold air comes in via the outlets, and there is a cheap fix for that at the hardware store: you can insulate them! Window trim might need caulking. When you have to do repairs on siding or walls, you can add insulation. Over the years you can make your house a lot warmer just by paying attention!

Develop the *art* of keeping cozy, and that is as much psychological as anything. Carpets and rugs on the floor feel warmer. Throws and quilts on the sofas help you resist the urge to turn up the thermostat. Candlelight—even one small votive on the table—feels magical when it's dark and forbidding outside. In the warmer weather, you can stow the cozy things away in trunks and benches. I knew some old-fashioned ladies who had different curtains and bedspreads for winter and summer! Maybe such an approach was easier when there was more household help to take care of it all, but it goes to show you how people really did take seriously the change of seasons.

As to the question of children's outerwear: let's please all use some common sense. If it's the middle of winter and in the single digits, don't plan on removing a child's coat to get in the car. Choose coats and jackets that are not overly bulky; get a warm one that allows freedom of movement. Then make sure that the straps of the car seat are secure, especially checking the chest adjustment to be sure it's in place.

At the same time, remember that children tend to get overheated in the car. You can turn the heat down a bit once the car warms up; or if you're on a long trip, take the jacket off—but do have it handy in case of an emergency that exposes him to the elements.

Remember not to let all the child's body heat escape as you are getting out of the car and spending time outside. Conservation of body heat—that is what we are after.

Everyone needs a jacket that goes below the waist to the hips (so that when you sit down, your nether regions have some protection from the cold), a hat, a scarf, and mittens. Put the scarf on *under* the jacket, around the neck; it won't offer warmth if it's worn outside the jacket! If the jacket has to come off, at least the chest is still warm. Choose a jacket with knit wrist cuffs to keep the air from going up the sleeves. For children, the wrist cuffs help mittens stay on securely. A cord for the mittens that goes inside the jacket works to keep them from getting lost, as do little clips.

Little kids don't need bulky sweaters. They usually hate them, won't wear them, and get overheated in them. Instead, choose lighter layers that trap their body heat without confining them: an undershirt, a regular flannel or thick knit shirt, and if anything extra seems necessary, make it a something like a light, soft wool vest or fleece pullover. If the child runs warm, even a thin shirt will work, as long as there is an undershirt long enough to tuck in underneath. You will spare yourself the grouchy, fretful parts of the day if you follow this advice, because the process of getting your body heat back up makes a person cranky.

Girls need real pants, *not leggings alone*, or corduroy jumpers over good sturdy tights or leggings. The ideal outfit for a little girl is tights, undershirt or camisole, long-sleeve cotton shirt, corduroy jumper, cardigan if needed. Warm socks in boots. And most of all, do not let their little middles be exposed to the air. Tuck that T-shirt in!

PART 7

On Getting Organized

Obviously, we need lists, notes, and systems to be organized. Over the years I have been impatient with my discovery that the project of getting organized can itself take time and resources. Just think of the sheer variety of note systems that are offered, both real and virtual—some of them not inexpensive. Mindful of the distraction from true organization that the attempt to organize can represent, and further taking into consideration varying temperaments and concepts of efficiency, in this section I offer some thoughts on a reasonably orderly approach.

Using a Sticky-Note System
for the To-Do List

I've finally figured out a list-making system for that helps me get things done, rather than a system that exists for its own sake. I've long abandoned those planners that require their own block of time to manage. As if managing *my life* isn't hard enough—I find I cannot muster the strength to manage the planner as well.

Every morning, this is the conversation between Mr. Lawler and me:

He: "So, Hon, what are you doing today?"

Me: "Oh, getting organized."

Every day, the same conversation! Will I ever be organized? I doubt it, but I know this: lists are our friends. Possibly, with enough excellent lists, we may someday get organized for good; I sometimes think I will have "Getting Organized" inscribed on my tombstone.

My preferred list-material is cut-up scrap paper. I like to grab a pen and a scrap of paper and make a list. For years, that's how I did my to-dos: just jotted them down. Side effect: many lists all over the house, stuck in books, at the bottom of my purse, on the counter by the door, and *not* at the bottom of my purse in the store. Still, I do default to this method, even if I sometimes do take a phone pic of the list after I write it.

There's nothing like a piece of paper that costs you nothing—that you are repurposing and recycling—that you are positively being virtuous by using! This scrap-paper method frees me from decision-making about whether the list in question merits the using up of an official piece of notepaper or page in a notebook. "This note seems so trivial—do I really need to take up my precious notebook with it?" seems to be my thought process.

Besides the frugality of the scrap-paper system, consider its portability. In theory, I can have my little scrap out on a counter or in my pocket and then just trash it—but then this ephemeral quality, which I regard as a feature, is precisely the drawback.

The system of a small notebook and sticky notes, which I will detail for you, has solved this conflict for me to a great extent. It's not as frugal, for sure (and thus I do still write my grocery lists on scrap paper). But it might help someone with my peculiar preferences, simply because, by its flexibility, it facilitates of one of the most important principles of time management: *have a short to-do list.*

Have Only Three Things on Your To-Do List

I read a business-management article arguing that the most effective corporate executive types have only three to five things on their to-do list. As a mother, I know that there are already many, many things that are already on the list before I even get started, such as laundry, making meals, changing diapers, tidying up, and I also have to have planners for homeschooling and menus. So I say *three* things on your to-do list each day.

The big question becomes how to figure out what those three things are?

You need a little chunk of time for finding the answer as you get started, and I recommend sneaking it into whatever you consider your prayer time. This is because what we do with our time is very much a spiritual issue. Although I am no spiritual director, I do consider it *prayer* to sit in God's presence and discuss with Him all those things that make up our day, including *what we should do.*

You might say that the to-do list is where the rubber meets the road in doing His will. Even going to the grocery store is His will for me, if it's what I need to do today. One of the most important questions we can ask each day (and each moment, really) is simply, "Am I doing what You want me to be doing now, Lord?" "Do You really want me to tear out that closet today, Lord, or is there something else on Your mind?" (Also, taking the list to prayer, spiritually and physically, makes it possible to be just a wee bit less distracted, if you are the distractible type, not that I would know about that. Instead of fixating on that important thing I just remembered I have to do, trying to memorize it, I can jot it down and go back to prayer.)

I don't say this is *all* we should pray about or always pray about; or that we should do all the talking in prayer. But I have found it a good practical way to offer God my time; to lay it all out before Him and abandon it to His will.

At first, to set up this system, and every once in a while (on retreat, for instance, or at the start of a new season of some kind), sit with God, pen and paper in hand. Make a list of ten or twenty-five or fifty or however many things you think need to be done. This will be the master list. It should have all the things: getting photos organized, cleaning out closets, calling the insurance company, prioritizing home repairs, figuring out a bill-pay system, planning your school year—all the calls, all the projects, all the commitments.

Now, looking at all those things, which are the top three that you could do today? It's very likely that besides "call the insurance company" and "grocery shop," the third thing may be "make list of household repairs." Maybe the insurance company simply must be called today. Maybe you have to go to the store, or everyone will starve. It's probable that you won't actually start on repairs today, but making a list of them is the first step and a big hurdle. On the list it goes!

There you go. Three things—in addition, of course, to all your other duties, which just get done whether they are written down or not. That is, unless they are out of the ordinary—say, there are four laundry baskets that must be tackled, or you won't be able to do your normal laundry. If you are really just beginning to be efficient in your day as a housekeeper and a mother, then list those "other duties" in the order you see them getting done for today. Cross them off as you go. But as you become more experienced in managing the flow of the household, you can just leave those things off the list, as it can be oppressive to see them there in black and white. Too many items on a to-do list is counterproductive.

Now, what I've discovered is that using sticky notes really helps and represents a significant improvement over the scrap-paper method. The improvement consists in giving a *visual*, which I find important, and also in allowing disposal of that which has been completed, which I find gratifying. I personally don't need an archive of notes that say "call doctor," so I am happy to toss them.

For this method to work well, it seems really important that the notes go onto durable pages. As I was thinking through what I would do, I was picturing a small spiral-bound photo album, the pages of which are smooth, heavy cardstock with a landscape orientation. You don't want too many pages, though, because that's too much pressure to multiply the tasks! We have enough tasks as it is. But I couldn't find what I was looking for.

The sturdiness is hard to find. In theory you could have a "notebook" that consisted of two stout covers—just a folder, really. You would open it up and there would be your to-dos.

I quickly realized that I might have three or however many things to do today, but there are going to be a lot of other things that need to stay near the top of the list. This is the difference between my system and the others. Most other systems have you looking at the whole list. Whatever doesn't get done moves to the next day. You are always "not doing" a lot of things, and it can be discouraging to be reminded of that. With the three-item list you are doing all the things you've realistically chosen for that day.

When they are done, they disappear; the next items move up from the master list onto new sticky notes, according to their priority. Obviously, something will pop up that isn't on the master list; it can easily become one of your few things to do on your main page.

So the prioritized items from the master list, a certain proportion of them (I usually have ten or fifteen), are on the "tomorrow" page of this notebook.

I saw I would need tabs. Fortunately, you can get sticky *tabs*. The main thing is that the ability to change this system around — its flexibility — is very appealing to me. I don't like my organization to be too dedicated. I like to be able to feel that I'm not a slave to it but, rather, that it's serving me. I guess I have commitment anxiety when it comes to organization.

Your master list — that long list of the overwhelming multiplicity of things you have to do (but fear you'll never get to) — can go in the back pages, perhaps under "master list." And you can have other notes under their own tabs. The page you open up to every morning never changes — only the stickies on it change.

On the inside of the cover are prayers and special intentions. When I open my notebook in my prayer time (as described above), I have my intentions right there.

On the right, on the first page, are the to-dos — *just for today*. Some days I need a sort of schedule and almost hourly breakdown, and that's when a large, lined sticky note comes in handy. I can write in the relevant hours very quickly and jot in what I want to do, and when.

But usually it's one task per small note. It works to put three things on one note, of course, but if the jobs are in very different categories, it can help to have the notes separate so that you can visually group them. They can also be grouped in action order.

If I need an archive, there's that master list, and I can cross out the items I've taken care of. But most tasks are not memorable!

On the inside of the back cover, I made a pocket very simply using cardstock (a recycled greeting card you particularly like and can cut down works very well) and glue. I can store a ready supply of various sticky notes there, replenishing when needed.

Other pages in this notebook are for jottings as they occur to me: crafting hopes and dreams, gift ideas, writing notes, and so on. I have other notebooks and an index card file for more extensive thoughts and notes into which these quick notes can be easily transferred; for to-dos, this sticky-note system is the way that works the best for me.

There you have it. I've always wanted a to-do system that's flexible, portable, simple, and visual. I've tried many, many others. This is it for me. I still jot things down on scraps of paper (especially as I say, shopping lists), but now I put most of my thoughts on sticky notes in this little book when they become official to-do items.

Notes on To-Do Notes

If you have a new baby, a houseful of sick children, or are otherwise in a slowdown, know that you must have a to-do list, but your sanity depends on what is on that list. If your to-dos are "wash face, brush teeth," "change diapers," and "defrost chicken broth" then that's a good day's work in my book.

When I first conceived this sticky-note idea, I felt that its drawback is that Post-its are ridiculously pricey (also I'm not a fan of the colors). But knockoffs are fine, and once you get started, keep your eye out for the ones put on clearance in various places. Soon you will have a stash of them. I decided it was worth it to use what turns out to be at most about three a day (usually I put like items together on a note) for me to have a sense of peace about how my day was going. I figure you can buy a lot of marked-down sticky notes for the price of one expensive planner.

Additionally, you can buy a glue stick of the sort of glue that makes sticky notes and make your own sticky notes! This has a strange appeal to someone who cares about paper weight and color.

Grocery Lists

The only effective way to make your grocery list is *in order of the aisles*. You are going to forget things, even things written down. Make it less likely that you will forget by using the layout of the store, rather than the order in which the things occur to you, to organize your list.

Some people suggest having a master list with items you frequently buy, pre-printed and organized by aisle. They suggest that you check or circle the items you need. I have tried this system but quickly abandoned it. Different stores are arranged differently; you quickly memorize the layouts and can jot down items based on the store you are going to. I find that having all the things printed out is distracting and causes me to overlook things. The effort necessary to have a supply of these master lists printed out and to get one before dashing to the store, when you have scrap paper *right there*, makes it not worthwhile to me. I think that having *one* master list could work if you are a consistent item-forgetter; check it before you finalize yours.

Even if you are writing out a list as items occur to you (or have such a thing on a family blackboard, for instance), rewrite it in aisle-order.

The Honey Do List; or, the Psychology of the Individual

What about your to-do list for your husband—that is, those things you would like him to accomplish? I don't know how my husband gets me to do things, but I get him to do things by making a Honey Do list. Somehow, if it's written up there on our kitchen blackboard, he will get it done. If it's not, it becomes one of those things that are just part of the landscape. It's like the bare bulb at the top of the stairs. When you move in, you say, "Wow, how could those people have lived with a bare bulb at the top of their stairs? I mean, every day they saw that thing, didn't they? What was wrong with them?" Then, ten years later, you go to sell the house, and you think, "We could just say 'as is' and then we wouldn't have to deal with stuff like that bare bulb," *if* you even see it anymore, which is unlikely.

Now, the thing about the Honey Do list is that I don't always remember how well it works. But if *I* remember to put something on it, my husband will get to it on chore day. He loves the satisfaction of crossing jobs off his to-do list. Since nagging is not pleasant or even a good strategy, we find that this method is the best way to communicate and still be peaceful.

On Organizing
Household Information

To paraphrase Aristotle, we ought to have right order, which includes putting in the proper amount of time into achieving right order—the time itself must be ordered. In other words, I find that I often fail at my efforts to organize because of two things: I just don't (I am disordered), or I put an *inordinate* amount of time and energy into doing something that doesn't merit it.

Also, know thyself, because if you are the type to go down the rabbit hole of organizing systems, you may never emerge to, you know, get things done.

There is no one master system for complete life organization in list or any other form. It's a collection of various strategies (and they will always fall short due to Original Sin). I will tell you what works for me in the different areas, and perhaps that will help you evaluate the methods you come across and help you find the system that works for you. Just keep in mind the principle that order means that the system itself serves the order, not vice versa.

Menu Planning

In the food and menu chapters, I have offered a really foolproof method of getting the food organized, shopping for it, and keeping notes about it. I like to use a physical binder; among other things, it allows me to archive those scraps of paper that turn out to have valuable information about menu plans that succeeded, shopping lists that need not be replicated every holiday, and notes for recipes I've developed. I include in it the very best recipe for the things our family likes best—the best brownies, the best butter cake, the best lasagna.

My binder has such oddities as cardstock templates for gingerbread houses, along with the best method for icing that holds them together. Having those things all together saves me a hunt through my cookbooks or online. That's just one random example. Basically, the binder is a record of my food brain.

Thoughts and Events

For deep thoughts, I use notebooks, journals, and an online site that captures links of articles I don't want to lose. (I had used Evernote; I now use Pocket—no doubt by the time you read this, something different will have been developed.) I don't save all the links. Just the truly good things I want to return to—bits of info that, back in the day, you would have clipped and put in a filing cabinet.

One very pretty journal holds the birthdays, christening days, and other info on my grandchildren. I use my best handwriting in it. I agonized about how many pages to leave in between each child.

A more battered one is a journal for thoughts, events, and quotes, kept over decades. I have several of these that I have started over the years, and I am not sure what is in them.

Then there is the five-year journal. Let me try to explain the difference: I always thought I would remember the important events of my life (the events themselves, as opposed to how I felt when they happened and my deepest, most intimate thoughts about them), but the years go by, and I don't remember many of them, much less the year they occurred. Things like the names of the couple who befriended us in Rome, or even meeting anyone on that trip, or what my favorite restaurant was, or the sequence of events that time the sale of the house fell through, or what the lawyer's funny secretary said at the meeting. Ever wonder how, in their memoirs, people remember all those names and incidents?

Well, many of them had what amounts to a log. A five-year journal is that for me. It has one page for each day of the year, and that page has five divisions, so that each June 7 in that five-year period has its own section for quick notes on facts of the day.

Any time is a good time to start yours. It could be kept by more than one person in the family, or each member could have something like it when he expresses interest. The point is to log what happened—and that is why, in historical records, you will find "bought six carts of hay" along with "Father died," which seems heartless but—that's the kind of record it is. You write in it, just a little, every day.

Phone Log

Another very good sort of log for family life is the phone log. Now that we have cell phones, causing the central phone for the house to be somewhat superfluous or even nonexistent, this log might not seem that important, but I will tell you how it operated for us and you can figure out if you like the idea and can adapt it.

I had a small notebook and a supply of pens and pencils near the phone in the kitchen. I am the person who used it the most, but others made entries as well. Mainly, it was for information that is important at the moment, information for which you are not ready to make a determination as to whether it will continue to be important in the future.

If it is, you can transfer it elsewhere—to a contact list or an online file. It's for jotting down the number of the plumber your friend is giving you as you chat about her day. It's for recording the names of physical therapists the receptionist at the doctor's office gives you, so you can look them up.

Especially in a big family with many activities, it always seemed like someone was always giving me a little tidbit of information. Where to store it? When the coach tells you which field the practices will now be held on, you can write it down there. The name of a wine you liked, a recommendation for a book, the number for the friend who is picking up your child (but may never again) ... I found it very useful because my short-term memory is not as good as I think it will be, but I didn't want some number that might not turn out to be useful to be entered in a more permanent place. I found I often flipped the pages back a few days or weeks to find that little thing I had quickly noted. What *was* the name of the painter we didn't end up using but maybe should call now? It was in the log, so no problem.

When the doctor is giving you extra information about how to treat a sick child (information that might not be on the prescription bottle), you can write it in the log. Once the child recovers, you won't need those notes again.

The most treasured use for this log turned out to be recording funny things people, children and adults alike, said that we wanted to remember. Our Christmas letter developed into a hilarious collection of these quotes, all thanks to the log, because one wouldn't want to interrupt the conversation to pull out a phone or go hunt down some more permanent journal.

When the log fills up, you have the opportunity to transfer any really important information to more permanent place and then simply throw the log away.

Index Cards

Finally, I learned that, for purposes of writing and giving talks, I need quotes and references on index cards. So now you know how hopelessly old school I have become, reverting from digital efforts (that failed). There is no substitute, I have found, for going through those note cards and being able to handle them, put them in the order I want and need, and then file them back away.

I also learned—too late, alas, but trying to make up for it now—that it's a good idea to write in your books (one of the many good thoughts I learned in *How to Read a Book*, by Mortimer Adler). I used to be very much opposed to marking up a book; it seemed sacrilegious somehow. But I have found that you don't want to be forced to reread all your books in order to remember what you thought at the time. You want to have a conversation with your future, possibly busy-because-she's-preparing-a-talk-or-teaching-a-class-or-simply-making-a-point self. Underline and make notes in the margin in a way that doesn't make the text unreadable.

Online Calendar

The online calendar is a great boon to parents. You can see your recurring and one-time events *and those of your spouse and anyone else you add to it*. If you are both on the go, online is best. Ditto pulling all your calendars together. In the olden days, I had yet another binder for all the sports and activities calendars, and I'd have to transfer them all onto my big kitchen calendar. Now, that activity's calendar can be added to yours. You can color code them, and it's amazing. I used to wonder *why* my husband didn't know that we *always* had soccer on Tuesdays until I finally realized that just because it was engraved on my mind, there was no reason to think he had any awareness at all.

Pinterest

This online visual filing system can help you train your eye and become a better maker of your home. Pinterest can replace binders full of magazine clippings, and if you are working on a design project, whether it's building a house or trying to visualize a more efficient closet, Pinterest can help you zero in on the details that work.

I've used it to find images that help me with a specific problem. If your countertops are brown granite and you want inspiration for trim paint that looks best with them, putting that into a search and pinning the images that you like to a board called "Brown Granite Color Scheme" will help you find your answers. If you need ideas for built-in shelves in a corner, make a board specifically for the images you love that feature shelves in the corner.

Homeschooling

Each child gets his own binder, unless you are doing two in one grade level. The details for this binder can be found in volume 2. The homeschool binder will serve you well through the years.

Efficiency Can Be
Taken Too Far

A good planner and to-do list are indispensable, for sure. I do want to say that it might perhaps be misguided to wake up in the morning very, *very* goal-oriented, or at least very aware that everyone *else* is goal-oriented and we are, by comparison, falling behind.

Amid achieving things and decluttering things and making sure we are bursting with explosions of creativity—all of which, of course, I endorse—we might pause each day to think about how much it means to those around us to find us peaceful.

The drive to check off all the boxes can make normal things seem like obstacles. I'm here to report that, for instance, babies are not efficient—but that this inefficiency is what makes babies so wonderful and precious.

In other words, I offer for your consideration that the seeming pointlessness of daily life in making a home may be a result of our not having the vantage point necessary *to see the whole.* And these circumstances of life that seem so, well, not fabulously indicative of our self-realization and, on the contrary, positively derail it, may be God's way of helping, not hindering, us on our path.

At this strange point in history, we have very little direction from our spiritual leaders to help us see that we are here on earth not to perform to some worldly standard and become all we can be, *our best selves, this instant,* but simply to do God's will and be with Him in Heaven.

And yet, each day is *also* full of things we need to do!

Today as I write this, the Office of Readings (from a letter of Pope St. Clement I to the Corinthians) explained the paradox well, and suited my theme:

> It is obvious, therefore, that none of these owed their honour and exaltation to themselves, or to their own labours, or to their deeds of virtue. No; they owed everything to God's will. So likewise with us, who by his will are called in Christ Jesus. We are not justified by our wisdom, intelligence, piety, or by any action of ours, however holy, but by faith, the one means by which God has justified men from the beginning. To him be glory for ever and ever. Amen....
>
> What must we do then, brothers? Give up good works? Stop practising Christian love? God forbid! We must be ready and eager for every opportunity to do good, and put our whole heart into it. Even the Creator and Lord of the universe rejoices in his works. By his supreme power he set the heavens in their place; by his infinite wisdom he gave them their order.
>
> Your peaceful work is a gift to others.

ASK AUNTIE LEILA

Setting Up Housekeeping, Making a Home

Here's a question I received. I hope the answer might help young wives recover this vision of peaceful orderliness and calm wonder I'm speaking of:

Dear Auntie Leila,

How do I organize a new house and new things obtained from our wedding registry? How do I set up housekeeping, and what do I do to keep it all running smoothly? What do you wish you had known when you were young and just setting up house? I'm not married yet, but two weeks from today I will be, and I'm feeling a bit overwhelmed at the prospect of having to make so many decisions about how things will be done! My mother was never the best at keeping house, so I don't have her example to follow.

A New Bride

---

ear New Bride,

This book is an attempt to answer just that question! But to put it in capsule form:

Enjoy the honeymoon! Don't worry. You are already far, far ahead of the game just by identifying the *need* to set up housekeeping and indeed be the arbiter of how your house is kept, as opposed to the victim of it.

In fact, since it takes most of us at least a decade or two to figure out that there is anything to be identified, let alone that we are the subject of this identification, you can take some time off while patting yourself on the back. Good job!

As soon as you get home—yes, your new home!—make your bed with the pretty sheets and bedding you received as gifts. If you can possibly wash the sheets first, do, but if not, don't worry; just do it soon. Remember, your bedroom is the sanctuary of your marriage. So this is your first lesson in housekeeping—ordering things correctly. Military wives know to hang your pretty things on the wall right away, not putting it off. This may seem like the reverse of correct order, but they have experience in what makes a new place feel homey.

Put a pretty tablecloth on the table, and make a nice supper, having provided yourself with what you need for supper, even if it means paper plates for now.

As you open your gifts, consider returning the items that don't make your heart go pit-a-pat, even if they are things you registered for. There's no shame in realizing that perhaps, for some of the items, you might have succumbed to a combination of enthusiasm for getting all the stuff, inexperience about what is truly helpful for you in your circumstances, and the store's capitalization on those two states of mind.

I'm not talking about making rash determinations about unusual gifts. Sometimes it takes time to assimilate those unique items. Sometimes they fit a need or desire you don't yet know you have, but the givers are more experienced, and often the gifts are not returnable in any case. But sometimes the return window is small, and it's worth admitting that you need to use it.

Before you completely open every box after unwrapping, be honest about whether the things will fit in your new home (which I will assume is going to be modest, in the approved newlywed mode). Remember, the gift was given for one reason: to make you happy. You might get, instead, something different or scaled down — for instance, only three of the twelve pots and pans in the set. But that is all you will need until such time as you have a baseball-team number of children — at which point you won't need three sizes of sauce pot; you will need one twenty-quart stock pot.

Another way to distinguish what makes your heart go pit-a-pat from what doesn't is this justly famous quote we reflected on earlier from William Morris: "Have nothing in your house that you do not know to be useful or believe to be beautiful."

Ponder the things you have each brought into the house from your previous lives apart as you find places for them. Again, don't do anything rash, but ask yourself if you have done what so many of us do, which is simply move things because they are things and moving is what you are doing. That box of T-shirts from high school? The collection of souvenir mugs from basketball venues? Maybe it's time to say goodbye.

Have lots of conversations about your future together and how you want it to be. Talk about what you really love about homes you have experienced. Get to know each other's hopes and dreams. Don't let people's exhortations and misplaced urgency about enjoying your newlywed state rob you of *this* enjoyment. Yes, you only live once. Yes, there are lots of fun things to do as newlyweds. Yes, you may someday find yourself owning two minivans and incapable of thinking beyond the children's activity schedules. But still, the real fun of this period in your life is hoping and dreaming. Do what *you* want to do to get ready for your future — not what other people deem appropriate, which ends up putting off that future.

In the course of these wonderful talks, use some of the time to set priorities, especially about how you will spend your money. Housekeeping is all about living well, within your means, and using your resources with wisdom to achieve your goals.

I wish I had done that — really thought through what would be important to me five, ten, and twenty years on, and then worked to make those things happen. Some goals I think are worthwhile: a home of your own; the education of your children, should God grant you children; and the environment you want as they are growing up. I wish I had made it a priority to find a modest place to vacation, where the children would make good memories and have a lot of freedom. Think of an enjoyable activity that you, your husband, and your future family can all do together, in terms of recreation, if you don't already have one.

Education here does not mean saving for college, which I think is pointless for most people of modest means. I am talking about having a good home library, musical instruments, opportunities for interacting with interesting people, and access to nature. Now *those* are worth investing in.

Carve out some space for creativity. Use your ingenuity to make it happen where you are. Think about how your creativity can serve your future. If you are imagining a home filled with quilts or knit blankets, or your own paintings, or refinished furniture, see how you can make yourself a little corner to do those things in and a budget for what you will need.

Read. Now is when you have time to read about how to cook, how to clean, how to do those creative things. You can learn more about education, philosophy, and gardening for that someday when you have a little plot to call your own or can access a community garden; you can learn to be frugal! Now is the time to read good novels and to get those thousand good books that John Senior identifies, the solid reading of childhood and youth, under your belt so that you aren't rushing when you suddenly need to get your children's reading in order—and to get a start on the hundred great books, the great and often demanding classics of Western civilization—so that you yourself can join the Great Conversation (that interaction of great minds that transcends time and space), if you haven't already. Now is the time to invest in worthy books and the time to read them.

Use Pinterest, or whatever design and inspiration app that's current, well. Does that sound frivolous? I firmly believe that it's a great tool for the homemaker. Back in the day, we cut pictures we loved out of magazines and kept them in a file. Now there's Pinterest. The Internet is a boon for homemakers, as long as you don't get caught up in fantasizing about perfection. Use it to record how others in your situation *solve problems* and reach their goals. As you seek answers to your questions, keep a record on your inspiration boards of what you find interesting, helpful, and beautiful.

Have a particular problem? For instance, are you wondering what shade to paint the kitchen walls when you have counters of a certain color? Are you gardening with a very specific challenge in your landscape? Do a search for the exact issue, and pin the results that spark your imagination. Go back and edit often. Pay attention, and it will really help you train your eye and learn to find solutions.

Try replacing the category of "decorating"—procuring things to beautify your home—with "putting your pretty things around." For those of us with limited means, the thought that we can't have something perfect makes us think we can't have anything at all. For a long time, I worked that way, assuming that if my dwelling couldn't be architect designed and professionally furnished, well, what was the use? The perils of very high standards!

I would tell myself that "someday" I would have everything "decorated," but "for now" I wouldn't bother, since I couldn't afford what I really wanted. Ah, that "someday"! What a wasting thought! I don't "decorate," although I might occasionally use that word. I just try to make things the way they are, only cleaner, prettier, and happier.

I believe that our homes should serve this goal: to make a proper place for the life of *this* family—one that we, together, think is beautiful and fitting, and one that offers to anyone who visits us a warm, loving welcome.

Remember, you can do a lot in an hour. You can do what *you* want to do and think should be done—especially if you are showered, have a plan for dinner, and have the laundry process under control (this one perhaps won't be as much of an issue for you now, but cast a thought in its direction anyway).

You can also look at your hours and think about how to make them orderly, bringing time into contact with God's inner life. This is liturgical living. Make your Sundays different and set apart, and you will find that everything else falls into place.

Enjoyment and doing what you want to do as a couple are mysterious realities: this week you don't have sanctifying grace to participate in the life of Christ with your true love—next week, after the wedding, you will. It's not up to Auntie Leila to do more than brush you off, set you on your feet, and give you a little push. You will run the race *your way.* And a marvelously unique way it will be!

You are making your home—your contribution to the world, a great adventure! There are means, and you will discover what they are, because you are clever and have an inquiring mind. And those means will lead you to the end: nothing less than God's kingdom.

Hope for When You Regret the Past

We have looked at how to set up housekeeping—and a real home—when starting out married life, but maybe some of you had a pang if, like me, you are already down the road without having done much of the practical or spiritual things I talked about; without realizing what was important until it was too late.

I know some of you do get these pangs, because you have written to me in this vein:

> It makes me tear my hair out to think of how I spent my twenties so foolishly, so disordered toward the faithful family life we are creating now.

Why didn't anyone tell me this before?

I do have a little to say about this regretting of the past, and *what might have been*. Whether it's regretting not realizing the importance of what you do in the home, not having true devotion, or having taken wrong turns, I want you to know what kind of hope God has for you.

Some of you are good with the past and are good with how you've used your time, and, well, God bless you. That's what the Irish say when they *really* mean "You're crazy"—as in "You have seven children? God bless you!" Or sometimes they *really* mean "Are you for real?"—as in "You have no regrets about the past? God bless you."

As for me, apart from the really awful things I've done pretty much on purpose, and all the stupid and ridiculous things I've done out of ignorance, there's just all the falling short and wasted time and serious ways in which I have not been kind or sweet or any of those things that I've recently discovered are important.

One day I discovered the remedy for this feeling—a little lifeline of hope. Not in the "Jesus died to save me from my sins" kind of way, which is, of course, at the back of everything I'm going to tell you—no need to mention it. Not even in the "Heaven will be our reward" kind of way, although sometimes that is all that keeps me going.

It's more a specific prayer that helps me with the actual, specific feeling of having *wasted time and ruined everything*.

Now, feelings are quite separate from objective facts, so even if we've repented and confessed and made reparation, we can still be so frustrated at the feeling (which, after all, is based on fact) that we've *not done what we ought to do*, and now our life is falling short in all these ways. This really is just life, and no one should be surprised that I, at least, wasn't able to wrestle all of it into the shape of my dreams.

Not that there isn't always much to be grateful for, for many are suffering much worse things than I (or you). It's just the defeat of it all ... way back when; some of which may not have been our fault. Sometimes we suffer misfortune, and what could be termed crop failures of the soul: floods and droughts, real and metaphorical; events not necessarily of our own making. And some things very much of our own making.

Sometimes the bitterness is hard to overcome. Especially when we get to that place where we see that things might have worked out, *if we had known then what we know now!*

This hope, this lifeline I'm speaking of first came to me in the form of a little scrap of Scripture: "And I will restore to you the years that the locust hath eaten" (Joel 2:25, KJV). It's a promise from God. He will restore the years.

Now, the chapter in the book of Joel from which this verse is taken is about many things. It's a prophecy about the redemption of Israel. It's apocalyptic and earth shaking and concerns the whole revolution of the universe in the day of the Lord. Its imagery is vivid: the blackness, the fire, the horses, the vats overflowing with wine and oil. The message is not a rosy, fairy-tale one.

And yet there's a tiny bit of comfort there for the *here and now*, for our own interior parched land, and for the desolation of the past. It's not *just* that He will take us from here, leaving behind the mess, and deliver us to a better place (although He will do that if we rend our hearts and not our garments, as He mentions).

He's specifically saying that *He will give back the years.*

Later, as I began doing the Office of Readings, I noticed how often we pray Psalm 90 (89 in some versions). Read it for yourself. Try the Revised Standard Version to get the full effect of what I am trying to say.

The first part of this psalm is about what I've been trying to say here. It's a lament for how short man's time is compared with God's time, and how futile things can seem—even our efforts. The psalmist sees how even our objective successes seem to us, in this light, like the children of men returning to dust; like grass withering. Have we done what we ought to do? This is what worries us, because we can sort of see the answer.

Then He puts the words in our mouths, words *we* should say to *Him*: "Make us glad as many days as thou hast afflicted us,/ and as many years as we have seen evil" (v. 15). Just as we say to our children, "Say, 'Mama, please give me the cherry,' and then I will give it to you," God is saying to us, "Say, 'Teach us to number our days aright. . . . Give me back the years. Make it up to me.' And then I will."

Now, we aren't babies, so we have to have the right kind of vision to see what He will do. We also have to have gone through those years of the dry times (so it's not a prayer that can be prayed too soon). And it's not that if we have faith, we will prosper—not according to how the world thinks of prosperity, most likely. Certainly, He didn't make His own Son to prosper. On the other hand, there are His words. We must trust and hope.

Pray this prayer of Psalm 90:15 and then have hope, let go, and trust. Remember Joel 2:25, when the memory of the locusts bites. He will restore the years, just as they ought to be, and the work of our hands will grow. And we will be the ones to tell the others of His goodness—we alone, who experienced it in just this way.

Make Something Beautiful

Do you have some handwork that you love to do, or some other creative outlet?

I've been quilting for about twenty-five years. I don't have many quilts to show for all that time, because I was learning when my kids were really little and had to take breaks because I was too pregnant to cut material out on the floor, or had a nursing baby in my arms all the time, or just couldn't get to it.

But you know, it's very fulfilling to be making something—to do something loving and creative even when you feel as if you are too busy. I have found that scheduling the time necessary to set myself up with a project yields major dividends in finding myself prepared later, at unexpected moments, when I can reach for my quilt bag and pull out my handwork. It's the setting up that's difficult. But with some thought, it can be done.

We need to learn to enjoy our days, to take satisfaction in small acts of beauty, however humble.

The recovery of this sense of satisfaction will lead us to be better to the people around us: kinder, more patient, and more affirming. I say "recovery," because I think that before the feminist revolution, the great majority of women, simply and without much fanfare, led quite satisfied lives, in no small part thanks to the little touches they gave their homes, without too much regard to the high fashions of the day.

I know that my grandmother, who raised seven children (without indoor plumbing for a good deal of the time), made lovely objects that were part of daily life at home, and she wasn't alone in doing so. I think this is why I'm drawn to crafts and styles from her day. I am drawn to the idea that women put so much creativity into their homes, with so little to work with. Quilting does have the advantage that the materials are not difficult to come by.

The problem with keeping the household is that many of the things we do each day are ephemeral. Worthwhile, but quickly undone! The same dishes get dirty again, sometimes within minutes. A clean room seems to attract little people with crayons, clay, and grand visions of sofa-cushion-fort architecture. Even a lovely meal doesn't have a long life.

If you have been sort of drowning in the riptides of your life, I encourage you to ask yourself what makes you feel really happy in a homemaking kind of way. Getting the knitting needles in your hands? Making a bag? Doing crewel embroidery?

I have a friend who tells me how energized she feels walking into her sewing studio, and I concur. It's a bracing feeling. And you don't need a whole studio! What if your sewing machine were on a little table in a closet, under a window, or in a corner? Mine is in my pantry on an ugly old office desk that I spray-painted black. I've seen a perfectly tidy, well-appointed little master bedroom with a sweet little sewing machine table against one wall in a corner.

There are many ideas online for creating a craft corner, and I find the visuals extremely helpful. The key is to make it pretty! If your machine is out, you won't dread it. It's only when your crafting items encroach on your main living spaces in that perched way that creativity turns burdensome.

If it's something like working with furniture, pottery, or sculpting, you may also want to take up needlepoint, only because it's hard to throw a pot while watching a baseball game or sitting outside of dance class. You can get a lot done in those hours here and there, just sitting and waiting. I like to talk to other moms—I think most of us are starved for conversation, aren't we? But I don't like to just sit there with my hands idle.

Remember the Middletons in *Sense and Sensibility*? "He hunted and shot, and she humoured her children; and these were their only resources." At least Sir Middleton had the advantage of a warm personality; Lady Middleton was cold. And, as Jane Austen tells us, she has nothing to do.

In contrast to this figure of mindless leisure are the women in *The Quilters: Women and Domestic Art, an Oral History*.[15] These pioneers give an inspiring example of creativity in the midst of astonishing activity: days of backbreaking work in the cotton fields in West Texas that put our soft situations to shame, although they seem not to complain much. And they made the things because they needed them, yet what they made transcended utility.

I enjoyed every moment of reading about these lovely women and their clever melding of their social and work lives into a beautiful and productive unity. Their communities seemed to thrive along with their creativity. I also love how the book reveals the men's interest in the women's handwork and their support for and participation in it (often surreptitiously!). Making beautiful things is a necessity in living the good life.

---

[15] Patricia Cooper and Norma Bradley Allen, *The Quilters: Women and Domestic Art: An Oral History* (Lubbock, TX: Texas Tech University Press, 1999).

Final Thoughts about Keeping Your Home

Wonder (joy and peace) cannot be obtained without Order. The temptation is to set out for perfection; the result of doing that is dissatisfaction. Instead, be willing to ask of yourself the minimum, which, in the case of housekeeping, is food and clean laundry!

When you suddenly feel very busy, I encourage you not to abandon your planning, but to take a little time to plan your menus *around your activities*—easy meals on running-around days, more labor-intensive ones on days you are at home. The truth is, only you can do it, because only you know which days you are running around and which days you are able to spend more time cooking. Only you know you have half a ham in the fridge and sweet potatoes in the pantry. Only you know that on a certain day, everyone needs a bigger meal than usual, but on another day a pot of soup will fit the bill.

But figuring these things out is not difficult if you use my methods. Go back and read how to get this done once and for all, using not *my* ideas of what *my* family likes but your very own family's tastes and preferences and special diets. In fact, your family does the hard work for you! No other method offers you that.

Save a step and tuck a few key things in your freezer as you go, as I outlined in the menu-making section. Personally, I just get very tired if I have to do too many things in one day, or if I have to be on my feet for too long. I can't manage a marathon in the kitchen, but I *can* do a little extra preparation a few days a week to make my life easier most of the time.

If you go from on-the-fly shopping to planning menus, even without shopping your store's specials or employing the really intensive saver's store-hopping method, I foresee that you will cut your grocery bill by at least one-third. That doesn't even count the money saved from eliminating emergency takeout and restaurant indulgences. But even more than the money saved is the peace of mind that comes with knowing that your children are not subsisting on spaghetti and pizza alone.

Once you have made the effort to get to the bottom of your laundry room (literally, to be able to see the floor), staying on top of the washing, folding, and putting away according to my plan (which has you spread out the process rather than impose the impossible task, in a large family, of doing it all at once), you will experience the freedom offered by minimal competence.

Keep your home reasonably clean as I have outlined. Your bedroom is the place to begin (not the kitchen). Every day, leave it with the bed made and things picked up. When you start your cleaning routine, start there. This can be life-changing because your bedroom represents the bedrock of your marriage.

If you do these two things, know what's for dinner, and know that you will get through your house at least once a week—oh, and the laundry: can't forget that, as if the piles won't be their own reminder—yes, if you do these *three* things, you will begin to experience a deep satisfaction in your home life. Your worries, frustrations, and discontents will abate. You will not yell as much. (Did you know that you yell because you think someone else should be dealing with the situation? You think your kids should deal with the disorganization of your life.) You will have at least this much peace, the peace of knowing that things are not irredeemably messy and that there's something to eat and clean underwear to put on.

The Reasonably Clean House is not about perfection, but about competence, about trying to have a minimum of order so that we can experience Order and Wonder—order in the home, order in our days; wonder in our time together as family and friends and with God.

You can't have one without the other, but don't let obtaining them disrupt your spirit. Approach everything with peace, with a sense of confidence that, having understood the mess, the dirt, the hunger of the little ones, or the piles of laundry, solutions will be forthcoming under the gaze of God. Resolve to do the minimum, the least you can do, with a good heart.

Pope Pius XI spoke of the woman's "truly regal throne to which she has been raised within the walls of the home by means of the Gospel." She ascends this throne only by desiring it and by being willing to serve and love and, yes, grapple with all she finds along the path to it. My hope is that these volumes offer encouragement in the journey and, above all, the perspective that our true home is not here on earth: it's with the saints and angels in Heaven, with God.

Appendices

APPENDIX A

Breakfast Recipes

Buttermilk Baking Mix

Make your own mix, and store in the refrigerator. Halve the recipe at first to see how you like it. It's versatile, and the pancakes it makes are very light and good!

Ingredients

10 cups unbleached flour

1 cup whole wheat flour (or just add another cup of white flour, making 11 cups)

1 cup oat flour (process regular oatmeal in the food processor or the blender until finely ground; one cup of oatmeal will give you one cup of oat flour) or 1/2 cup oat bran

1/2 cup wheat bran

1/4 cup wheat germ

1/2 cup flax meal

1 1/2 tablespoons salt

1 tablespoon sugar

2 tablespoons baking soda

6 tablespoons baking powder (I have used as little as 4 tablespoons when I have found myself short of baking powder)

3 sticks (12 ounces) butter or 2 sticks butter and 1/2 cup coconut oil

Feel free to substitute various flours and meals, using all flax meal if you are out of bran, and so forth.

Directions

You can process your baking soda and baking powder with your oatmeal to remove any lumps and facilitate distribution in the mix.

Measure all the ingredients except the butter into a large bowl. Stir to mix.

In the food processor or a large bowl, cut together several cups of the flour mixture and a stick of butter until it resembles coarse cornmeal. Set aside and repeat with each butter stick. Then mix the batches together before you divide for storage or use.

Store in the refrigerator in tightly a covered container or in a ziplock bag with the air pressed out. A large, slim, rectangular container is the most space efficient for the refrigerator. I use a plastic container meant for bulk cereals. It holds about two quarts and is large enough for all this mix.

To use, spoon, don't pack, the mixture into a cup. Unless you've used all coconut oil, be sure to refrigerate the leftover mixture so the butter will not become rancid.

Biscuits

Serves 4 to 6 as an accompaniment to a bowl of soup

Ingredients

2 cups Buttermilk Baking Mix

2/3 cup milk

Directions

No need to measure precisely. Measure the cold mix (cold so that the butter will stay in lumps) into a bowl, add about 2/3 cup of buttermilk (or a combination with some milk if you like), little by little, until you get the proper consistency, which is somewhat dry—not like a batter but closer to a pie crust; dry enough to be able to knead. Turn the mix out on your clean counter and gently knead it about six times or until it just holds together. Roll the dough out roughly, cut it in half, put one half on top of the other, and roll it out again to the thickness of an inch. Cut your biscuits with a round cutter or simply cut rectangles (this method eliminates the problem of scraps). Put biscuits in a greased pan and bake for about 8 minutes at 425 degrees or until puffed and golden brown.

Note that the gentle kneading and stacking gave you nicely layered biscuits!

Pancakes

Serves 4 to 6

Ingredients

2 cups Buttermilk Baking Mix
1/2 cup flour (whole wheat or all-purpose)
2 eggs
2 cups buttermilk

Directions

Combine the mix and the flour in a large mixing bowl. Make a well in the center. Add the eggs and lightly beat them in the well.

Add the buttermilk and lightly incorporate it into the mix. Avoid beating the mix, which will make your pancakes tough. Instead, keep the part that's mixed very wet as you pull in all the dry ingredients gradually. Stop before you think you are done.

Your mixture should be lumpy and light and battery. As you make your pancakes, you will give the batter a gentle stir each time you dip in your spoon, so allow for that.

Ladle by scant half cups onto a sizzling griddle. Allow small bubbles to form on the surface, flip, and cook until done.

Scones

This mix makes a fluffier kind of scone.

Ingredients

3 1/2 cups Buttermilk Baking Mix
2/3 cup sugar
1 cup nuts or dried fruit
2 eggs
1/2 cup light cream
1/2 cup buttermilk

Directions

Combine the mix, the sugar, and the nuts or dried fruit.

Combine the eggs, the cream, and the buttermilk, and add the mixture to the dry ingredients.

Turn the dough onto a clean, floured counter and gently knead it by folding one side over onto the other using a bench scraper or a spatula, give it a few pats, and repeating until it holds together somewhat.

Divide the dough into four pieces and form each one into a round. Gently roll each round until it is about one and a half inches thick. Using your bench scraper, move each round onto a baking sheet; all four should fit fine. Cut each round into six or eight wedges, pulling the wedges apart slightly.

Brush with more cream and sprinkle with sugar (raw sugar gives a good crunch). Bake at 425 degrees until golden brown, about 15 minutes (less for a convection oven or for smaller scones).

Waffles

These waffles are light, crispy, and tender.
Serves 4 to 6

Ingredients

2 cups Buttermilk Baking Mix
1 cup flour
1/4 cup cornstarch
1/4 cup sugar
2 eggs
3 cups buttermilk
1/2 cup milk

Directions

Preheat the waffle iron.

Combine the dry ingredients (the mix through the sugar) in a large mixing bowl. Make a well in the center. Add the eggs and lightly beat them in the well.

Add the buttermilk and the milk and lightly incorporate them into the mix. Avoid beating the mix, which will make your waffles tough. Instead, keep the part that's mixed very wet as you pull in all the dry ingredients gradually. Stop before you think you are done.

Your mixture should be lumpy and light and battery.

As you make your waffles, you will give the batter a gentle stir each time you dip in your spoon, so allow for that.

Lightly grease the waffle iron, if necessary (the more you grease, the less crispy the waffles, counterintuitively). Pour in the amount of batter your waffle iron's manufacturer recommends and bake.

Place cooked waffles on a rack if you are not serving immediately. You can hold them in a warm oven if necessary; the rack will help them remain crisp.

Night-Before Breakfast Casserole

*There are many recipes like this out there. I prefer mine
somewhat on the substantial side, so I like this one.*

Ingredients

1 1/2 pounds bread (I use homemade; raisin bread is lovely), cut
into cubes
cooked bacon or sausage
12 eggs
2 1/2 cups whole milk (add more milk for a lighter texture; I like
mine substantial)
1 teaspoon vanilla
1/2 cup sugar (if you want it a bit more like French toast)
1 teaspoon salt
2 teaspoons cinnamon
1 cup shredded cheddar cheese (optional)

Directions

The night before you intend to serve this casserole, butter a large lasagna pan. Fill the pan with the bread cubes to within an inch of the top.

Add up to a pound of crumbled cooked bacon or sausage. This is a good way to use leftover breakfast meat (in the unlikely event you have any). Even a sprinkling of bacon bits is appreciated. A good hearty portion of sausage is heaven.

Whisk together the eggs, milk, vanilla, sugar, salt, cinnamon, and cheese, and pour this mixture over the bread, distributing the cheese evenly.

Cover with foil and keep in the fridge overnight.

In the morning, bake the casserole at 350 degrees for 40 minutes (30 minutes for a convection oven), or until the casserole is puffed and browned.

Serve with maple syrup.

Leftovers can be kept in the refrigerator and microwaved for a quick breakfast the following day.

Granola

These amounts are approximate.

Ingredients

8 cups oats

1 small package of flaked coconut (sweetened or not), about 2 cups

2 to 4 cups chopped nuts

1 1/2 cups brown sugar (This seems like a lot, but this recipe makes many servings. You can start with a smaller amount at first if you like. You can also substitute honey, molasses, or maple syrup.)

1 cup water

3/4 cup oil (try coconut oil for a delicious flavor!)

1 tablespoon cinnamon

1 teaspoon salt (don't omit: salt is important to wake up the taste buds)

1 teaspoon almond extract (if using almonds)

2 cups of any combination of the following: dried cranberries, chopped dates, raisins, chopped apricots, to be added after the granola has baked

Directions

Preheat the oven to 325 degrees.

Combine the oats, the coconut, and the nuts in a large mixing bowl.

Combine the rest of the ingredients *except* the dried fruit in a saucepan, bring the mixture to a boil, and simmer for 5 minutes, or until the sugar is dissolved and the syrup is slightly thickened.

Pour the syrup over the ingredients in the bowl, and mix well until all the oats are coated.

Pour the mixture into shallow pan (a lasagna pan works well), and bake for 30 to 35 minutes, stirring every 10 minutes, until the mixture is evenly browned.

Remove from the oven. Stir in the extra ingredients at this point.

Cool completely without stirring, for clumpiness, and store in airtight containers (and the granola can be frozen).

Oatmeal Porridge Like Mother, Like Daughter

This method is similar to the way I cook all grains (except pasta)—namely, with a bit of fat at the beginning to coat each grain and produce a delectable separateness and lack of stickiness or objectionable gumminess in the texture. Try the same method with rice, couscous, barley, and bulgur. Stock up on grains and keep them in jars or in ziplock bags in the freezer so that they do not get stale or rancid. If you are using steel-cut oats, soak them the night before.

Ingredients

    1 cup oats (if steel-cut, soak in 2 cups water)
    1/2 cup Cream of Wheat (quick-cooking farina)
    1/4 cup Wheatena (Do you have this where you live? It's basically
        toasted finely cracked wheat. If you don't, add more farina or
        cornmeal.)
    1 tablespoon butter
    1/4 teaspoon salt
    1/2 cup sugar, brown sugar, honey, or maple syrup

Directions

Bring 4 cups of water to a boil (use half if using soaked oats). Add the butter and salt.

Stir in the oats, the Cream of Wheat, and the Wheatena.

Cook for about 20 minutes, stirring. If the consistency is too thick, add water; if too thin, add more Cream of Wheat. I like to make the consistency quite thick so that cold milk can be added at serving. This cools the porridge down and adds protein. If you like to cook your porridge in milk but get annoyed by how it tends to boil over, try stirring instant dry milk (up to one cup for this amount) at the end of the cooking.

Add the sugar, brown sugar, honey, or syrup. I like to sweeten the porridge in the pot to a moderate degree of sweetness so that only a little needs to be added at the table. I have found that if I serve it completely unsweetened, children tend to add too much.

Serve with maple syrup and milk. Add a tablespoon of peanut butter or chopped pecans for heartiness. The nuts will make this breakfast last until lunch. You can also stir in a well beaten egg for the protein challenged; the heat will make it into a custard.

Papa's Special

*I have found out that many families have something
they call Papa's Special, or sometimes Daddy's Special!*

Ingredients

English muffin
butter
honey (Use real local raw honey; grocery store honey can contain
    corn syrup! Of course, if you have a child under one, don't use
    honey at all.)
peanut butter (Use real peanut butter made from ground peanuts;
    major brands have a lot of additives and sugar in them.)

Directions

Toast the English muffin. Butter both sides (technically, this makes it a Mama's Special, because Papa doesn't butter the peanut-butter side). Spread honey on one side and peanut butter on the other. Sandwich the sides together.

Plain Cooking: Surviving Morning Sickness and More

Quick disclaimer: I rarely had more than little waves of nausea while pregnant. Before you hate me, I want to tell you that my observation, backed up by multiple studies (or, maybe not), is that those with easy pregnancies often have difficult deliveries, and vice versa. Does that make you feel better? I'll wait while you run to the bathroom. Poor you.

But I have some strategies for you to cope with morning sickness, and some tips. With my admittedly scant experience and surveys of truly morning-sick friends, this post will help. The main issue is how to feel a little better—but also, how to feed everyone when you feel lousy. The answer is to fall back on Plain Cooking, and that is something you learn to do so you can pull it out without thinking too hard about it.

As I see it, we have these levels of morning sickness—call it the Defense Readiness Condition (Defcon), but for pregnancy (or other state that may benefit from preparedness and emergency procedures regarding food supply).

Defcon 5: You are still on Pinterest and can manage to layer dips, garnish salads with edible flowers harvested from your garden, and handle recipes embedded in other recipes. You can stomach the sight of raw chicken for a short time. You are not too tired to have a garden. Good for you! We'll be over for supper.

Defcon 4: You walk rather fast past the chicken case at the grocery store. A dish of squid you mistakenly ate in week 9 has put you off squid forever. Never again will you eat squid. You can barely type the word. Your family wonders why chicken has disappeared from the menu, although some of them aren't sad about this (they are the four-year-old). Ways to make ground beef are not finding any appeal, but you're sticking with it. As long as the six-year-old keeps you supplied with little fizzy hard candies from the corner market, you are going to make it, although your teeth will be the worse for wear. By week 20 you are feeling okay, as long as you have one nap a day. (This may or may not have been me—at my worst. I said I was sorry.) You're doing fine, really, and the troops are fed.

Defcon 3: Dragging from sofa to bed, bed to sofa, barfing along the way. Wishing you had the energy to strangle the next person to tell you to drink ginger ale. Subsisting on saltines. Here is where perhaps we can be of help.

First, let's look at how to feed your family in this case, and, of course, I think your friends and family should be supplying you with generous meals, but for one reason or another, that might not be the case. So let's figure out a strategy.

I think rules are in order, don't you? Thinking and understanding is so hard when you are suffering from morning sickness. Rules have the virtue of standing there, ready to be followed, when thinking isn't an option. So here are three warm-up rules and then on to Plain Cooking.

Rule 1: Get the medical part of it squared away.[16] Have your blood tested for iron. The iron in your prenatal vitamin is probably not enough. Take your Floridix (or Blood Builder—easily swallowed, reasonably sized pills—if you don't think you can handle swallowing the liquid).[17] Iron can worsen

---

[16] Nausea that starts in late pregnancy can be a warning sign of preeclampsia. Check with your doctor or midwife.
[17] Needless to say, check with your doctor or midwife before taking any supplements.

nausea, but so can anemia. Try to take it later in the day when you've eaten something (nondairy).

If you can eat red meat or liver, do. Try liver pâté; either make a simple one with onions and prunes, or buy it. Liverwurst isn't bad, spread on crisp crackers; you may find you crave it when you're anemic. Liver + prunes = iron and may be helpful with consequent digestive issues. There are combinations of vitamins that can help you. Ask your doctor or midwife. But above all, don't get anemic on top of everything else.

There are safe medications for morning sickness. Many ladies swear by the vitamin B6 plus Unisom[18] combination (if you know you get sick, start as soon as you can; you can split the pills to spread the anti-nausea effect over the day, if that's more affordable for you; and there is a prescription version that is slow release) or Zofran, or both. You need to bring it up with the doctor—I've heard too many stories of ladies needing IV fluids more than once, yet the doctor *still* doesn't bring up medical relief. Getting dehydrated is far worse for Baby than taking the (safe!) medication!

Rule 2: Rest. You are making a baby. That's pretty important and amazing. If this is not your first child, you are making a sibling for your other child(ren)—the best gift you will ever give them, besides your marriage. You don't have to do anything else for them in the way of activities, entertainment, and so forth; and your kids will not only survive but will thrive, because they will do for you the things you are not able to take care of. You will see. When you can't, they will.

Sometimes I think this is obvious, to rest, but then I see ladies running around and realize that unless you have my voice in your head, you might not know that you can just lie down. (But if you literally can't move, you might be anemic. See number 1.)

Remember, you might not look all that pregnant, and thus you might think that people are judging you (or you might be judging yourself) for

---

[18] But as with any medication, even if prescribed by a doctor, keep an eye on how you react. Some find that the Unisom can lead to personality changes. The B6 by itself might do the trick.

feeling bad, but all the hard work of making fingers and toes is taking place right now! No wonder you can't cope!

If your other child is only eighteen months old, then it's tricky to have to check out of your daily energetic routine, but you'd be surprised how little an eighteen-month-old needs. If you are skeptical, remember this anecdote a friend once told me when I was lamenting a bout of incapacitating sickness: "Once I was so sick and no one was there to help me. I basically lay on the sofa and held out a banana. The [little] kids ran around in circles in the living room, stopping as they passed for a bite." I don't know how much lower the bar can be, so just think of that and congratulate yourself for holding it together.

Get a fence and let the kids run around outside. When people ask what you need, tell them you need a fence.

Auntie Leila hereby gives you permission to lie on the sofa for as long as you are able.

Rule 3: When you *can* do something, try to do it fast. It's better to do something really quickly and then go back to the sofa than to move slowly for a long period of time. Train yourself to visualize the fastest way to do a particular task, and then do it that way. A sweet reader with severe morning sickness to whom I wrote this thought commented:

> Thank you so much for that advice. It was actually more helpful than you may realize because I can be a sort of "slow to get moving" type of girl. The reminder to work quickly when able is most applicable.

Rule 4: Familiarize yourself with Plain Cooking. When you are able, just cook the food. Do not Pinterest it, do not "Julia Child" it.

Everything is fine with butter and salt.

Cooked meat lasts a couple of days in the fridge and cooked vegetables last for longer than that (but fresh ones don't, so better to cook them).

Boil or bake potatoes. Heck, microwave them. I laughed when I saw a *New York Times* article about "the right way to bake a potato." There is literally nothing easier than baking a potato. Turn oven on. Put potatoes in (you don't even need a pan!). Bake. Place on plate. Cut open. Add butter and salt.

Yes, there are entire cookbooks for how make chicken breasts interesting. But you can also get a pan, melt butter in it, throw the breasts in, and cook them. Salt and eat.

Roast a whole chicken. Just salt it and put it in a medium oven. Roast it for 15 minutes per pound. Take it out. Hack pieces off it. Put it in the fridge. Take it out. Hack more pieces off it. Repeat until nothing is left. If you can muster the energy, throw the carcass in a pot, cover it with water, and make stock.

Put chuck roasts and pork shoulders in the slow cooker (respectively) with some tomato paste and dried onion and salt. You don't need to add water to the pork. You can add a cup or two of water, wine, or broth to the beef. Cook until the meat is tender, six hours or so. If it's not tender, cook it some more. If you can't open a can of tomato paste, don't worry. It will be fine.

Get pork chops. Melt butter in a pan. Brown the chops on one side. Turn them over. Salt. Cover and cook on low heat for 8 minutes (depending on the thickness, more or less). Eat.

Sometimes you need to know that you can open a jar of sauce. Boil pasta. Brown ground beef and add salt. Open jar of tomato sauce (store brand is fine). Pour over the beef. Heat the mixture, and pour it over the pasta. Serve with parmesan cheese or even grated cheddar.

Brown ground beef. Add dried minced onion and salt. Serve over potatoes. Put a dollop of sour cream on top if you want to be fancy. Or put it in a tortilla. Anyone who can open the fridge can get some things to add to that.

Truly, a child can do any of these things. You have only to tell him about washing his hands and the counters with soap. If your child is too young, even your hard-working husband can take ten minutes and do them. If necessary, you can give directions from the sofa.

Just think "meat, starch, vegetable, bread." If all else fails, bread and cheese.

To get slightly more complicated in case the fog clears or someone is there to help:

- BBQ sandwiches with the cooked meat: leftover braised (as above, in the slow cooker) meat, BBQ sauce, rolls
- Ground beef, BBQ sauce, potatoes
- Cooked pork (pulled apart), BBQ sauce, rice

Get the bottled BBQ sauce that is made with sugar, not high-fructose corn syrup. Always have some of that handy, along with bulky rolls in the freezer.

Make a pot of rice and put your cooked meat and vegetables on top, and tell a child to get the soy sauce.

Get a ham (have your husband pick it up for you—one with a bone, pre-sliced or not, but not sweetened), bake it at 325 degrees in a pan with sides. In the same oven, put sweet potatoes on a baking tray lined with foil. (Do not omit the foil, because we don't want you scrubbing pans.)

After two hours, take the ham out, turn the oven up to 425 degrees, and continue to cook the sweet potatoes until they ooze sugar, about another half hour. Boil some green beans.

Open the sweet potatoes and serve them with butter and salt. Once you taste roasted sweet potatoes, you will love them. I literally made it through childhood without eating one green item, thanks to sweet potatoes.

Have a kid take the peels off any leftover sweet potatoes and put the flesh in a container in the fridge. This can be quickly reheated in a bowl or by frying it up in a pan with eggs.

Another day, have ham sandwiches—just bread, butter, and ham, fruit or pickles, and chips on the side.

Another day, soup made with the ham bone—pea soup couldn't be easier. Throw the peas with the bone into the slow cooker, add dried minced onion, and two quarts of water. If you feel fancy or have a child who can help, cut up a carrot and one stalk of celery to add to the pot. Add salt at the end.

Another day, cook some pasta, and add the ham and green beans to the cooked pasta with butter and cheese.

In your pantry you need dried minced onions and dried garlic powder. You can add some of those to whatever you're cooking plainly.

If the defcon level can be downgraded:

Put that chicken carcass that's been picked clean in a pot. Throw in dried onion flakes. Add water, and boil. Strain. Cook noodles in it, maybe a chopped carrot (cook the carrot pieces before the noodles). Shake some dried parsley in.) There you go. Lots of bread and butter.

Caesar salad: send someone out for a big package of Romaine lettuce, parmesan cheese, anchovies (really—you might find you crave anchovies), and Italian bread. They could break Auntie Leila's rule this once and buy Caesar salad dressing, although it's just oil, vinegar, mustard, salt, and garlic (we'll leave the egg yolk out of it for now). Put the leftover chicken next to this salad, and you're good to go.

The main thing is to use your limited cooking time well. If you can do it, cook as big a roast or as many chicken parts as you can manage so that you can put some in the freezer. Have plenty of ziplock freezer bags on hand to make this as easy as possible.

Make a big pot of pasta, and toss it with olive oil. You can have many meals that are pasta, cheese, pieces of meat, and vegetables. All of that has been in your fridge; just microwave it. The same can be done with potatoes or rice.

Don't worry, you will get through this. Someday you will cook with recipes again. For now, just aim to have some cooked food on the table.

Tips for Quelling the Nausea

I realize that so far I've suggested liver and anchovies, but if you are still with me, this advice could help:

Eat whatever you can eat. If that means pastries or ice cream or cheeseburgers or salted nuts, that's what you should eat. You need calories. Don't try to choke something down if you have an aversion to it. We women have been conditioned to cling to the notion of salad as our one healthy option, but salad might not be for you right now. (I suspect that we shouldn't fight an aversion to salad, as raw greens can harbor bacteria that can be quite dangerous when you're vulnerable.)

Try eating before *lifting your head up off the pillow.* Ask your husband to bring your snack right to you, handing it to you so you can eat while prone.

A cooler by your bed or even a dorm-sized refrigerator in your room might be just the ticket during this time.

Try to eat something with protein if you can. Yes, salty crackers can help, but you need quickly to follow up with (or go straight to) cheese, yogurt, pieces of cooked meat, or nuts. You might be able to eat a sharp, salty cheese like feta.

Eat and drink at frequent intervals. Your aim is to keep your blood sugar level even. Drinking a lot of water is vital. Think of it this way: the reason you feel terrible is that hormones are coursing through your body so that Baby will grow. (You may also get headaches for the same reason.) You need a good fluids balance to have the hormones at the proper levels. If ever you were going to aim to increase your water consumption, now is that time.

Sometimes water doesn't seem to fit the bill. I always drank quantities of homemade iced tea, even knowing that experts frown on caffeine for pregnant women; however, I frown on pregnant women getting dehydrated. Some ladies like the bubbles of seltzer with a little juice in it. It's more important to drink a good amount than to fret over what it is that you are drinking. I would only say, avoid diet sodas because artificial sweeteners are really poison (my husband wrote a book about them!)—and aspartame is the worst of them all, affecting the kidneys and crossing the brain blood barrier. If real ginger ale is too pricey or strong for you, try cutting it with seltzer.

If you can, try to avoid sugars (although I stand by eating what you are able to eat when things are dire). Fats are good. You're aiming at a balance so that your insulin is steady. *Eat at the times of day when you feel less sick.* Set a timer if necessary, because you might be tempted to use your less-sick hours to power through, when what you need to do is eat something during that phase.

Try not to smell the things. This makes the crockpot a bit trickier, I realize, although the advantage is that you can put it out in the garage or on the deck while the food is cooking.

On the other hand, Deirdre suggests sniffing a cut lemon; it has helped her. I found that sniffing a tea bag helped me. Mint works wonders for some. You can keep it in herb, lozenge, or tea form.

Sometimes you can eat something if someone just puts it in front of you. Don't say you can't eat it until you really know for sure. Thinking about it might be worse than eating it. The time I was sickest, I couldn't stand to hear the words "ham," "broccoli," or "cheese sauce," but when handed a plate of just that, I could eat it. Whatever is the thing you can most see yourself eating, just serve that as simply as possible or ask to have it served to you.

Magnesium and vitamin D really help with feeling better, and magnesium is best absorbed through the skin. A foot bath or actual bath with Epsom salts is soothing and delivers the magnesium—far better than in pill form. You can get a big bag of Epsom salts at the drugstore.

Taking cod liver oil can help with the vitamin D. Yes, this is a two-edged sword for sure, and there are capsules. The issue is burping. Deirdre suggests taking it before bed so you are asleep when you burp!

Sometimes nausea is actually from acid reflux, so try to get that under control. Relieve constipation (the sweet potatoes really help with that, as do flax and dates, which you should be eating anyway for your labor). Try Tums or Zantac. Nausea can also be due to low acid, so taking an apple cider vinegar drink or lemonade can help—if you are craving lemonade and it helps, then go with that.

There's still Defcon 2—walking around with a little suitcase containing IV fluids. This is so hard. Please rest and be cared for. I don't know what to say, other than maybe look at the tips above and see if you can manage them or pass them to your husband.

And Defcon 1—hospitalization: Auntie Leila is so sorry and has even less to tell you, other than to direct your husband to this chapter, which will also help anyone who isn't able to be very handy around the kitchen, even if not pregnant. (Hence, the "more" in the title of this chapter. It's just good to remember, for lots of dire circumstances, that you—or someone else—can keep it simple.)

A possibly consoling thought, when anxiety about the rest of your family is making things worse: A friend who does get morning sickness told me recently about a real upside to her most recent pregnancy, and this relates to meal planning directly. She decided she just had to keep it simple and not cater to her other children's pickiness (they were all under six at the time)—because she just could not. She got what she could on the table and that was that, and it was usually the same thing many days in a row.

And you know what? Her children became very hearty eaters!

If none of this helps, let it go, just let it slide. What helps one mom might not help you, and vice versa.

Please join or form a St. Gregory Pocket as soon as you can (I say more about this in volume 1). We all need a community to help us through these times. We can't do it on our own. When you've been through it, you know what to do—which is more than I can say for most people. Be there to help others, and they will help you.

In any case, everyone has his fight to fight, and I want you to know that we all have those times when things fall apart. Do your best, and know that God sees you and loves you. Sometimes I think that we have these times in our lives so that we learn humility and that we aren't meant to be "perfect." How else will we ever empathize with anyone?

Work fast when you can; do the minimum; stock up on good videos and books for the kids. Remember that offering up your suffering is the way God asks us to be united with Him. It isn't wasted—you will never know until you get to Heaven how your lonely, silent suffering helps others. But it does.

APPENDIX C

Bland-Diet Tray Meals

A big part of being a Mom is knowing how to take care of a sick person with love and skill. I think that training in nursing should be required of all women, just as home economics used to be. We need both. Now we don't have anything, and so we have a book like this one.

Early on in my mothering path, of course one of my little ones got sick. I checked with the pediatrician, and he said, "It's the flu. Plenty of liquids and keep him on a bland diet. Call me tomorrow."

So I called him the next day, and he asked, "What did he eat?"

"Spaghetti with tomato sauce and cheese," says I. That honestly seemed bland to me!

"WHAT!" Yes, he was shouting. "What have you done to me!" Yes, that's what he said! What have you done to *me*?

Okay, then, what *is* a bland diet? I asked, and I got an answer, which I put together in the following section. I printed it out and keep it taped to the inside back cover of my personal menu and recipe binder. If you have someone who needs to stick with this sort of regimen, it's useful to have the information written out where you can refer to it as long as you need to.

When Mr. Lawler and I were first married, we didn't have a dining room table. We ate our meals off trays. I still have those trays, almost thirty years later! They have certainly saved the day for feeding sick people: you can't help feeling better when your meal comes on a tray.

The Bland Diet

Bland diet: What to eat when you (or someone you love) have an upset stomach, vomiting, diarrhea, the flu, or the doctor says, "Put him on a bland diet."

Sometimes someone is sick, and he knows what he does and does not want to eat. My experience as "field nurse" to my crew is that there are certain stomach bugs that must be treated very carefully or getting over them will take so long that the risk of dehydration becomes real. When the stomach just can't take anything at all, here are some things you can do.

If *nothing* is tolerated, try giving *nothing* for a few hours, up to six. The stomach needs to rest completely. Keep a sharp eye out for the signs of dehydration, in which case you need to go to the hospital for IV fluids. You can ask the doctor if you are not sure.

If it's possible to give something, try the suggestions on the following page (we placed this list so that it's easy to make a copy of it to keep inside your cabinet door or in your food binder).

Bland Diet

During the Crisis, for Hydration

Give liquids by the spoonful, slowly (every five minutes or so), cutting back if it's not tolerated. Don't give plain water, as it doesn't sit as well as something a little sweet; don't give food, other than a plain saltine if it can be tolerated.

- Black tea with sugar and no milk
- Peppermint tea
- Ginger ale (be aware that big-name brands don't actually have ginger in them, but do have high-fructose corn syrup. Consider stocking up on real cane-sugar soda with real ginger during the flu season.)
- Diluted juice
- Popsicles

During the Recovery

- No fats
- No dairy
- No raw vegetables or fruits
- No beans, seeds, dried fruits, or other high-fiber foods
- No spices
- Soft-boiled egg
- Poached egg
- Very ripe banana
- Applesauce
- Toast—no butter, but honey or jelly is okay
- Saltines, not Ritz (too oily)
- Beef broth (be aware of the non-nutritional nature of canned beef broth, as well as the MSG, and maybe keep some homemade stock in the freezer)
- Plain chicken breast
- Chicken noodle soup
- Chicken rice soup (use white rice)
- Rice (salt, and a tiny amount of butter can be tolerated after a bit)
- Mashed potatoes (without milk—mash with potato water and salt)
- Popsicles
- Apple juice mixed with water
- Black "real" tea—sugar, no milk
- Peppermint tea
- Ginger ale
- Tonic (not for pregnant ladies as contains quinine—but good for malaria, I suppose)

Introduce dairy slowly in the form of plain yogurt sweetened with a little jam or honey. (Ice cream is usually well tolerated, at least by our family!)

APPENDIX D

How to Patch Jeans

I have been a mother for decades and decades. I have three of the male sex and four of the female. Can you imagine how many jeans we have had? Can you further imagine how many holes in the knees we have had? Many.

It's hard to describe to someone who hasn't been through the exigencies of providing that many children with clothing on a tight budget just how defeating, and yet how very common an occurrence, it is when a child puts a hole in his jeans. The jeans themselves might have cost you very little (other than the "human toll" of hours spent in a thrift store with babies in tow, careful labeling of boxes in the attic, and reassuring of wary youths that the style and cut of the garment are correct). But replacing a particular pair of jeans at a particular time is heartbreakingly dear.

(A digression regarding jeans that are sold "distressed" and full of holes. How insulting they are to those of us who need clothing that will look presentable for as long as possible and to the original jeans wearers: thrifty people who have holes in their clothes because they are actually doing hard work that would kill a fancy designer outright. I can't stand the thought of handing over good money for such a thing. How the designers must be scorning us all the way to the bank! How stupid they must think we are!)

In all those years with all those hole-producing children, I never really figured out how to patch jeans. I've done them by hand, I've used iron-on patches (most unsatisfactory), and I've just let the children run around being all "holy."

Honestly, my "solution"—and it's not a bad one—was that, for many years, I rarely bought the boys a pair of shorts. In the spring, I just took whatever pants they had, cut the bottoms of the legs off, and hemmed them! Either the pants had holes in the knees or were going to be too worn out (thus un-pass-down-able) the following year anyway.

But finally, in the twilight of my mothering career, I have figured out how to put a stinkin' patch on a pair of jeans.

Patch Fabric

You could use any pretty or handsome, sturdy fabric for a patch. Cut two pieces the same size, allowing extra for ironing under the edges for a neat look. Putting a patch right across the width of the leg (rather than making one to cover just the hole or the worn part) will alleviate centering issues. Just scoot the folded-under edge of the patch right up to the unopened seam. You should probably do both knees, even if the hole is in just one.

You can also keep some old denim around (either cut up a pair of jeans that are truly dead, or pick up a random pair in the same color denim at the thrift store clearance; you might as well get an extra-large pair and cut it into pieces as large as you can for your repair stash). Rather than making a bulky patch by turning under the edge, just use a more solid stitching to finish off the raw edge. It will take a bit longer, but it will be worth it for comfort.

The Trick for a Durable Patch

The trick is to patching jeans is to break down and open up the seam that isn't double-stitched—the seam on the outside of the leg. Using your seam ripper and scissors, open up the seam a good eight inches or more beside the knee. It will have another seam under it, the one that finishes the raw edge inside, so yes, it's a little tedious. Sometimes, once you have made an opening, you can just rip it. But don't rip the fabric!

Now you will be able to sew on your patch. Using that now open seam, you will be able to sew not only the verticals of the patch, but also the horizontals! This is what was keeping me from sturdily patching the jeans on the machine, the fact that there is no way to maneuver the foot to sew parallel to the hem.

Use a setting on your machine that will give you a durable double-stitch, or, if your machine is super basic, do a close zigzag. It won't take but a moment to sew up the seam you opened, simply by turning the pants inside out and pulling them flat. Just stitch on the line left by the original stitches.

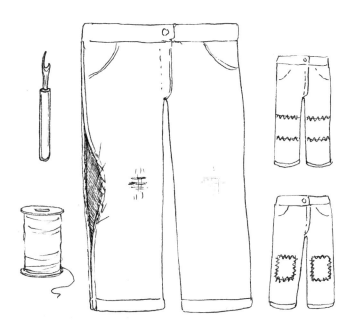

APPENDIX E

Visible Mending, a Satisfying Way to Make Do

I'd probably need another volume to do justice to the idea of mending, patching, and generally making do with household objects, but I thought maybe a little example would convey a great deal, as well as being amusing.

So many times I was ready to throw away an Icelandic wool blanket; they were all the fashion in the seventies when my mother very kindly gave me this one as a Christmas gift when I was a teenager. Some years later, when it was in use on my own child's bed, our dog ripped a hole in it.

I wavered: I shouldn't keep something that has a big hole in it, but I didn't want to ditch it either, because it was of such good quality. But there was a *big hole* in it.

Finally I figured out what to do. I cut a patch from another blanket that *was* pitch-worthy (it was fairly moth-eaten) to make this patch, thinking that the path to keeping the Icelandic one was to embrace the hole.

I patched both sides with a blanket stitch, using yarn. For the inner sewing, I cut what had been a jagged tear into a neat circle.

I'm glad, because if I had ever seen someone else's story of this kind of patch, I would have been mad at myself for throwing a good blanket away.

APPENDIX F

Beeswax Finish for a Butcher Block

H ere is how to finish a butcher block that you plan to use *as* a butcher block, as well as a cutting board or a tabletop. I use it on my coffee table. You will need beeswax[19] and a food-grade oil. I prefer mineral oil because vegetable oils become rancid after time and some more stable oils are not food grade (but would work fine if your board is not coming into contact with food, of course).

Melt the oil and the beeswax together in a jar, in a ratio of about four parts oil to one part wax. (This sounds precise but is actually guesswork. Do the mysteriously knowledgeable people whose directions one follows mean parts by weight? Volume? I used volume.) To melt them, heat water in a small slow cooker or pot, and place the jar in the water. Stir the oil and beeswax with a wooden skewer or spoon (which will then be nicely

---

[19] We now have our own beeswax because we keep bees, but it's easy enough to order. It's an amazing substance and well worth owning. You won't need much; you can even use stray beeswax candles that may not look as fresh as when you got them. Simply melt, strain, and use according to my directions.

waxed) until the beeswax melts and the whole mixture becomes as one. (I tell you these details in case you are like me and would really like to know.)

As the hot mixture cools, it will become a thick paste that can be stored indefinitely. To apply it to your wood, warm up the jar in the same way, in simmering water. Meanwhile, prepare the wood surface by wiping some of the plain mineral oil on it; using a clean rag, rub it in, letting it soak in for a few minutes, and then rub off the excess. Using the same rag, rub on your warm beeswax paste. After applying the paste, let it cool and then buff it with another clean cloth. These processes (rubbing on oil, then oil and wax paste) may be repeated as needed, and you can store the original rag right in the jar of paste so as not to waste any of it.

INDEX

Index

Index

decluttering with, 154–156
for toys, 258–259
shopping, 59–63. *See also* grocery
shopping
emotional spending, 293
as entertainment, 293–294
non-retail, 295
praying about, 295
quality and, 297, 299
for Thanksgiving, 200
sickness. *See also* health
bland diet, 378–380
morning sickness, 368–374
nausea remedies, 374–377
sideboards, 137–140
Sidetracked Home Executives (Young
and Jones), 132, 159, 202
silverware
drawer for, 249
for travel, 91
single-income households
frugality and, 293
homemaking in, 300–301n
thriftiness and, 290–292
sinks
beauty over the, 233–234
cleaning, 238
flow in the kitchen and, 213–216
slippers, 318
snacks
breakfast and, 83
price comparisons, 62
soaking
during meal preparation, 245
for stain removal, 121–122
socks
purchasing criteria, 108–109,
112
for winter, 318

soup. *See also* stocks
accompaniments for, 75, 360
bean soup, 91
in Dutch oven, 226
frozen corn for, 78
grocery lists for, 54, 58
leftover meat for, 68, 69, 72, 76,
77, 94
for Lenten meals, 49
for lunches, 51, 52
in Plain Cooking, 373
in recipes, 42
during recovery, 380
Save a Step preparation, 71
for Thanksgiving, 198
in thrifty menus, 40, 41
in weekly menus, 46, 48
special-occasion menus, 43–44
spices
during cleanup, 245
during recovery, 380
storage of, 72
spills
bins and, 258–259
cleaning, 240, 241
two- to four-year-olds, 178
while traveling, 91
spiritual detachment, 291
sponges, cleanliness of, 235–238
squash
in regular menus, 42
in special-occasion menus,
43–44
stash of, 78
in Sunday menus, 44
for Thanksgiving, 196, 199
in weekly menus, 47
St. Patrick's Day, weekly menus and,
49

Index

ILLUSTRATOR'S NOTE

T he illustrations for this work were drawn from life, from imagination, and, in the case of a few images, from photos or other reference images. They were rendered first in pencil on drawing paper and then redrawn with either Staedtler or Micron pen.

Some of the domestic scenes were captured in the home of our friend Therese Cross, to whom I express my gratitude for welcoming me for an afternoon of perching myself around her charming home with my drawing pad for this purpose.

My husband, artist John H. Folley, patiently provided consultation and image scanning and editing, as well as nigh-solo parenting of four little ones during my all-intensive week of work on this project.

My thanks to my mother, the author, for entrusting another work to me for visualization, enabling me to pursue my humble vision, and for continuing to tolerate my art supplies strewn around the house. Faithful readers of hers will recognize vignettes of her home in many of these drawings.

My gratitude extends also to Sophia Institute Press and Carolyn McKinney for their accommodating and respectful partnership.

I dedicate these illustrations in loving memory of my grandmother, Elizabeth Day Edwards, who taught me how to draw.

— Deirdre M. Folley

ABOUT THE AUTHOR

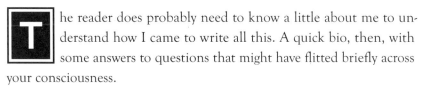he reader does probably need to know a little about me to understand how I came to write all this. A quick bio, then, with some answers to questions that might have flitted briefly across your consciousness.

My name is pronounced "Lye-la"; "Lay-la" is also fine, as it's the Arabic way. Without intending it, my Egyptian father and (mostly) Welsh-background American mother chose the one name that the two cultures have in common. It's also my Egyptian grandmother's name.

I'm the only child of parents who divorced when I was three; wife of Phil, who is American (Irish, and a little German), mother of seven children, grandmother of sixteen with, God willing, more to come.

I'm a convert to Catholicism from vague secular humanism, with a brief, completely uninformed and unconvincing stop as Muslim, sometime in middle school when I was desperately seeking a spiritual home and thought I could find it in the cultural milieu of my father (who was himself agnostic, an appreciator of the good things in life, and a solver of problems, good engineer that he was).

My childhood took place during the upheavals of the sixties and their aftermath; feminists were calling the shots by the time I was in high school. My father had come to this country to do graduate work in the field of engineering. He held academic life in the highest regard. Many are not aware that upper-class women in Egypt had by that time entered professional life, having benefited from Western-style secondary education. My father definitely had the highest expectations for my career.

My father had come to the United States by way of Hungary, where he worked as an engineer in the railways on behalf of Egypt. His experience in Hungary convinced him that communism was terrible and that no one should ever be subject to that system, which he simply described as a police state.

My mother, though rebellious in her personal life when I was young (she later became a devout Catholic), through her reading had become staunchly antitotalitarian. The books and magazines at home (with her) ranged from texts elucidating the most extreme versions of psychoanalysis to the best, most energetic defenses of Western civilization (exposing the ideological flaws of the former category). I also had access to the classics of child and adult literature.

My voracious reading habit led me to the Catholic Church. In high school I met my future husband, who is ten years older than I. He was a journalist working in the same office as my mother, and he had a decisive influence on my life. (I tell a lot of this story in an episode of *The Journey Home* with Marcus Grodi.) And though I had a long road to travel to learn what virtue is and how to get it, I knew in my heart that I wanted to make a home with Phil—that I didn't want a career.

I was nineteen when we married. Being a young wife from a confused background during the early feminist years, in a city where the women my age were definitely *not* getting married and having children, I was isolated and incompetent at what I set out to do. I simply had no skills and no share in the collective memory that had sustained those who had gone before me.

I call how I got from there to here "the journey of a girl who didn't know how to sweep the floor," and I wrote a good deal of what I learned on that journey first on my blog, *Like Mother, Like Daughter*, and then here in this book. My hope and prayer is that it will benefit you in some way, dear reader.

Sophia Institute

Sophia Institute is a nonprofit institution that seeks to nurture the spiritual, moral, and cultural life of souls and to spread the gospel of Christ in conformity with the authentic teachings of the Roman Catholic Church.

Sophia Institute Press fulfills this mission by offering translations, reprints, and new publications that afford readers a rich source of the enduring wisdom of mankind.

Sophia Institute also operates the popular online resource CatholicExchange.com. *Catholic Exchange* provides world news from a Catholic perspective as well as daily devotionals and articles that will help readers to grow in holiness and live a life consistent with the teachings of the Church.

In 2013, Sophia Institute launched Sophia Institute for Teachers to renew and rebuild Catholic culture through service to Catholic education. With the goal of nurturing the spiritual, moral, and cultural life of souls, and an abiding respect for the role and work of teachers, we strive to provide materials and programs that are at once enlightening to the mind and ennobling to the heart; faithful and complete, as well as useful and practical.

Sophia Institute gratefully recognizes the Solidarity Association for preserving and encouraging the growth of our apostolate over the course of many years. Without their generous and timely support, this book would not be in your hands.

www.SophiaInstitute.com
www.CatholicExchange.com
www.SophiaInstituteforTeachers.org

Sophia Institute Press® is a registered trademark of Sophia Institute.
Sophia Institute is a tax-exempt institution as defined by the
Internal Revenue Code, Section 501(c)(3). Tax ID 22-2548708.